Coping with Change in
the Modern World

Coping with Change in the Modern World

Diarmuid Ó Murchú MSC

THE MERCIER PRESS
and distributed in Britain by
FOWLER WRIGHT BOOKS LTD.

The Mercier Press Limited
4 Bridge Street, Cork
24 Lower Abbey Street, Dublin 1

Fowler Wright Books Limited
Burgess Street, Leominster, Herefordshire, England.

British Library Cataloguing in Publication Data
O Murchú, Diarmuid
  Coping with change in the modern world.
  1. Social change—Philosophy
  I. Title
  303.4   GN358

  ISBN 0-85342-827-1 (The Mercier Press)
  ISBN 0-85244-144-4 (Fowler Wright Books Ltd.)

With gratitude and love, I dedicate this book
to my Parents and Family
who befriend me in a special way on the
changing journey of life:
JOHN & MARGARET
JOE, PAT, MARY, ANN

Printed by Litho Press Co., Midleton, Co. Cork.

Contents

Acknowledgements

The publishers and author gratefully acknowledge permission to reprint, granted by:

Associate Book Publishers Ltd,. for diagrams from T. C. McGinnis & J. U. Ayers, *Closed and Open Lifestyles*, Routledge & Kegan Paul, pp. 16-17, 115-116.

Charles Knight Ltd., for illustration in Paul Rogers (Ed.), *The Education of Human Ecologists*, p. 10.

Butterworth Scientific Ltd,. for reproduction of the figure 'Schematic Ecostructure for a Megapolis' in *Futures*, 16(1984), p. 354.

Gower Publishing Group, for diagram in G. Burrell & G. Morgan, *Sociological Paradigms and Organizational Analysis*, Heinemann, p. 29.

Marianists of Ohio, for the reproduction of 'The Vitality Curve' from Lawrence Cadia & Alia, *Shaping the Coming of Age of Religious Life*, Seabury Presss, p. 53.

Pergamon Press, for material taken from Michael Cazenave (Ed.), *Science and Consciousness*, p. 368.

The St. Andrew Press, for reproduction of material in Roger Clarke, *Work in Crisis*, pp. 28, 81.

Viking Penguin Inc., for use of material from Stephen Bliss (Ed.), *The New Holistic Health Handbook*, The Stephen Greene Press, p. 17.

Introduction

The way to do research is to attack the facts at the point of greatest astonishment. – ANON

As I peer darkly outward and inward from this mortal tapestry of life, it comes to me more and more that the most fundamental facts of existence are the ones I am least sure of. Indeed, about all I know is that we seem to be surrounded and imbued by mysteries and immensities – GUY MURCHIE

Every person needs to learn to trust his or her own images. It is precisely out of this trust that the artist in us is born – MATTHEW FOX

When I began writing this book my intention was to provide a manual of practical skills, enabling the reader to cope more effectively with the momentum of change in today's world. The plan seemed simple and straight-forward: begin with *perceptions* of what is happening, to be followed by *interpretations* of those perceptions and conclude with *prescribed skills* to cope with the ensuing reality. Already a number of writers (in the vein of Alvin Toffler) had analysed the data and explained the nature of contemporary change. I saw no point in repeating what was already accomplished with a degree of lucidity and expertise which I could not hope to emulate. My task, therefore, was to provide a compendium of *coping skills* for the changing world-scene outlined by others.

I began with what was intended to be a resumé of the changing trends of contemporary life. What was envisaged for a few pages became a whole chapter, progressively unfolding into a whole book. The neat, conceptual plan proved to be more of an obstacle than an asset. It seemed so logical, self-consistent and obvious, but the more I tried holding on, the more it seemed to elude me. I was frustrated and confused.

In the midst of my darkness, however, there emerged an alluring vision: the more I reflected on experience and analysed my observations, new questions and challenges began to impinge from all directions. It was not that former descriptions of change were wrong, or even superficial; they were simply *inadequate.*

They did not present the *total* picture, or rather they presented it in a *limited* and *limiting* perspective.

Then came the revelation and the breakthrough. Initially, it was hard to accept, but I suppose every new discovery is! I had been emulating the technocrats of my era; *faithfully* and *rigidly*, I had been operating out of my blinkered conditioning and limited consciousness. I had been trying to manipulate and control the world of change. My frustration was that I was trying to impose rational and utilitarian interpretations on a reality that transcends all these categories. *I was trying to control change when, in reality, change controls me.* I had to relearn what my spiritual peers so often proclaimed: *surrender* is the supreme freedom. How I resist that word 'surrender', but gradually its profound mystical truth is penetrating my heart.

The change I write about in this book is the one we all experience in our everyday lives; it is also the one we spend most of our time running away from through resistances and rationalisations. I do not write about some special type of change peculiar to mystics, sages or freaks. What is unique about this book is its *interpretation* of change. Contrary to most other books on the subject, it begins with the assumption that change happens and will continue to happen for the benefit of humanity. Try as we like we cannot halt, control or modify change. That does not mean that we are its helpless victims. We can use it to our advantage precisely when we surrender to its flow and momentum.

The book falls naturally into three sections. In *Part One*, I seek to explore the nature and impact of change at a global, universal level. To many readers, this section (which I consider to be the most important) may be irritatingly vague and general; the interpretation of change I adopt presumes both an *evolutionary* and *spiritual* basis to the world of our experience. Without incorporating these dimensions I would be unable to explore the subject of change in the unique manner presented in this book.

I use the term *evolutionary* to describe those changes in science and religion, in international affairs and global developments which signal the approach of a new evolutionary leap. These observations (detailed in *Part One*) are based more on *intuition* than on objective verification. But cumulative evidence, from a variety of people in all the different disciplines, obliges us to take the evolutionary theory seriously. Having explored the evidence we may choose to dismiss and ignore it; the chances are we'll accept rather than reject it and then we'll know for ourselves what change means in its depth and profundity.

People who warm to an evolutionary understanding of life tend to be spiritually motivated. This does not necessarily mean that they belong to a formal religious system or go to Church regularly. It does mean that they have learned to transcend the merely rational and observable; they feel a sense of being connected with an inner power at work in their own lives, in their dealings with associates and in their relationship to the cosmos. They are open to mystery, to the new, to the eternal future. Faith is perceived not so much as adherence to one or other religious system, as rather a call to exploration and new discovery of that reality which grounds our life and our world.

The reader who resonates with our global reality, as explored in *Part One*, will readily identify with its social implications (*Part Two*) and its personal ramifications (*Part Three*). In seeking to interpret and cope with change, most people tend to begin with their immediate reality, at a personal and/or social level. This may be an appropriate starting point, but for many people it has proved to be frustrating and discouraging. Having done everything that was possible and reasonable, people wonder why they have not achieved a more amenable outcome, that is to say, why they haven't succeeded in changing or (more frequently) in dampening the effects of anticipated change. Often they proceed to blame themselves and under-estimate their potential, a response which further diminishes their enthusiasm and coping skills.

The thesis I wish to present is that the appropriate starting point is not our *immediate* reality, but our *global, universal* context. The most powerful waves of change in today's world take place at the broadest and deepest levels of our experience, creating a ripple effect in our social institutions and in our personal lives. Instead of microscopic navel-gazing – looking from within outwards – we need to cultivate a macroscopic stance: looking from outside inwards! We begin to see things very differently and many dimensions of our experience, which otherwise remain estranged and fragmented, begin to form a fascinating and intriguing pattern. Such is the vision presented in this book, one cryptically expressed by John Shea (1978, pp. 43-44) in these words:

It is at the limits of human power that the quest for meaning becomes most acute. When we cannot explain the events which engulf us, when we cannot endure the suffering which overwhelms us, when we cannot bear the evil which defeats us, we do not become submissive but highly imaginative. We formulate symbols which account for and even celebrate the darkness and ambiguity. The effort is not to deny the undeniable – that there are unexplained events, that life hurts, or that rain falls upon the just – but to deny that there are inexplicable events, that life is undeniable, and that justice is a mirage. The instinct to meaning will not be denied.

Part One

Global Change

1: Living in a Time of Transition

Every scientific methodology is involved in a constant search to define the upper limits of what is possible. – JEREMY REFKIN

And because we are slow to liberate ourselves, the world has come to liberate us from our history. – C. S. SONG

We live in a moment of history where change is so speeded up that we begin to see the present only when it is already disappearing. – R. D. LAING

In 1952, a strange event took place on the island of Koshima in Southern Japan. A young female monkey, of the species *Macaca Fuscata*, decided to try a new recipe for lunch. Instead of eating her grit-laden, unwashed potato, as she had been taught by her ancestors, she decided to take it down to the sea and wash it. And she liked the new flavour, spiced by the salty water. It took some time to teach the new trick to her associates. Beginning with the young members, her fellow-females acquired the new skill with greater ease than the male counterparts; after some time the elderly were convinced and joined in the new adventure. The initiator had earned herself a reputation and scientists named her *Imo*. That was in 1952!

By 1958 something even more dramatic was taking place. Monkeys throughout the entire colony had acquired the new behaviour. It was readily established that there had been no *physical* contact between Imo (and her associates) and the rest of the group. So, what was going on?

To explain this strange phenomenon, scientists use the term *Morphic Resonance*. The theory states that when a certain percentage of a group acquires a new behaviour, then the awareness accompanying that discovery 'automatically' informs the entire group (the morphogenetic field) exerting on it a transforming effect (cf. Sheldrake, 1981, 1985). There exists a variety of scientific opinion on what the 'certain percentage' might be. It is certainly not higher than 10% and some venture to suggest that a threshold as low as 1% is adequate to create the qualitative leap.

A New Evolutionary Leap

The timing of this event is highly significant. Many new movements – political, scientific, religious – with international and global impact, began to emerge during the 1950s and, in not a few cases, 1960 marked the point of breakthrough. In 1950, over 40% of the world population lived under colonial control, but only 3% in 1970 and less than 1% in 1977. In 1960 alone *seventeen* African nations achieved independence. That same year Pope John XXIII announced the Second Vatican Council. It was also a time of major developments in outer space exploration: in 1958, Russia launched its first Sputnik satellite while the USA formed the National Aeronautics and Space Administration (NASA), launching its first astronaut in space in 1961. The early 1960s marked the beginning of modern computerisation and the technology of knowledge which reached an apex in 1977 when, for the first time in history, the majority of the American workforce was employed in processing knowledge and information.

Already in the 1940s, Teilhard de Chardin predicted a new revolutionary breakthrough: the *physical* development of the human species seemed close to completion; further growth would take place not so much in the realm of the *physical*, but primarily in the domain of *psyche* and *spirit*. If de Chardin is correct, *Homo Spiritus* is outrunning *Homo Sapiens*. Even if one disagrees with this perception, few can deny that the cumulative impact of knowledge and information (non physical processes) in the past twenty to forty years is, indeed, impressive and marks a profound change in our perception and understanding of life.

A brief look at how we handle knowledge and information verifies de Chardin's prediction. From the beginning of the Christian era up to the dawn of the scientific revolution (c. 1600 AD), our 'quantity' of knowledge doubled that of the three-to-five previous thousand years; between 1600 AD and 1900 AD, it doubled again.

It took only *fifty* years for another quantitative leap (up to 1950), followed by yet another shorter span of *twenty* years, up to 1970; then *ten* years (up to 1980) and currently the quantity of information is duplicating every *three* years. We need to remember that this process is not taking place merely in academic institutions or in centres of learning. It is a human and global phenomenon; we are *all* causing it and our lives are being transformed by it.

Alongside the expansion of knowledge we note a parallel effort to store relevant information. To scan just the past few hundred years, we witnessed a progression from *museums* or *laboratories*, where data was restored in material and physical form, to *libraries* where information could be stacked in smaller space because it was now in *written* form. We then invented *microfilms* to contain masses of information while simultaneously finding new ways of communicating it, by means of television and subsequently the video boom. Then came computerisation, culminating in the *microchip*, which in itself can contain a whole library of information.

It is now clear that as information increases our means of storing it becomes progressively smaller (in physical and material terms). I submit that we are very close – perhaps, within *ten* years – to the point where we can no longer contain information in a physical or material object. The microchip serves a *symbolic* as well as a *functional* purpose. Our physical means of *coping* with knowledge has been our way of *controlling* it. Computerisation is the last stronghold of the 'will-to-power', a sophisticated and highly competitive means of controlling, manipulating and ultimately exploiting the resources of creation. But its days are numbered and its time is running out.

We are rapidly approaching the hour when information will be contained in *consciousness*, a 'non-physical', spiritual receptacle. In this way, knowledge becomes everybody's gift. It becomes synonymous with human awareness, power from within that will be unleashed at the appropriate evolutionary moment. When that time comes, our relationship with knowledge will be such that anything we can *think* we can do, and any problems we can put into words, we can solve.

An Idea Whose Time Has Come

This new quality of consciousness is neither alien nor superior to our current human awareness; it is simply a latent propensity awaiting its hour. Its awakening we can trace briefly to the beginnings of the eighteen-century when Gothfried Wilhelm von Leibniz suggested that our material universe, along with our human concepts of time, space, mass and motion, were secondary reality, the real world being an underlying, non-material life-form which held all the individual parts together in a creative, holistic synthesis. Only in the *twentieth* century, however, did we begin to explore the 'intelligence' behind the universe in its ultimate depth. This exploration followed two parallel lines at *global* and *personal* levels.

We can briefly trace the development in chronological order:

1902:   Psychologist, William James proposed that '. . . the definite images of traditional psychology (i.e. explicit forms) form the very smallest part of our minds as they actually live.' (McDermott, 1967, pp. 254-255)

1905:   Albert Einstein published his special theory of relativity (and subsequently, the quantum theory) creating a radically new way of perceiving reality, especially in the space-time continuum.

1908:   Sigmund Freud visited the USA (at the invitation of Stanley Hall), thereby gaining international recognition for his theory of the individual subconscious: that dimension of inner experience over which we have little or no control but which determines much of our human thought and behaviour.

1929:   Alfred N. Whitehead outlined his theory of *process*; dualisms such as mind/matter are false; reality is inclusive and interlocking and it unfolds in a progressive, holistic, self-organised way. That same year Karl Lashley published his research, demonstrating that specific memory is not to be found in any particular site in the brain, but is distributed throughout.

1936:   Carl Jung outlined his thesis of the *Collective Unconscious*[1]. Contrary to Freud, Jung maintained that personal consciousness was largely governed by universal, psychic forces, basically benevolent in nature and recapitulating all the past experiences and future aspirations of mankind and accessible to all humans.

1955: Teilhard de Chardin died. Posthumously, his works were published and translated into several languages. As early as the mid 1940s de Chardin suggested that human, physical evolution had, by and large, run its course; mankind was approaching a new threshold where psychic, evolutionary growth (including mind and spirit) would predominate.

1960: A burgeoning of transpersonal psychologists, exploring inner states of being and frequently linking with oriental meditation practices, began to flourish in the West, especially in the USA.

1969: Karl Pribram of Stanford University proposed that we should view the human brain not as a machine composed of independent parts but as a *hologram*, in which specific information, and memory in particular, is not located in any one part, but distributed throughout the brain and even throughout the nervous system. (The *hologram* is described on pp. 80-81).

1971: Physicist, David Bohm of London University, who had worked with Einstein, proposed that the universe itself is a *hologram*. All that unfolds before our eyes is merely an external, fragmentary manifestation of an underlying, unbroken wholeness. Both Bohm and Pribram published their theories.

1975: Fritjof Capra published *The Tao of Physics*, outlining an important and unprecedented dimension in the new scientific paradigm, namely, the attempt to combine the insights of Western science and Eastern mysticism, in an effort to discover the ultimate meaning of life.

1980: Erich Jantsch published *The Self-Organising Universe*, probably one of the most thorough analysis of the *Gaia hypothesis* (see pp. 48-49) which maintains that the universe evolves at a *micro* and *macro* level through an inherent process of self-renewal and reorganisation. Just as the individual mind contains the dynamics for self-renewal at a personal level, so there exists a type of universal mind for global self-regeneration.

1984: Dr Carlo Rubbia and his team at CERN (Geneva) nailed the sixth quark, thus concluding a twenty-year pursuit in the most recent attempt to discover the 'ultimate building blocks of matter'. Contrary to popular expectation, however, the scientists had not isolated the 'building blocks'. Instead, they were confronted by a new mysterious and baffling reality: quarks were not 'things' existing in isolation but rather energies that funtioned only in relationship with each other and with related particles. The implications of this discovery are far-reaching and, as yet, are poorly understood, even by the scientific community itself.

The above list is both limited and selective, but adequate to highlight a convergence of insight, pre-empting an evolutionary breakthrough where *spirit/mind* rather than *matter* becomes the governing principle. Never before did we know so much about the human psyche and, most baffling, of all, is the amount we yet have to learn. Carl Sagan (1981, pp. 50-51) captivates our sense of progress along with the immensities awaiting discovery.

Human DNA is a ladder a billion nucleotides long. Most possible combinations of nucleotides are nonsense: they would cause the synthesis of proteins that would perform no useful function. Only an extremely limited number of nucleic acid molecules are any good for life-forms as complicated as we. Even so, the number of useful ways of putting nucleic acids together is stupefyingly large – probably far greater than the total number of electrons and protons in the universe. Accordingly, the number of possible individual human beings is vastly greater than the number that have ever lived: the untapped potential of the human species is immense. There must be ways of putting nucleic acids together that will function far better – by any criterion we choose – than any human being that has ever lived. Fortunately, we do not yet know how to assemble alternative sequences of nucleotides to make alternative kinds of human beings. In the future we may we be able to assemble nucleotides in any desired sequence, to produce whatever characteristics we think desirable – a sobering and disquieting prospect.

Peter Russell (1982, p. vii) captivates the new evolutionary mood in the opening pages of *The Awakening Earth*:

Humanity could be on the threshold of an evolutionary leap, a leap which could occur in a flash of evolutionary time, a leap such as occurs only once in a billion years. And the changes leading to this leap are taking place right before our eyes, or rather right behind them – *within our minds.* (Emphasis mine).

Global Consciousness

Personal growth in consciousness evokes great interest today. No less unique and spectacular is the expansion in global consciousness, the cumulative impact of human awareness on international and global events. Ever since the dawn of the industrial revolution, a cultural wish for deeper and broader understanding has pervaded the human psyche. The nineteenth century alone produced such momentous thinkers as Auguste Comte, Herbert Spencer, Charles Darwin, Sigmund Freud, Louis Pasteur, Gregory Mendel, Karl Marx, Nicolai Danilevsky, to mention but a few.

A rapidly expanding body of technological skill and wisdom has helped to create the new global awareness. No longer are humans prepared to be the capricious victims of fate and circumstance. Advances in all fields clearly point to the possibility of controlling and manipulating almost any alien force affecting human and earthly life. And one doesn't wish to deny the permanent human urge towards greed and the will-to-power, demonstrated most potently and perniciously in the creation and use of the Atom Bomb.

When representatives of fifty nations gathered in San Francisco, in April, 1945 to launch the United Nations, few could deny that the emerging global consciousness had reached a new depth of maturity. Although previous attempts to unite governments and nations – the Achaean League and the League of Nations – had failed, the dream for a new world order refused to dwindle. Even before the cataclysmic atom bombs were dropped on Hiroshima and Nagasaki, it was already clear that nothing less than a global government would generate a true and lasting peace.

As stated in the opening paragraphs of its Charter, the UN set itself the primary task of maintaining international peace and security. It represented something of an universal repulsion for war, and a widespread desire for co-operation and friendship between the nations of the earth. With hindsight, one detects a deeper, symbolic meaning in the establishment of the UN: a statement of intent by representatives of all mankind that there is but one earth – our earth – for which we are all responsible and to which we owe our livelihood and survival. The global consciousness symbolised by the UN far exceeds issues of war and peace;

it also encapsulates a desire for greater harmony and integration at all levels of human existence. In a word, it marked the arrival of the global village!

The turbulent situation arising from the Second World War set the immediate context for the establishment of the UN. For the second time in less than thirty years the Western world was engulfed in warfare. Things were getting dangerously out of hand. Yet, it was a crisis with a strange destiny, best understood, perhaps, by employing the Chinese term 'chi' which means both *crisis* and *opportunity*. One could say that the war represented the crisis, the divisions, bitterness and hatred: and the UN, the opportunity, the possibility of a new global order.

Since 1945, the global political scene has changed dramatically. The UN itself has expanded from a membership of *fifty* in 1945 to *one hundred and fourteen* in 1965 (of the *sixty-three* new member states, *fifty-seven* were from the Asian/African block) to *one hundred and fifty four* in 1984. As already noted, the colonial empires have all but disappeared. Although two superpowers dominate the Northern hemisphere (USA and USSR) and both seem to be striving for mastery of the earth (and of outer space), a new global consciousness shared by millions of people in all continents indicates a desire to move towards a different reality.

The UN itself, sadly, has succumbed to the bureaucracy of power and consequently has lost much of its potential for the creation of a world government. Moreover, the superpowers seem to usurp any UN initiatives aimed at progress and peace. Despite these setbacks, world govenment is coming as the culmination of a long evolutionary process outlined by Guy Murchie (1979, p. 584) in these words:

> World government has become such an obviously essential step in Earth's present development that it must be considered one of the factors in planetary germination although it hasn't yet happened. . .
>
> An evolution of many thousands of years is involved here, starting with families, then small clans that gradually yielded to larger, stronger tribes, led by chiefs or priests. Next appeared village and town governments that grew into city states that eventually amalgamated into nations, federations, empires, grand alliances and super-powers – with only the final step of a true world federation still lacking.

National consciousness is on the wane. Tribal, ethnic and religious differences are seen by many to be enriching rather than divisive. A realisation that the earth has the potential to nourish and support all its five billion people and many more – provided the superpowers of the Western world cease their ruthless exploitation of the world's resources – creates a new human bond, transcending time, place, culture and nationality. Increasing numbers of people believe that the earth is ours – the whole earth – our one and only home!

It is an idyllic picture and a long way from the divided world we know only too well today. It may not be as far-fetched as it seems! There is increasing evidence to suggest that the old world order is in disarray, rapidly declining and ultimately facing extinction. In the poetic words of Arthur Clarke (quoted in Ferguson, 1982, p. 65):

> We are living at a time when history is holding its breath and the present is detaching itself from the past like an iceberg that has broken away from its mooring to sail across the boundless oceans.

Walter Schubart (quoted in Sorokin, 1950, p. 125) in his study on the rise and fall of different civilisations, concludes with a somewhat similar observation:

> Especially breathtaking are the periods when one prototype dies out and a new one begins to emerge. These periods are the intermediary, apocalyptic moments of humanity. In such periods people feel that everything is crumbling and the end of the world is coming. In fact, such moments will be repeated many times in the future.

The Rise and Fall of Civilisations

Western civilisation[2] is crumbling, decaying, dying! Western values no longer serve the revitalisation of life and culture: hence, the pain, suffering and political anarchy of the African and South American continents, long subjected to Western domination and now striving to articulate their own status and identity.

Slowly and painfully, the West is losing its grip on the world. Population trends in Europe and in the USA reveal an increasing age group with declining birth rates, especially in the big cities. Western values, based on industrial production and technological progress, are now being rejected even by Westerners themselves. The political clarion call for democratic freedom (hailed by successive American presidents) is openly rejected in favour of Marxist/Socialist ideology. The christian church, the power and glory of European culture, has all but lost its influence in the Western world, while a new quality of religion[3] is beginning to arise in Africa, South America and Asia.

The rise and fall of major civilisations is amply documented by a number of well-known scholars. Already in the eighteenth century, Giovanni Battista Vico claimed that each nation had three ages: an initial 'heroic' age, characterised by a 'barbarism of the senses', gradually refined into a national lifestyle marked by unity and moral integrity before entering a phase of decline characterised by intellectualised decadence, what Vico calls a 'barbarism of the intellect'. Paul Ligeti, Nikolai Danilevsky, Oswald Spengler, Arnold Toynbee, Pitrim Sorokin, Walter Schubart, Alfred Kroeber, F.S.C. Northrop and Nicolai Berdyaev have all provided comparative analyses of up to thirty different civilisations, most of which are now extinct.

A broad resumé of their findings appears on p. 21; the similarities are impressive and sufficiently concurrent to extrapolate guidelines and principles governing the growth and decline of each major phase. Of particular interest to the contemporary Western reader are the dominant features marking the *Breakdown/Disintegration phase*. These clearly signal the imminent decline of our Western civilisation and, that being the case, we also need to study the conditions and forces which revitalise a culture; otherwise, we condemn ourselves to a futile and meaningless death.

According to de Beus (1985, p. 23), the picture painted by most of the authors of the last phase of civilisation shows the following striking resemblances:

A concentration of power in two or three centres

A period of large-scale wars conducted by means of mass armies and using engines of mass destruction between ever larger units, until one of them gains the upper hand

An universal yearning on the part of the masses for world peace and world order

A loss of creative force

A search for new religions or for an universal Church

PHASES/STAGES IN CULTURAL EVOLUTION: MODEL ONE

Phase/Stage	*Features*	*Leading Theorists*
Launching	Sense-perception dominates: life tends to be disorganised and tribalistic. Struggle and hardship elicit a creative, enthusiastic response.	Arnold Toybee; Nikolai Danilevsky; Oswald Spengler P. Ligeti (architectural), P. Sorokin (ideational), W. Schubart (Ascetic-Messianic), A. Kroeber (first religiously dominated culture), F. S. C. Northrop (dominantly aesthetic), N. Berdyaev (Barbaric religious).
Expansion	Creative minority spearheads new life, growth and values.	Toynbee; Spengler; Danilevsky, Ligeti (plastic), Sorokin (idealistic), Schubart (harmonious), Berdyaev (mediaeval-renaissance type).
Stabilisation	Values become formalised: legally, morally and institutionally. Expansion is at its maximum. Individuals and movements seek total control; subtly, the seeds of corruption are sown.	Danilevsky; Spengler Ligeti (Malerisch), Sorokin (sensate), Schubart (Heroic or Promethean), Berdyaev (Humanistic/secular), Northrop (theoretic), Kroeber (secular, intellectual-artistic culture free from religious domination).
Breakdown	Dominant groups vie for power. Institutions become introverted and self-perpetuating, no longer serving the best interests of their members. Greed and self-aggrandisment dominate all round.	Toynbee Danilevsky Spengler
Disintegration	Crime, violence and apathy predominate. People begin to abandon the system and set-up alternatives, while the ruling institutions feverishly hold on to power that becomes progressively meaningless and ineffective.	Toynbee; Danilevsky Spengler (?)

Sources: Kroeber (1944), Sorokin (1950), Spengler (1961) and Toynbee (1960)

Antithesis or schisms in society
A loss of style, evident in the arts as a 'sense of promiscuity'
The rise of dictators, demagogues and warlords
And, finally, a return of society to a primitive state without living civilisation.

All these features, and some others of a distinctively destructive nature, are widespread in the West today. Added to the breakdown of traditional values is the 'cultural shift' which accompanies each new evolutionary leap. It may peak in one or other part of the globe, but as history verifies it has global, universal repercussions.

Cultures influence one another and the decline of one may mean the upsurge of another with far-reaching effects on the whole civilisation. Today, we are the victims or beneficiaries (depending on one's perception) of major world changes. We are engulfed by those changes and often can feel quite helpless. The greatest threat is felt by those who fail to understand the nature of this global transition: we can neither prevent it nor modify it, but we do not have to be absorbed by it. We can flow with its rhythm and impulse; in that way we become co-creators of the new and emerging World order.

PHASES/STAGES IN CULTURAL EVOLUTION: MODEL TWO

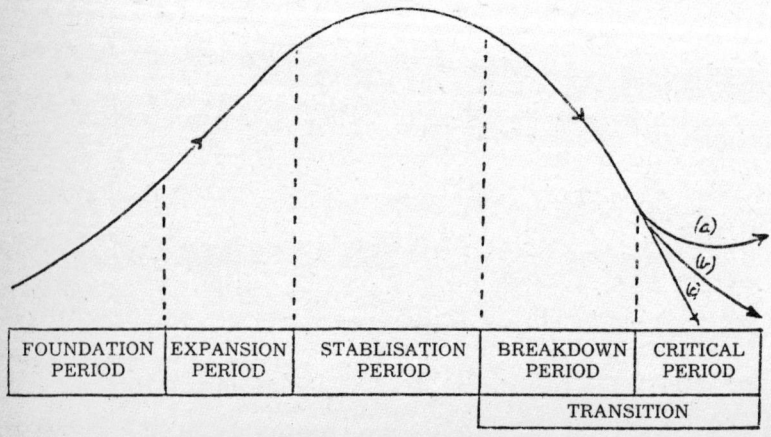

Critical Period: (a) Revitalisation (b) Low Level of Minimal Survival (c) Extinction

Sources: Based on Cada and Alia, 1979, p. 53.

Moving from the Old to the New

Our ability to cope with change depends on how we *perceive* the transition taking place in our world today, how we *interpret* the unfolding process in both its positive and negative dimensions and how we choose to *respond* to new developments. The *quality of response* merits much attention and will form the basis of this book. People may respond positively or negatively; in both cases there is a degree of awareness and a measure of choice; but many, perhaps, the bulk of humanity, expend much time and energy in *avoiding* rather than in *making* a response. Hence, the extensive apathy and indifference, with consequent crime and violence, which dominates society today.

FEATURES OF CULTURAL DECLINE

1. International and national power struggles
2. Wars, violence, crime
3. Economic disarray
4. Fragmentation of relationships
5. Moral corruption
6. Religious indifference
7. Polarisation and entrenchment
8. A sense of 'promiscuity' in the arts
9. A return to neo-tribalism
10. Rapid development of urbanisation
11. A loss of creative force
12. An universal yearning for peace and new order.

FEATURES OF REVITALISATION

1. The rise of creative minorities
2. A return to nature: a new wave of ecological consciousness
3. The exploration of alternative lifestyles
4. Novel scientific paradigms
5. Traditional polar values (e.g. science and religion) interact in new ways
6. A renewed interest in spirituality (especially mysticism)
7. New models of family life
8. Neotribalism: recapitulating our cultural origins
9. A new story (myth) begins to unfold
10. New evolutionary shift (perceived retrospectively).

Readers avid for answers and solutions may expect quick remedies or a condensed version of the way forward. Frequently, we hear the remark 'We know what the problem is; what we need to be told is how to solve it.' This may well be the major blockage to change in our world today. We have a superficial understanding of the problem; we fail to realise that the seeds of the solution are to be found in the problem; this is true of both individual and cultural growth. Without an in-depth understanding of the problem, the 'solutions' we proffer may be inappropriate for our new evolutionary age.

Throughout this book we explore, side by side, the nature of the problem and what may be appropriate resolutions. Without an in-depth analysis of the problem, we cannot hope to understand the transition from the 'old ways' we must leave behind to the new world view we are invited to embrace. Nor should we consider the problem to be something external to us; we are part of society; *we* are society. We have created and continue to create the problem and we only succeed in changing our reality when we acknowledge its total context, positively and negatively.

The way forward, however, is not *totally* dependent on an analysis of the problem. We are not the first of the human species to experience a cultural shift. We can learn from the problems of the past; we can also benefit from the wisdom of our ancestors and their often ingenious manner of coping with catastrophe and turning a breakdown into a breakthrough. In his study of the change from one scientific model to another, Thomas S. Kuhn (1970, p. 79) writes:

> The transformation from a paradigm in crisis to a new one from which a new tradition of normal science can emerge is far from a cumulative process, one achieved from an articulation or extension of the old paradigm. Rather it is a reconstruction of the field from new fundamentals, a reconstruction that changes some of the field's most elementary, theoretical generalisations as well as many of its paradigm methods and applications. . . When the transition is complete, the profession will have changed its view of the field, its methods and its goals.

The 'solution', therefore, consists not in correcting the faults of a former system as one might replace worn-out parts in a machine. It is as if the 'parts' themselves were demanding a new body within which they could function anew and survive. There is something drastic, even extreme, in this quality of change. In rather poetic terms, Kuhn (quoting Herbert Butterfield) describes it as 'picking up the other end of the stick'. The key to comprehending this *quality* of change may be in Kuhn's own words quoted above: '. . . a reconstruction of the field. . .' What is this *field*?

The field refers to *consciousness*: the quality and quantity of thought, feeling, perception and intuition in today's world. The way we comprehend and understand contemporary life is profoundly different from that of twenty years ago. Imbued with the new consciousness we are, almost in spite of ourselves, beginning to live in novel and different ways. This shift is exemplified in the growth of knowledge and information, outlined at the beginning of this chapter.

Only a small proportion of people have been endowed with this new wisdom; yet we are profoundly affected by it. Many people perceive it to be threatening and disturbing and try to diminish its impact. An expanding minority welcome it – some cautiously, others quite openly – it depends on how one feels about the process. What seems inescapable is the fact that a programme of change is under way; we are all affected by it. Whether it transpires to be for our benefit or destruction largely (if not totally) depends on how we perceive, interpret and respond to what is happening.

In the major studies on the transition from a declining culture to a newly emerging supersystem,[4] the following features seem to mark the breakthrough:

 a) A creative minority are inspired by a new vision. They tend to comprise a diversity of people from different backgrounds, frequently disenchanted members of the middle-class rather than revolutionary figures of the oppressed or deprived sectors of the community.

 b) The new vision is more a fascination with novel possibilities than a reaction to, or even a solution for, old problems. Consequently, the creative minority is often dismissed as being 'airy-fairy', 'dreamers', 'unreal', 'superficial', 'a passing fad'.

 c) The initial enthusiasm may dwindle and occasionally is smothered by the moral condemnations of Church or State (sometimes, both), but tends to revive, survive and eventually assume a leading role. Belonging to a creative minority entails pain, misunderstanding and often outright rejection.

 d) What was initially a dream now becomes a new paradigm. It tends to be characterised by:

i) a deeper quality of human relationships, based more on trust and mutual recognition of differences and complementarity;

ii) a tendency to abandon the dominant institutions of the former model to a form of neo-tribalism (see pp. 154ff), sometimes chaotic and disorganised, but eventually leading to forms of social and political organisation;

iii) a revitalisation of spirituality, though not the highly developed, moralistic type envisaged by Toynbee, but rather of a God perceived and worshipped in nature, characteristic of pre-historic times;

iv) a predominance of sense perception (as outlined by Sorokin); intellectualisation and rationalisation tend to be abandoned in favour of a direct, non-judgemental and uninhibited experience of life as lived in daily interaction;

v) a closeness to nature, marked by a strong ecological consciousness.

In the above process, one cannot deny the risk of regression in the tendency to abandon the sophistication and integration which contemporary lifestyle and structures seek to embody. In fact, without the oft-quoted Christian maxim, 'you must become like little children', the enterprise seems bizarre and absurd. Our difficulty with it, of course, is that its underlying meaning is so difficult to grasp. Why? Because we are dealing with a *primordial, archetypal experience*, with the basic fundamental desires of human life, the original simplicity (which may also be our final destiny) to which human beings forever aspire and which they seek to re-instate culturally in the transition phases of major civilisations. In the course of subsequent chapters, I'll strive to spell out this profoundly complex phenomenon. Suffice to note at this juncture, that the revitalisation of a culture (which tends to be concurrent with the birth of a newly emerging subculture) marks a *recapitulation* of human growth and experience. The forward leap is energised by mobilising resources from our past, at both a conscious and unconscious level.

Faced with the experience of cultural transition, the human species subconsciously seems to check with the collective wisdom of the past to ensure it goes forward in the right direction. The innate simplicity of our origins, our childlike dependency, our tribal identity, all come into play. And this is not regression! The very recapitulation of the old is happening in a new way, with a new purpose. It is, in the cryptic words of Bede Griffiths (1976) a 'return to the centre', to that focal point where past, present and future coalesce, creating a new human response that is at one time consistent with our origin as a species and yet radically new by contemporary standards.

In trying to explain this phenomenon, we are delving into the realm of mysticism and immediately we recall that mystics all over the world, and in all ages, highlight the inability of human language to explain and expound the meaning of life. Yet, we *are* creatures of meaning; unknowingly, we seek meaning unceasingly and strive to impose it where it doesn't exist (Frankl, 1959). If human language fails us in our search then our challenge is to create a new language, a new medium of exploration and that is not entirely a far-fetched idea as we shall see later.

Change takes place around us all the time and in every conceivable situation. Coping with personal and social change is something we take for granted, often under-estimating our ability to deal competently with the situation. Change at a more universal level is scary and threatening until we take the courage to explore it. Then we may begin to realise that change is of the essence: without it life atrophies in a sea of morbidity. Moreover, we ourselves are so designed, individually and collectively, that we can only reach our full potential in a world open to change and in the on-going discovery of each new revelation made possible by the altering nature of universal life.

2: Parting with Old Ways

It is the business of the future to be dangerous. . . The major advances in civilisation are processes that all but wreck the societies in which they occur.

– A. N. WHITEHEAD

Western civilisation has entered into a profound and irreversible crisis.

– JOE HOLLAND

Great confusion and unrest usually arise before a new paradigm emerges.

– KENNETH R. PELLETIER

We need to think about extinction in a meaningful way. – JONATHAN SCHELL

There is something vast and vague in the idea of global change, demanding a great deal more than the proverbial stretch of the imagination. However, the negative connotation is easily established and the features of destructive change in today's world are all too well known. They include the following:

a) An economic recession in which the relationship of capital and productivity has been seriously eroded; multinational corporations rule the roost often leaving governments helpless in the face of international monetary swings;

b) An expanding gap between the rich and the poor while millions of pounds are spent on armaments each day;

c) Extensive warfare both north and south of the equator;

d) The threat of nuclear extinction, or, at least the threat of short and long term effects of nuclear pollution in a variety of forms;

e) The manipulative power and potential of modern technology, posing a real threat to human freedom and dignity;

f) Political corruption has been a feature of many governments in various parts of the world in recent times;

g) A rapid increase in petty crime, violence and drug-trafficking, accompanied by moral permissiveness and promiscuity – on a global scale;

h) Mass unemployment in all parts of the world, with its accompanying meaninglessness, hopelessness and despair;

i) Fragmentation in relationships, family breakdown and infidelity in long-term commitments, especially in the West;

j) Progressive irrelevance of institutional religion, in universal proportion, although quite differently expressed in various cultures.

This list depicts a world in chaos. It is an ugly, fragmented and depressing picture. We no longer ask: 'What went wrong?', but depressingly wonder: 'Can we ever hope to get things right?'

'Bringing down inflation', 'creating more jobs', 'more effective measures to combat crime', 'aid for the Third World' are among the impressive slogans used by governments to allay our worst fears. But the slogans are wearing thin; it is clear to everybody that things aren't getting better. Many European countries have cut the level of inflation to single figures, but this has not improved the life-quality of the rank-and-file of society; new jobs are created, but redundancies continue to outgrow them. Despite all the rhetoric and good will, the gap between rich and poor was never greater. And, finally, the arms race: the money spent on arms' production each week comes to *seventeen billion* US dollars, enough money to feed the earth's population for a whole year! What a tragic waste of resources and energy, and how helpless we all feel in the face of such gross immorality!

It is a grim picture which the majority of people either ignore or try to explain away. Turning a blind eye is an understandable human reaction, but it only exacerbates the problem. Humbly and honestly, we need to acknowledge that we are engulfed in a cultural, global crisis. The old order is dying, crumbling, falling to pieces.

Faced with crisis it is customary to displace hurt feelings and lay blame at the feet of the 'guilty' ones – the multinationals, the American dollar, the price of oil. For the contemporary world scene there are no valid scapegoats, because the corruption has arisen from within the system itself. Just as aging and senility are features of human personhood so decay, decline and death are endemic to civilisations. We humans contribute to the decline; in a sense we *are* the decline, although we may never acknowledge that fact. Nobody sets out to arrest or kill a civilisation, yet, we all contribute, frequently through passivity or lack of concern. With good reason, Sorokin (1950, p. 117) can claim that civilisations perish through suicide rather than through murder.

Try as we may, we can neither arrest the dying process nor reverse the downward curve on which twentieth century civilisation is well and truly set. We can *accept* and *facilitate* the painful transition and, strange as it may seem, that is our only way of coming to grips with it.

Our Cultural Death-Wish

In today's world nobody wants to think about *death*, in any sense of the word. Yet, we are surrounded by it. Despite the longevity promised and made possible by medical progress and improved living standards, millions die before the age of *fifty*. The escalating rate of violence, the thousands of unborn children aborted each year, the perpetual threat of nuclear disaster, reveal not merely ambivalent attitudes about the sacredness of life but a distinctive frivolity about *death* itself. It has been suggested that our world suffers from a cultural death-wish, exemplified in the declining birth-rate of western nations, noted particularly in urban populations, with reductions of 10% in both London and New York between 1971 and 1981 (de Beus, 1985, p. 50).

The cult of pleasure has accentuated our tendency towards self-destruction. So much human life is wastefully consumed in alcoholism, drug abuse, cancer, coronary ailments and sexually transmitted diseases. In many cases, these illnesses are self-induced. In other words, our value perception is so exclusively focused on *pleasure* (as distinct from *happiness*) that the pleasure principle itself has now become a death instinct (Freud, 1955). Perhaps, the real genius of Sigmund Freud is that he articulated this phenomenon in the early 1920s. A prophet before his time?

Nowhere is the cultural death-wish more apparent than in the arts, the supreme, symbolic expression of our culture.[5] Modern literature, art and music are absorbed in nihilism and bawdiness; no longer are our symbolic constructs capable of projecting a symbolic vision to lift us out of our morass; even our artists have succumbed to morbidity and inertia and like all 'well-adjusted' humans have rationalised their position with what is becoming yet another well-worn cliché: 'The task of the arts is to mirror reality as it is, not as it should be.' This, I submit, is a functionalist approach rather than a creative one.

A new pessimism pervades artistic expression in today's world.

Polak (1973, p. 278) claims that modern art is chiefly characterised by the loss of an ideal image of God which reinforces the suppression of an ideal image of man:

> Modern art. . . robs the world of radiance. God is dead and man is at best a robot, made up of lines, surfaces, angles and spheres without life and without soul.

In seeking to portray life as it is, thus absolutising a death-infested present, the focus often tends to be on the nonsensical, the perverse, the demonic, the negative. Disintegration, fragmentation, morbidity, obscenity, bestiality are dominant themes. The casual visitor to the modern art gallery can scarcely avoid the feeling of despair in the face of visual voids, confusion in the face of portrayed chaos, and perhaps, a total lack of feeling on viewing flatland surfaces devoid of structure or perspective.

Instead of illuminating our chaos, thus enabling us to deal with it, modern art draws us into a vicious downward spiral of self-destruction, an incoherent, aimless trail, a form of enslavement and addiction, feeding its craving by reproducing ever grosser representations of a reality itself becoming ever more fragmented.

Modern music is submerged in a similar malaise, typified in the quip from Derek Jarman's film, *Jubilee* (1978), on punk culture: 'We keep the music loud so that we can't hear the world falling apart.' Modern music tends to belong to that genre which seeks renewal in demolition, pandemonium and cacophany, without any original, creative power and without positive symbolism. A contemporary disco vividly portrays the disenchantment and disillusionment of today's youth, engulfed in hysterical frolics amid diminished light and distorted sound and the occasional modified odour of cannabis, alcohol or some other mind-altering drug. The scene has anarchy and disintegration written all over it. And, yet this is the highlight of a good week for thousands of young people.

Finally, a brief review of modern literature: Samuel Beckett's cryptic phrase probably says it all: 'I have nothing to say and I'm saying it'. This sense of emptiness, vagrancy, randomness and waste are dominant themes in the poetry of such nationally diverse writers as Ezra Pound, T. S. Eliot, André Breton, Paul van Ostayen, Sylvia Plath, Peter Porter and John Cooper Clarke. Like their associates in art and music these poets register a strong protest against a society that is totally unworthy of humankind. This is an admirable task but can become counter-productive when the protest is turned against the poetic medium itself in the rejection of punctuation, syntax and symmetry, of rhyme, rhythm, and meter, of ordered prosody and melodious harmony:

> In outward form, poetry has been shredded into unrelated image-fragments, detached word and sound combinations, a stream of vibrations which does not crystallise as a melody, a series of image-flashes juxtaposed in deliberate disorder. Each separate image is elequent enough, but together the images are a triumph of inarticulateness. (Polak, 1973, p. 285.)

Samuel Beckett's *Waiting for Godot* is a classic dramatic expression of aimlessness, lack of meaning, direction or purpose. (Other examples from contemporary drama include Eugene Ionesco's *Amédée*, Arthur Adamor's *Professor Taranne*, Edward Albee's *The Zoo Story* and Christopher Fry's *The Lady's not for Burning*.) Even the quality of the dialogue is an insult to human dignity and can scarcely be considered as *communication* in any reasonable sense of the word. Verbiage, devoid of content or feeling, also features in the works of such well-known playwrights as Pinter, Stoppard, Brecht, Ionesco, Orton, Anouilh, Hare and Berkoff, while the American playwright, David Mamet encapsulates the thoughtless but powerfully exploitive use of four-lettered words to a degree that would nauseate any sane theatre-goer.

Cohen-Richards (1973, p. 89) describes modern literature as

> . . . primarily one of disorientation and despair. This literary disposition towards the demonic mirrors the tendency towards nihilism in the existential position. The egocentred nature of the existential quest falls short of the integration of the whole man; it is the growth process seen only from the one-sided viewpoint of the limited ego. It is the quest which, searching for man, only embraces him passionately and then leaves him isolated and alone in an alienated world.

Malcolm Bradbury (1977) provides a useful critique of the contemporary novel. Quoting Gerald Graef, he claims that literary culture assumes a posture acknowledging its own futility. In former times, the novel was built on fictitious characters in a highly imaginative plot. But the nature and pace of contemporary life outwits the novelist, leaving him/her deflated, disorientated

RECURRING THEMES IN THE CONTEMPORARY ARTS

Theme	*Explanation*
The Nonsensical	The representation of the meaningless and the irrational as the normal face of human society. Analogies with neurosis, narcosis and nightmares. The portrayal of the fundamental disintegration and incoherence of human life.
The Existential	The ultrarealistic answer to the challenge of our current trends of thought. Identification with science and technology. Utilitarian, calculating attitudes. The portrayal of man as completely alone, forsaken by God and his better self.
The Perverse	The preference for the morbid, the obscene, and the ugly. The salacious portrayal of excess and abnormality.
The Demonic	The evocation of the forces of darkness and evil. The regression of humanity to bestiality: *Satan conduit le bal.*
The Negative	Development of the themes of chaos, wasteland and death. Images of damnation and moral impotence.

Source: Fred Polak (1973), p. 278

and even exhausted. His only hope for survival and relevance is to succumb to a 'fixation on the present moment', in which a society avid for sensationalism (i.e. innoculation against reality) contrives and contorts daily experience into a whirlwind of pleasure and power. Novelists in this vein would include such fast-pace thriller writers as John le Carré, Jackie Collins and Jeffrey Archer while authors such as William Golding, Graham Greene, William Faulkner, Norman Mailer, John Wain, Anthony Burgess, Salman Rushdie and J. P. Donleavy provide us with a statement about the despair of 'serious' contemporary writers to find shape or coherence in modern life.

A substantial number of contemporary writers are in danger of becoming enmeshed in a dilemma they wish to resolve, but know not how. The symbolic medium of expression, in this case, the written story, can be so disjointed and unfocused that it fails to engage the creative imagination. The message is lost (if, indeed, a message exists at all), thus alienating further the seeker-after truth. In not a few cases, the artist has become something of a parrot, re-echoing the cultural groans of death and despair. The imagination of the symbol-maker has been replaced by the mechanical, photographic representation of a deluded prophet.

We may bemoan the decadence of modern music, art and literature, and in our passion for a structured, neat frame of symbolic reference, may strive to patch up the collapsing system. In this way, we run the risk of totally missing the point. Contemporary culture is not dying or declining because of external, overt forces, but because of a deep-rooted internal malaise. In a sense, it has become redundant and is no longer capable of containing or articulating the aspirations of the impending new age. The literary genre called *deconstruction*, exemplified in the writings of the late B. S. Johnson, Jacques Derrida, Harold Bloom, Paul de Man and others claim that language (especially in the written form) jeopardises and even destroys the range of *meaning* expressed in words, although it remains always more extensive and encompassing than words can convey (cf. Atkins, 1983).

The deconstructionists are opposed to structure and to what they term *logocentricity*: the belief that sounds are mere representations of meanings already present in the speaker's mind. The opponents of structure, in line with many contemporary 'critics', are loath to offer alternatives and, in their writings, steer clear of such speculation. Paradoxically, this may be a most creative and responsible stance, although extremely irritating to the rationalistic, solution-seeking academic of our time.

In conjunction with other theorists of our time, the deconstructionists draw attention to the fact that contemporary structures whether state institutions, social models, scientific paradigms or literary genre are becoming increasingly deficient (or inefficient) as means of embodying and articulating the aspirations of our age. What alternatives will emerge is far from clear and perhaps more important, are likely to be the fruit of a new evolutionary consciousness rather than the invention of human beings. In this light the reticence of the critics, their unwillingness to offer alternatives, may be a gesture of profound intuitive wisdom. The ability to pose the right questions rather than offer practical resolutions is a supreme prophetic quality for a time of transition. (On the literary genre, *deconstruction*, see Sim (1982)).

Coping with Death

In the present century, few people have come face to face with death as perceptively and creatively as the psychiatrist, Elizabeth Kubler-Ross (1970, 1982). Her initial research is based on the experience of death taking place in the lives of terminally ill patients. In more recent times, her insights and findings have been used to interpret the death-process (sense of loss, bereavement, decline, decay, etc) taking place at any level of existence, personally, institutionally or, even, culturally. Her conceptual framework can be applied to the material under consideration in this chapter.

Kubler-Ross outlines *five stages* in the experience of dying, each of which we will consider in some detail:

1. *Denial.* The initial sense of shock elicits a tendency to rationalise the fact of imminent death: 'I can't be happening to me'; 'No, it's not true'; 'It must a wrong diagnosis'. At an institutional or cultural level the denial tends to take the form of turning a 'blind eye' to the impending decay and decline. A whole range of defence mechanisms are employed, consciously or unconsciously (usually the latter); unknown to ourselves we are forever trying to ward off the inevitable. Individuals, organisations, even governments adopt the same language: phrases like 'economic

recession', 'the oil crisis', 'mass inflation', 'the floating dollar' become clichéd rationalisations of a crisis for which many people genuinely suspect there is no *real* solution.

Western nations continually acclaim an economic recovery, but *there is nothing to recover from.* Ever since the dawn of the industrial revolution, the ultimate goal of technology has been the creation of a human life style where work becomes so highly mechanised that human beings are set free for leisure and creativity. Unemployment and mass expenditure on state benefits are the by-products of noble and sublime human aspirations. An old order is dying because, *culturally*, we have arrived at a new point in human evolution. It is inappropriate to hold on to the old order. No matter how painful the parting, we must learn to let go.

Another common reaction of the denial state is that of *individualism* 'If the system cannot be rectified or salvaged, well, at least, I'll safeguard my own niche'. Some people call it the survival instinct. It has motivated the Swiss government to provide every family with underground accommodation in case of nuclear catastrophe, the naive assumption being that humans can survive on a 'dead' earth. Such individualism is the product of the Western capitalistic mind-set and, indeed, may be a major contributing factor in the current fragmentation of Western society. Contrary to popular opinion, it is not a characteristic of our prehistoric ancestors, nor is it an appropriate value of the 'new order', where personal survival (and growth) is inconceivable apart from ecological, environmental and global well-being. More on this topic in subsequent chapters.

Of all the resistances to the death-process, especially at an institutional or cultural level, this first stage of *denial* tends to be the most rigid and prolonged. In Western society in particular, we are scared of losing, letting-go, giving-up. Our technological, mechanistic attitude to life has left deep imprints on our cultural psyche, characterised by ethnic, national and even religious superiority. We have a deep need to be 'in charge', in control, capable of dissecting, re-assembling and manipulating all dimensions of life as we do with the *machine,* the single most powerful symbol of western technology. Any talk about death, decay, letting-go, even *change* (which implies a break from cherished values) is perceived as submission to forces incapable of being mechanised and this is deemed to be weakness.

Defence mechanisms can be very powerful and extremely difficult to confront. Any effort to analyse them, never mind modify them, tends to meet with resistance. In some cases, the defences cave in because the underlying psychic infra-structure can no longer uphold them. This, we typically call 'a nervous breakdown' – which can exhibit a range of psychotic behaviours – popularly explained as people being totally out of touch with reality. Could it be that these people were always essentially that way, under the guise of strongly held defence mechanisms? In other words, the denial process serves no useful purpose either for appropriate personal growth or for an integrated perception of one's role in the world.

With adequate and appropriate support, we can outgrow the denial stage. In the case of personal death or grief, this demands tactful and prolonged counselling with a lot of reassurance and understanding from close friends and associates. At a social/cultural level, the process is obviously a great deal more complex and may not be resolved successfully until some of the other stages have also been experienced and negotiated. So, let us review the other stages of the Kubler-Ross model.

2. *Anger.* In the case of personal loss, feelings of rage, envy and resentment tend to be directed at others, displaced on to the surgeon, the nursing staff, relations perceived to be negligent in procuring medical care, or on to God. The intense emotional feelings usually elicit a response and this enables the person to articulate further their resistance to death.

This stage is more easily identified than the denial phase – at both a personal and social level. Institutionally, stage two operates mainly through the medium of *blaming*: trade unions blaming management and visa-versa, people blaming governments, governments blaming the money market, the oil crisis, etc. The church and educational system are blamed frequently for the breakdown in cultural and moral values.

A great deal of anger is projected into the environment, a common feature in contemporary society, expressed in terrorist activities, escalating crime rates and a generally destructive attitude to life and property. Urban riots (as in Britain, 1985) indicate something of the cultural anger, bottled up in our contemporary dying civilisation.

The anger tends to be misunderstood by both the authorities and those exhibiting the feeling. The former tend to respond by new and 'more effective' control measures while the angry demand better and fairer services and opportunities; both groups, subconsciously, are trying to patch-up an outdated system and, consequently, are still operating at the *denial* level. They yet have to learn the painful lesson that the better future to which they 'angrily' aspire, is to be found, not within the system they know, but in a reality as yet unborn.

In time, many 'angry young men' (John Osborne) become frustrated both by their own anger and the clear awareness that their destructive attitudes and behaviour only compound the mess in which, already, they are enmeshed. Even the conviction that the destruction of the capitalist system is a prerequisite for the utopian communist state, where all share equally in the good things of life, loses something of its euphoria and appeal. Then the anger tends to 'freeze'; it moves inside and coagulates creating a new quality of resistance or response, popularly known as *depression*.

I do not wish to suggest that all forms of depression can be equated with 'frozen anger', but I wish to submit that the link between the two is stronger than traditional psychology was prepared to acknowledge. Kubler-Ross does not draw immediate connections between these two states, inserting the third phase, *bargaining* between anger and depression. This order may be more directly applicable to personal death or grief; even then the stages may not follow each other in strict order, and the feelings present at any one time may be a mixture of some or all of the five phases. In the case of social or cultural death (decay or decline), however, the *bargaining* phase may succeed the *denial* rather than the *anger*. We will now explore Kubler-Ross's third stage.

3. *Bargaining*. In the case of the terminally-ill person, this phase is frequently marked by a tendency to bargain with God: 'If I am spared or get a reprieve, I'll pray more' or 'If I change my ways, God may spare me'. Resisting the death is not as absolute as at the denial or anger stages; its inevitability is more easily accepted. A degree of inner freedom is achieved, acknowledging that only some higher power can prevent the dreaded outcome. This may be the first step in accepting one's death with dignity and

equanimity.

At a social and cultural level the bargaining stage is a great deal more complex although easily identifiable. Things have got so bad that many can identify the inevitable demise, be it that of a movement, institution or nation. Members may even talk about and discuss the inevitable perdition, but in resorting to action a different type of logic prevails: 'Perhaps we can change our way of doing things. . . if we use another approach. . . if we play the cards differently. . . things might not turn out quite so bad.' Superficial change at the external, surface level may ensue; obviously it will not offset the inevitable; apart from anything else, reform has come too late!

Nowhere has the bargaining mentality been more widely and destructively used in recent years than in Trade Union strategy, particularly in the effort to save jobs. In the face of impending closure of factory, shop or business, often necessitated by the outdated nature of old, high-cost technology or precipitated by modern, marketing demands, unions frequently adopt a stand of 'digging-in one's heels', thus prolonging the inevitable outcome by a series of negotiations for short-term gains which are perceived to salvage individual jobs, but with little thought or concern for the overall common good.

Meanwhile the misguided negotiating process tends to be accompanied by stoppages and strikes, all of which only exacerbate the decline and decay. When the closures eventually happen, workers may be bitter and even distraught because 'false promises' have got them nowhere. Occasionally (perhaps frequently), workers feel pleased because of the 'lump sum' their union successfully negotiated. Amid this air of personal greed few consider the social or cultural damage caused to the many, so that the few may benefit. Elsewhere in the economy, the negative and destructive repercussions have a ripple effect. In time, not just a few factories, but a whole productive economy may be grinding to a halt. There are indications that this is happening today right across the developed nations.

What our trade unionists need is the insight, vision and creativity to accept the inevitable outcome and redirect their time and energies towards the exploration of alternative work-options. Trade unions have adopted very negative attitudes to entrepreneurs and to people with pioneering spirits within the

DEATH-STAGES OF KUBLER-ROSS
APPLIED TO SOCIAL AND CULTURAL DECLINE

Stage	Dominant Response	Typical Reaction
Denial	Rationalisation	'It can't be happening to us' 'I don't believe a word of it' 'All this "new age" rubbish!'
Anger	Displacement and blame	'Western governments have a lot to answer for' 'The Second Vatican Council destroyed the Catholic church' 'Feminism is the curse of this generation'
Bargaining	An attempt to defer or deflect the crisis	'Suppose we make some changes, we may get a reprieve' 'There must be a way out of this dilemma' 'These things may happen in the third world but not here'
Depression	Hopelessness, helplessness and guilt	'Everything seems to be falling apart' 'The end of the world must be approaching' 'After all our trouble. . .' 'Why bother – there's no point!'
Acceptance	A glimmer of hope; a willingness to let-go.	'If you can't beat them join them' 'Pulling-up roots is so painful, but it seems to be our only option' 'Where do we go from here?'

traditional industries – often in the name of preserving jobs. Such gross selfishness and manipulative greed has doomed to extinction many enterprises which otherwise might have survived with the aid of new talent and fresh approaches.

The trade union movement prides itself in being the voice of the rank and file. The movement has achieved a great deal in bringing status and dignity to the worker. However, in recent times, the unions have frequently exceeded their brief. In this capacity, they represent an upsurge in the power of the ordinary people, noted as early as 1967 in the French student protests and in recent times by the rise of laity in church life, feminism, a better status for handicapped people, etc. The right to bargain and the power to do so are admirable achievements of modern culture, but the corresponding *duties* have been conveniently ignored or underrated.

I do not wish to suggest that the type of bargaining outlined above is the only or main feature of Kubler-Ross's third stage as applied to social and cultural institutions. In my opinion, it is one of its clearest and most powerful applications. No less clear and, perhaps, even more lethal is the swing to the right in both political and ecclesiastical life. The bargaining stance goes somewhat like this: we need strong, clear-headed leaders who will outline the rules unambiguously, ensure they are applied and observed by all; in this way we hope to get order into the chaos and get things 'back to normal'.

'Normality' in this context means the stability and conformity of former times, a stifling and stultifying feature of life which served the old order well, but which is alien to the spirit and structure of the emerging culture. This quality of bargaining, basing its hopes on forms of leadership which come precariously close to being dictatorships, is obvious in such Western 'democracies' as the USA and Britain and also in religious systems such as Islam and Roman Catholicism.

The travesty in adopting a bargaining stance is that decline and disintegration are acknowledged but perceived as alien and to be avoided if at all possible. 'Bargainers' work out of a very functional and short-sighted frame of reference. And when one method fails they try another. Contrary to the experience of the terminally-ill, there is no guarantee that social/cultural resistance to death expressed in bargaining behaviour will lead eventually to the fourth stage of depression. At the social/cultural level, the bargainer is much more likely to become 'stuck' and remain locked in a perpetual search for 'ways to fix it'. One assumes that at some stage anger begins to erupt, providing the triggering-off mechanism for the fourth stage to which we now turn our attention.

4. *Depression*. As already indicated this is a more likely successor to *anger* rather than to *bargaining*, especially in the case of the social/cultural death experience. At this stage, the person facing death begins to face the inescapable. Resistances gradually diminish and a mood of hopelessness, helplessness and lethargy predominates. According to Kubler-Ross, there are two distinct phases: one of *reactive* depression, focused on what has to be left behind and one of *preparatory* depression, centred on what needs to be done before the end.

Both phases are also discernible in social/cultural breakdown and more specifically in coping with change. Faced with a new and altered experience people may spend much time bemoaning the 'good old days'. No longer do they talk in terms of getting back to normality; they have moved beyond that stage; in their hearts they know things will never be the same again. The old order is finished, much as they would like to resurrect it; all they can do is grieve about it.

As with the terminally-ill person, it is very important to give people experiencing such feelings much attention and acceptance. People need space and time to grieve about the things they cherished, the enterprises and institutions to which they may have given the love and commitment of many years. If people are given appropriate space and support to grieve at this *reactive* phase, then the *preparatory* is likely to follow in a much more integrated way.

In *preparatory* depression, the numbness and listlessness is left behind (in a large measure, at least) and energies tend to be directed on a course of making 'the best of what is left' or 'preparing for the future'. The terminally-ill person begins making renewed contact with others, allowing her own and others' experiences to enter her consciousness. In the social/cultural context people begin to query the new order (begrudgingly, at first), and explore what it might have to offer for their growth and enhancement. The way has been opened for the fifth and final stage.

5. *Acceptance*. Being able to accept one's own death (or the loss incurred through bereavement, unemployment, serious accident or failure) is a courageous and liberating experience and leads to increased self-reliance. Those who care for the dying in our homes and hospitals frequently witness the serenity and peacefulness of dying people especially when they have negotiated successfully the stages outlined above and this rarely happens without thorough, professional counselling. It is sometimes observed that people, in these final hours of life, seem to be controlling their own destiny as in the case of the person who passes on shortly after the last member of the family has arrived from some distant land. Relatives and friends can be immensely relieved, often feeling privileged to have witnessed such a death experience.

In the social/cultural realm, the acceptance stage marks the final parting with the old order. Former securities and familiar structures are left behind; a new and risky enterprise, often an 'unknown' is embarked upon. It is important to note that this final stage is not so much an *evolution* in which the old progressively gives way to the new. A new reality has been born with the trauma and ecstasy of every new birth. It is more a *transformation* than an *evolution*. The old is present in the new, but so transformed as to be virtually unrecognisable. In language, at once deeply spiritual and pragmatic, it is a *starting all over again*.

Death and Resurrection

Only spiritual/religious language can elucidate the nature of this transformation which is articulated with varying degrees of clarity in all the great religions of man. In the christian faith, we speak of *death* and *resurrection*. The mystery of Christ's dying and rising again becomes a great deal more comprehensible when interpreted in the light of Kubler-Ross's paradigm. So often our preachers tell us: 'Christ had to die. . .', and we wonder why? The answer quite simply is: because he was a powerful agent (prophet) of transformation.

Jesus came to set up a new Kingdom (i.e. inaugurate a new order of events). It could not happen until the old one died and in the torment, suffering and death of Christ is represented all that was passing away. And we find the resurrection so hard to comprehend! We seek to interpret it in the light of previous events and often we dismiss it as a mythical or legendary tale. It is the articulation of a new, a *totally new*, reality, a novel way of being, of living, or relating to the created order. Resurrection doesn't follow on death in sequential order (as the writer of John's Gospel succinctly perceives). Death and resurrection complement each other as *life-forces* at different ends of a spectrum.

Today, we live in a world engulfed by death. Globally, culturally, socially, an old order is fragmenting and there is nothing we can do to save it. In fact, the most liberating thing we can do is accept it, strive to understand it and be open to the seeds of resurrection which fertilise in the ashes of every death. I know of no model which explains so profoundly the nature of our contemporary cultural crisis as that of Elizabeth Kubler-Ross. To the best of my knowledge, Kubler-Ross herself has never applied her conceptual framework to the social/cultural context. It has been done by others, especially those in sociological and psychological disciplines aimed at interpreting and understanding the upheaval and chaos of modern life. Without referring explicitly to Kubler-Ross, writers such as Peter Marris (1974) and Elliot Jaques (1970, especially pp. 38-63) reinforce her many insights in their analysis of the human 'loss of meaning' in varous life-crises, unemployment included.

The scene outlined in the present chapter leaves little room for hope or optimism. Paradoxically, it engenders much hope and empowers people to comprehend and cope with an otherwise hopeless situation. For a start, it accepts the negative reality and does not try to rationalise or explain it away; in itself, this can be deeply liberating. It acknowledges the power and finality of death while poignantly demonstrating that death never has the final word.

Individually, socially, culturally and globally, neither ourselves nor the earth we inhabit, will accept extinction as our ultimate destiny. Some powerful inner voice keeps on saying: 'There is no such thing as ultimate death.' René Dubos (1976) and others indicate how rapidly areas of the earth devastated by the atom bombs of the Second World War regained the diversity of species and life-forms in existence prior to the destruction. From an evolutionary perspective we can surmise that in the event of

nuclear extinction, life on earth would return to its present richness and diversity within a thousand years, possibly in a time-span
much shorter than this, which, in either case is merely a few
seconds in the evolutionary time-scale.

The nature and impact of change hinges around death and
resurrection, two universal movements ever at play – at all levels
of life and existence. At the present time the death experience
predominates. In time, it will yield pride of place to resurrection
but already, I suggest, the seeds of new life are sprouting amid
the cinders of a dying civilisation. In the midst of darkness and
despair there are signs of hope and glimpses, however vague, of
what the new order looks like:

> Behind the impressive overlay of our technological Disneyland with
> its infinite opportunities for both creative and destructive play, we
> glimpse a wasteland. We sense and experience a wasteland of the
> human spirit, a purgatory of model personalities who, living in terms
> of a dead past, are lost and unresponsive to the potential in the present.
> We see the bleached bones of broken symbols, shattered ideals and
> dead ways of being in the world. But we at the threshold perceive,
> too, the possibility of a wasteland transformed and a world reborn.
> (Cohen-Richards, 1973, p.2.)

To that new vision we now turn our attention.

3: A New Vision of Life on Earth

It is, when one thinks of it, a rather substantial sin of omission to omit the cosmos itself. – MATTHEW FOX

Without mysticism, there can be no successful religion: and there can be no well-founded mysticism apart from faith in some unification of the universe.

– TEILHARD DE CHARDIN

We are sitting our final evolutionary examination for our viability as a species. – THE GAIA ATLAS

In the opening chapter we referred to de Chardin's prediction of a new evolutionary leap marked by a transformation taking place primarily at the psychic and spiritual levels of life. To many people, with a passion for scientific verification this is a wild, unsubstantiated claim. Indeed, every evolutionary leap defies rational explanation and only makes sense retrospectively. Nor can we subscribe too seriously to the theory that there have been major catastrophes throughout the course of evolution that strip the theory of progressive and cumulative progress of much credibility. Life does not unfold in a neat, easily-analysed progression, but intuitive observation points to a world-in-process, gradually unfolding in an ever-enriching complexity and destined for an ultimate flowering, probably some billions of years away.

Without such an evolutionary perspective it is well nigh impossible to interpret present-day reality in a meaningful way. We live in a rapidly changing world, but it is *change with a purpose*, the creation of a new global consciousness and the transformation into new realms of being. We have outlined the signs of death and decay, indicative of the old order. In the present and subsequent chapters, I wish to explore the emerging global vision with its network of relationships, popularly known as the *new paradigm*.

Object or Organism?

In 1969, for the first time in history, man landed on the moon. All over the world news media hailed the achievement with joy and admiration. What never hit the headlines, although often noted in books and journals, was the deep spiritual experience of the astronauts as they stepped on the surface of the moon and perhaps, more awe-inspiring, their view of planet earth, observed from outer-space. On returning home, they shared their experiences and observations, speaking at length about their perception of the earth from space. Somehow or other, it did not resemble the rock-like, objective, stable reality they had assumed it to be. Instead, it resembled a living, *breathing organism*, an embodiment of life, purpose and meaning. And the astronauts all felt a new bond with the earth, a relationship they express in a variety of words:

> The first thing that came to mind as I looked at. . . planet earth floating in the vastness of space. . . was its incredible beauty. . . a blue and white jewel suspended against a velvet black sky. . . The presence of divinity became almost palpable and *I knew* that life in the universe was not just an accident based on random processes. This knowledge came to me directly – noetically. . . an experiential cognition.
>
> (Words of Edgar D. Mitchell quoted by Murchie, 1979, p. 618.)

> You realise that on that small spot, that little blue and white thing, is everything that means anything to you – all of history and music and poetry and art and death and birth and love, tears, joy, games, all of it on that little spot out there. . . You recognise that you are a piece of this total life. . . And when you come back, there is a difference in that world now. There is a difference in that relationship between you and that planet and you and all those other forms of life on that planet, because you've had that kind of experience.
>
> (Words of Russell Schweickart, quoted by Russell, 1982, p. 4.)

> I really believe that if the political leaders of the world could see their planet from a distance. . . their outlook would be fundamentally changed. . . I think the view from 100,000 miles could be invaluable in getting people together to work out joint solutions, by causing them to realise that the planet we share unites us in a way far more basic and far more important than differences in skin, colour or religion or economic system. . . If I could use only one word to describe the earth as seen from the moon, I would ignore both its size and colour and

search for a more elemental quality, that of fragility. The earth appears 'fragile' above all else. I don't know why, but it does.

(Michael Collins, 1974, pp. 470, 471.)

Already in 1948, the astronomer, Fred Hoyle had written: 'Once a photograph of the earth taken from outside is available. . . a new idea, as powerful as any other in history, will be let loose.' Earlier still, in 1919, James Jeans had suggested that the universe should be perceived as a great thought rather than a great machine. In 1969, the cumulative wisdom of creation spirituality, as articulated by both mystics and scientists down through the ages, seemed to create a new morphic resonance. The journey to the moon was not merely a voyage to outer space; it also proved to be an expedition to the inner realms of the earth, the birth of a new cosmology.

Even rationally minded scientists were touched by this mystical vision. Could it be true that the earth is, in fact, a living organism? One of the first to explore this possibility was the British biochemist, James Lovelock, who suggested that the earth thrives and survives as a living biosystem with its diverse parts – plants, animals, fungi, humans, along with the atmosphere, the oceans and the soil, all inter-related and interdependent. Lovelock suggests that the creative interaction within the biosystem is poised in a delicate and intricate manner. Planetary homeostatis is maintained by an amazing and mysterious interaction of chemical components such as oxygen, salt, ammonia, sulphur, nitrogen, methane, among others. The ozone layer in the upper atmosphere seems to be the earth's gentle guardian, maintaining the amazing and fascinating matrix in a self-regulatory, life-giving balance.

With an apparent reservation, Lovelock suggests that we, humans, may be the nervous system of *Gaia* (Lovelock's name for the biosystem, derived from the Greek earth-mother goddess, *Ge*), a very different status from that envisaged in the Book of *Genesis* (Old Testament) where man is considered to be the master of creation, and an image totally at variance with Francis Bacon's model scientist who is to keep torturing nature until she reveals all her secrets.

According to the Gaia hypothesis, all life-forms are interdependent and inter-related. We humans do not have exemplary status, other than in the fact of being the conscious dimension of the cosmos. And that 'superior' awareness is not for self-aggrandisement, but to be put at the service of the creative process. Spiritual theories suggesting that man saves his soul by fleeing the world, or the prominent alternative that the human being is unique in creation because of a special relationship with God, are both inadequate spiritualities for the new global consciousness.

There are no privileged beings in the biosphere. Mother Earth nourishes and nurtures all her family (from humans to insects) according to the uniqueness of each member. Every organism, both animate and inanimate, contributes in an unique way to earth's growth and evolution, and *all* life-forms are essential to the well-being of Mother Earth. Life flourishes and flowers on the mutual interaction and interdependence of creatures, great and small. None has a superior status to the other; no one 'species' can claim rights over the other, nor may they exploit the others for the satisfaction of needs. In the words of Theodore Roszak: 'The needs of the planet are the needs of the person; the rights of the persons are the rights of the planet.'

The new order poses fresh challenges, among them being the invitation to let go of our manipulative and domineering urge to control and subdue, to exploit and jeopardise the resources of nature. We have ravaged the womb that sustains us and consequently, are engulfed in a death of our own making. The freedom to enter into a reciprocal relationship with the earth, as distinct from the role of the distant and unfeeling technocrat, is a first precondition for a place in tomorrow's world. But the needed conversion, the change of heart, is probably beyond the majority of mankind, conditioned into being mechanical functionaries; they will die with the old order. Their survival would mean the death of the earth, but the earth has a strange and powerful resilience (a corollary to Lovelock's thesis) in the face of which, humanity rather than the planet is likely to perish.

The Self-Organising Universe

Erich Jantsch (1980), a systems theorist at Berkeley University, California, explores the Gaia hypothesis from an evolutionary perspective. Here, the word, *evolution* means neither the random growth based on pure chance (Darwin's view) nor the progressive, stable, almost predictable quality of growth or progress.

Jantsch, along with his associates of the holistic paradigm, views the universe as an *open* system, vastly complex, with a continuous interplay between the emergence of the new and the confirmation of the old. In such a world *equilibrium* is the equivalent of stagnation and death. A high degree of non-equilibrium, which sustains the self-organising process is, in turn, maintained by a continuous exchange of matter and energy with the environment. The dynamic forces for such a globally stable, but never-resting structure Jantsch calls 'autopoiesis' (the propensity for self reproduction and self-renewal).

The process of self-renewal has neither beginning nor end. It is happening all the time especially in the interaction between what Jantsch calls the *micro* and *macro* levels of evolution. The former refers to the evolution of different life-forms ranging from the original single-celled organisms (prokaryotes and eu-ckaryotes) to complex creatures like humans; and the latter refers to the evolution of the biosphere itself. Jantsch claims that these two processes are interdependent. For example, the original pro-karyotes lived without oxygen since there was little or none in the atmosphere, but almost from the beginning these minute creatures began to modify their environment and after billions of years produced oxygen through photo-synthesis, augmenting in this way their own evolutionary growth (into eukaryotes) but also paving the way for the emergence of new life-forms. Meanwhile, the macroscopic biosphere creates its own microscopic life by maintaining a level of *homeostasis* – a state of dynamic balance characterised by multiple interdependent fluctuations. Consequently, new life or new growth is not simply a matter of an organism adapting to a given environment but rather from the *co-evolution* of both organism and environment at all levels of life.

Guy Murchie (1979, p. 15) provides a rather vivid example of co-evolutionary interdependence:

> While the bubble of life is materially concentrated in the fifteen-mile-thick earth skin of sea, soil and densest air, it is fuelled and fed from energy in the planet's core and mantle and from the sun and stars. And it is bound together not only by gravitational, electromagnetic and nuclear cohesion but also by a kind of surface tension of inter-dependency, of chemical and psychological needs and intellectual accelerations interlaced with mystic, sometimes explosive spiritual forces.

MODEL OF CO-EVOLUTIONARY INTERDEPENDENCE

COMMUNITY

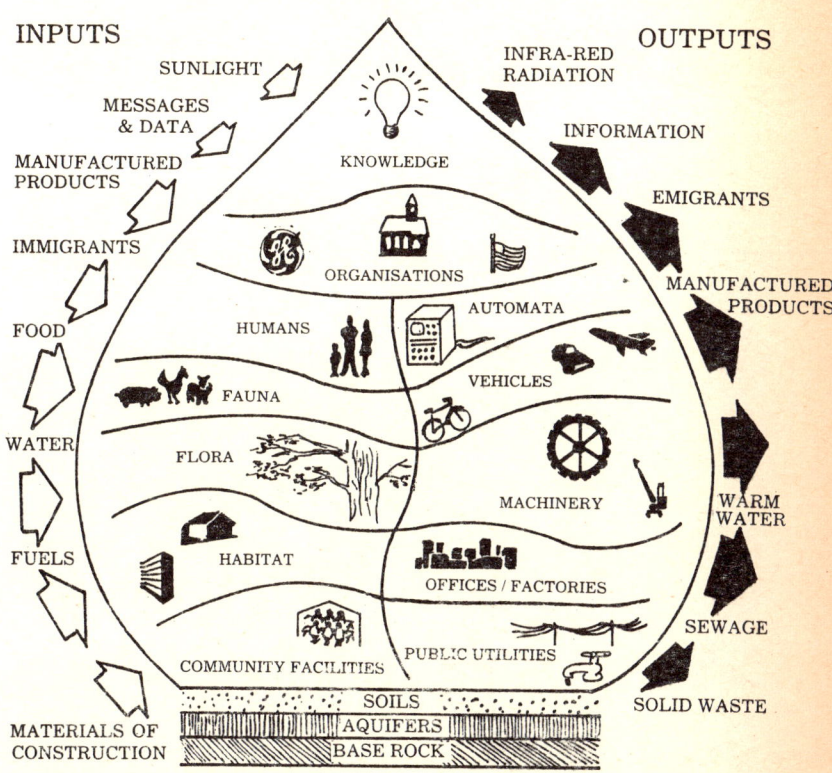

INPUTS

SUNLIGHT
MESSAGES & DATA
MANUFACTURED PRODUCTS
IMMIGRANTS
FOOD
WATER
FUELS
MATERIALS OF CONSTRUCTION

KNOWLEDGE
ORGANISATIONS
HUMANS
AUTOMATA
FAUNA
VEHICLES
FLORA
MACHINERY
HABITAT
OFFICES / FACTORIES
COMMUNITY FACILITIES
PUBLIC UTILITIES
SOILS
AQUIFERS
BASE ROCK

OUTPUTS

INFRA-RED RADIATION
INFORMATION
EMIGRANTS
MANUFACTURED PRODUCTS
WARM WATER
SEWAGE
SOLID WASTE

Source: Richard L. Meier, 'Energy and Habitat', *Futures*, 16 (1984), 351-371 at p. 354.

From a chemical standpoint alone, animal life without plants to eat would starve quicker but no more surely than most plants would die without animals. Even minerals would be drastically disturbed without both these higher kingdoms. It has been calculated that photosynthesis in present terrestrial vegetation would literally consume all the carbon dioxide out of the atmosphere within a year or two if it were not replenished by smoke from fires, engine fumes, and the exhalations of animals and other consumers or decomposers. (See Diagram, p. 51.)

Evolution is not a deterministic, progressive process, whereby organisms adapt (by change or by design) to create equilibrium. The working principle is *order through fluctuation*, creating an ever increasing complexity through which the *open* system survives and flourishes.

And yet, this is not a random process. It is characterised by purpose and a sense of direction, not so much in terms of a divine beginning or an ultimate end, but by virtue of an innate, ever-active, self-organising propensity which Jantsch calls *mind*; this quality he describes as an in-built, all-pervasive wisdom, facilitating order and harmony through the apparently chaotic and disorganised life of the unfolding universe. Hence his statement: 'God is not the creator but the mind of the universe' (p. 308), that creative force which confers *meaning* and *purpose*. The search for meaning expresses itself primarily in the *interconnectedness* of the various life-forms. It is the task of religion, says Jantsch, to discover and explore these connections; in this way, religion becomes '. . . the core of creative action' (p. 300).

Initially, Jantsch's highly elaborate exposé may give the impression that humans are swept along by an evolutionary drive, in some predetermined fashion. Quite the contrary! Human creativity forms an integral part of *co-evolution*. Humans are destined to become the conscious expression of those values best suited to the final destiny of the evolutionary process itself. Consequently, attention must not be on our *rights* as if somehow we were entitled to a privileged place in the universe. In agreement with Geoffrey Vickers, Jantsch maintains that '. . . rights constitute a static and defensive structure-oriented concept, whereas the acceptance of responsibility implies creative participation in the design of the human world' (p. 265). This responsibility in its ultimate expression means a growth in *self-transcendence*.

In other words, we are invited to cultivate a new attitude towards the earth and towards creation at large, whereby we acknowledge and accept the universe's own creative design, its own inherent growth-orientation which we must not change or manipulate for mere personal or material gain. Instead, we must foster a new relationship – in thought and action – with the universe of which we are a *part*, and not an external manager. Only with this renewed consciousness can we hope to tune-in with the 'mind' of the universe and thus enhance (rather than inhibit) the growth of creation which is also the goal and destiny of humankind. (Jantsch, 1980, pp. 183-184.)

In rather technical language, Jantsch formulates a theory of universal and earthly development to which scholars of many disciplines subscribe, namely, that life on earth does not thrive on a static, stable state of equilibrium, a framework which seeks to keep change to a minimum, but rather on a process of interdependence and interaction, based on fluctuation and fluidity, often marked by apparent randomness in its individual movements but congruent and unified at a higher unobservable level.

So often we humans, seek to impose meaning and structure and a degree of stability on what we can physically observe and control, largely because we fail to perceive the global, holistic (invisible) forces (what Lovelock and Jantsch call the *self-organising, dynamic principle*) which give unity and purpose to our world. The hardest lesson we, humans of the *twentieth* century (and the approaching twenty-first), have to learn is that we live in world of continuous, profound change; that this change is inherent to the world's and our own well-being; that we cannot arrest or modify this changing nature of reality, no matter how much we try. In other words, we cannot conquer or control the world we inhabit.

Positively, we can only contribute to the ongoing growth and evolution when we ourselves become attuned to the climate of change, and begin to feel at home in its richness, diversity and advance. And that is the major challenge facing us as a new evolutionary age dawns upon us.

Extended Relationships

The word *relationship*, as popularly used, has a distinctive, personal flavour. It seeks to describe those forms of human interaction which facilitate emotional, social or spiritual bonds between people. In the holistic paradigm, *relationships* are considered to be both the essence and purpose of life. Life evolves, not according to a predetermined plan following strict linear progression, but as a process that gathers momentum according as the diverse elements of creation begin to relate with each other in a more effective way. It is in the creative interplay of the elements that life unfolds.

Adaptation and natural selection is not based on a survival of the fittest, but more accurately on the *survival of the most sensitive*. It is those species which can adopt new behaviours, creating new and enriching interactions with other life-forms, that survive, and not just in a biological sense, but more particularly in the creative, innovative potential which marks all evolutionary growth.

The quality of relationships marking our next evolutionary leap will be characterised by *breadth* rather than *intensity*. Being deeply in love with the 'few' will yield pride of place to that love which seeks to connect us with all that is lovable in life. The exclusiveness of relationships, especially in the domain of human fellowship, will extend to include a wider variety of spiritual, human and ecological experiences. Intimacy will not be pulvarised, but greatly enriched, indeed, *transformed*, with a lifelong quality largely unknown in today's world.

Is this mere speculation? Readers in touch with the rising ecological consciousness of the past few decades can vouch for this new vision. Ecology, more than any other sphere of contemporary science, portrays how central relationships are to our growth and survival on planet earth. All living forms are interdependent (see Diagram on p. 55). *We absolutely need each other*, and we need each other's tenderness, love and care.

> Everything in this world is connected with everything else in a delicate and complex web of interrelationships. The best computer ever designed by humankind still cannot calculate even a tiny fraction of all the relationships that exist in the ecosystem of a simple pond. Scientists have tried it and have only thrown up their hands in despair after realising the complexity and detail involved.' (Jeremy Rifkin, 1985, p. 244.)

Our traditional ecology and cosmology, based on hierarchical

ECOLOGICAL INTERRELATIONSHIPS OF THE ECOSYSTEM

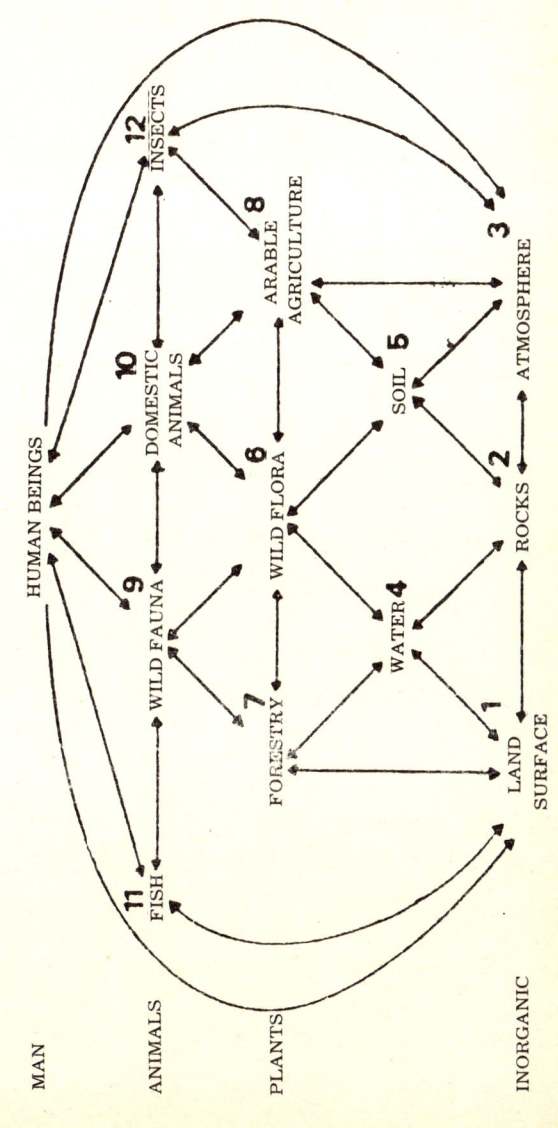

Source: Paul Rogers, 1972, p. 10.

priority of man over animal, animal over plant, living matter over
inanimate, is riddled with contradiction and has led to untold pain
and suffering on this earth. We may venture to suggest that the
accumulation of pain and misery in today's world is the result of
the cruelty that we, humans, have inflicted, not just on each other,
but on life at large.

We have ravaged the earth, polluted our air, ruthlessly killed
animals, poisoned the atmosphere, savagely and thoughtlessly
interfered in the pattern and flow of nature. And then we wonder
why children die of leukemia; why so many people die of
coronories and cancer; why so much meaningless suffering in the
world? The answer is quite simple: *we, humans, invent it.*

There is no mystery about suffering. Every major religious system has its 'mystery of the cross', which is largely a spiritual
rationalisation justifying humans in continuing their barbaric lifestyle, enabling us to cast our eyes to heaven so that we don't have
to look at the mess we have created on earth. When we begin to
treat nature in a nurturing, caring and healing way, nature will
nurture, care for and heal us. Within ourselves and within our
world are all the resources we need to be healthy, happy people.
But we are not connected *integrally* either with each other or
with the world we inhabit; that is the root of our problem.

The diagram (on p. 55) is a simple, ecological outline of the
interrelationships at work in the ecosystem. Poignantly, it portrays the interdependency of the various elements. Remove any
one element and the others are not merely deprived; their very
survival is seriously threatened. Ironic as it may seem the top layer
'human beings' could be removed without serious threat to the
survival of all the other elements. It is a sobering reminder that
the earth and its diversity of life-forms survived for some four-
hundred-million years without man. Our time-span as a species
on this earth, covering ten to fourteen million years is merely 7%
of the entire evolutionary time-scale. And yet, we act, talk and
think as if somehow we engineered the whole creative 'display'.

To unlearn our aggressive and arrogant attitude to creation is
the greatest challenge of our times; without this profound and
radical conversion we stand little chance of entering the new age.
It's a time for letting-go and letting-be. It's not the physical,
external control that matters anymore; it's the interior, psychic,
spiritual disposition that feels no need to affirm itself at the cost

of all other created phenomena. In this new outlook rests our greatest hope. We are confronted with a new quality of freedom which will not be won by *might* or *right*, but by a trusting surrender to the mystery we live within:

> But there is only one way to overcome the ignorance in the world: surrender. The only power the forces of ignorance have is the power we give them by our fears and resistance. When we agree with our adversary by total faith, total surrender, all false powers have nothing more to sustain them. (Walter Starcke, 1974, p. 104.)

Systems and Networks

The holistic, interdependent perception of life evokes a new mode of understanding, outlined in the interdisciplinary study known as *General Systems Theory*. The theory was outlined in the late 1940s when biologists such as Ludwig von Bertalanffy and Paul Weiss began to note the common properties underlying widely different phenomena. General Systems Theory, therefore, is not really a theory but rather a new way of looking at life through the combined insights of various disciplines without which we could not comprehend the connections and relationships which enable all systems to function in a creative and harmonious way.

A basic tenet of the *General Systems Theory* is that nothing can be understood in isolation; everything is part of a system. According to James Miller (1978), a leading proponent of this new approach, all living systems are composed of subsystems which take-in, process and excrete matter, energy or information (or combinations of these). And by virtue of an inner, self-organising principle, the various subsystems work in harmony for the good of the whole.

Specialisation has been and still is an outstanding feature of the Western value-system. Aided by bureaucratic technology it has served us well, but today, it has gone awry. Trade unionists bicker as to who may or may not perform a specific task; professionals demand exorbitant fees on the grounds of special skills, the educational system (of many Western nations) is largely geared to the 25-30% of the young population eligible to take degrees at a third-level institute; yet, it is imposed on the remaining 60-65% for whom it may be largely if not totally irrelevant.

The contemporary town-planner may serve as a good example

for whom a training based on General Systems Theory is highly desirable: he/she needs to be well versed in basic engineering, sociology, social psychology, ecology and health care. Many such tasks can no longer be done effectively by one person, or even by the few with individually, specialised qualifications; what is needed is a *team* whose members are all well informed in an interdisciplinary way.

To describe the teamwork envisaged in interdisciplinary co-operation, we employ the term *Network*. We may use the analogy of a fishing net with its intricate intersecting lines. The net is useful and effective when all the intersections are intact; as these snap or tear away, the net becomes progressively useless. In modern usage, *networks* consist of conglomerates of interconnections between people and resources so that *together* we can achieve with greater impact what would be less effective if achieved on an individual basis. But there is also a qualitative variable; each member/resource brings its uniqueness to the task in hand so that the complementarity of diverse elements can create a holistic outcome:

> A network is the total relational field of a person and usually has a space/time representation. Although a network has a low degree of visibility, it has a high degree of information-exchange properties. A network has few normal rules, but consists of relationships between many persons, some of whom are known to many others in the network, while others merely form a linkage between persons. (Speck & Attneave, 1973, p. 10)

Boissevain & Clyde (1973, pp. 9ff) indicate how the concept of (social) network has been employed in tackling problems of modern urban societies and of changing peasant and tribal communities, because of a dissatisfaction with the strictly structural approach. To cope with modern complexities we need a new strategy for utilising the diverse gifts and talents of the social community. What we cannot achieve in isolation we can attain through the social network. Society benefits from our cumulative wisdom and we ourselves are invigorated by the creative interaction of the network system.

The development of the social network marks an important departure from the control and manipulation of the isolated individual to a new social and holistic consciousness reminding us that we each need the cumulative wisdom and mutual support of our fellow men and women if we are to negotiate successfully the transition into tomorrow's world.

Mysticism and Holism

Psychic/spiritual evolution knows no individual building blocks, except in their relationship to each other and to the ecosystem which they serve. It may seem a *totally* new vision. It signifies a notable departure from the past and present, but it is not as original as it seems initially, nor is it without historical precedent. In every age and culture there are those whose vision and value-system ground them in a reality different from the prevailing ethos. Among such groups are *mystics*, who feature in all major world religions. Often they are misunderstood and may be considered bizarre, weird and totally out of touch with reality. Retrospectively, they are remembered for their holiness and heroic asceticism. Because of the extreme and exclusive nature of their sanctity they more readily win the admiration of monks and cloistered contemplatives rather than the approval of society's rank and file. Today, there is a revival of the mystical tradition, with a more favourable impression of the mystical impact on human and earthly civilisation.

In every age and in every culture, mystics are the guardians of human and earthly integrity. They jolt us out of our comfortable and routine existence as they remind us of our interconnectedness with the transcendent, within our own lives, within our world, and within the eternal scope of life itself. The mystics are the ones who supersede all categories and divisions, all barriers and legalities, all dichotomies and superficial distinctions. The following is a typically mystical perception, written by Honorius of Autun about 1125 AD:

> All in God's creation gives great delight to anyone looking upon it, for in some things there is beauty, as in flowers; in others healing, as in herbs; in others food, as in produce; in others meaning, as in snakes and birds. . . The supreme Artisan made the universe like a great zither upon which he placed strings to yield a variety of sounds. . . A harmonious cord is sounded by spirit and body, angel and devil, heaven and hell, fire and water, air and earth, sweet and bitter, soft and hard, and so are all other things harmonised. (Quoted by Matthew Fox, 1984, p. 70.)

Spiritually, we tend to depict the mystics in a role that suits our own limited consciousness: people of sanctity and holiness, immersed in prayer and contemplation, almost a class apart from the rest of humanity, with little interest in human or earthly affairs. We make them look so heavenly as to divest them of all earthly appeal. Walter Stace (1960), in a well known work, presents another view, a very necessary one for a balanced and complete picture of the mystical phenomenon. Stace differentiates *extrovertive* and *introvertive* mysticism. The former exhibits the following characteristics:

a) All things are perceived as one. Though the mystic sees trees, people, houses, etc., they mysteriously appear to be identical and/or rooted in some unity which lies behind them;

b) The world is experienced as alive or conscious; reality is perceived to be a 'living presence';

c) The experience is characteristically a 'sense of objectivity or reality'. It does not seem to be merely an inner, subjective state of soul, but on the contrary, appears to have 'objective reference'. Those who have the experience cannot help but suppose that it involved a perception of reality;

d) The mystic enjoys a feeling of blessedness, joy, happiness, satisfaction;

e) What is apprehended is deemed to be holy, sacred or divine;

f) Paradoxicality is another feature of the experience, typically described in terms which, if taken seriously, are contradictory, odd, strained, even bizarre at times;

g) The experience and its object are allegedly ineffable. The mystic claims that they cannot be described adequately in words.

Along with the characteristics outlined above, *introvertive* mysticism exhibits the following features:

i) the devotee ceases to experience time and space; (We note in passing that contemporary physics also question the validity of these categories, cf. pp. 82-84).

ii) It is an unitary consciousness, often explained in the following manner:

— the mind of the mystic is emptied of ordinary things. Awareness of the phenomenal world vanishes. The mystic no longer remembers, reasons or imagines. The soul is stripped of abstract thoughts and sensuous images. Everything is pure awareness in a state superseding that of sleep or unconsciousness;

— the mystic experiences a One (Unity) which may be identified with the transcendant self, Nirvana, God, an exalted state of being;

— the mystic experiences union or identity with this one. The experience may be ecstatic, but also marked by pain and intense suffering.

The *extrovertive* and *introvertive* represent two poles of the mystical experience. The cosmic dimension has received scant attention, while the spiritual aspect tends to be portrayed as a victory over, or a rejection of, worldly reality. True mysticism rejects all dichotomies and dualisms. Its dominant orientation has been and continues to be, unitary and holistic, aimed at convergence rather than distinction.

Contrary to popular opinion, mysticism is not a comfortable cop-out for religious freaks. It is a vocation with immense global responsibility and, at an universal level, there is really no distinction between Eastern and Western forms, other than the Eastern tends to be more widely available and is much more solidly rooted in its cosmic ambiance.

Mysticism holds a vital clue to evolutionary growth and development. The mystic is receptively tuned to the creative life-impulse within and without, expressing something of the primeval human will-to-meaning, of the inbuilt urge to impose and extrapolate meaning from the diverse, even contradictory, experiences of life. The mystic holds together the polarities and opposites of existence, maintaining simultaneously an inner relationship with the mysterious, unchanging and all-powerful God and a sense of being at home with the changing, fragmented reality of daily life. The mystical pursuit is one of integration, holding together the diverse energies of universal life.

The popular perception that the mystic abandons the world and devotes her life to penance, prayer and austerity is not without foundation. However, it is merely one dimension of mysticism, by no means representative of either the essential nature of mystical experience nor of the universal expression of mystical holiness. In the West, we have inherited a very one-sided view, one cultivated by a culture so deprived in self-worth and healthy self-appreciation that it tended to admire heroism and the anti-world polemic portrayed in the lives of outstanding people. The limited impact, geographically and influentially, of this brand of mysticism is noted by the late J. A. T. Robinson (1967, p. 120):

> It is hardly surprising that the mystics have had a limited appeal. Yet, I am not convinced that this one-sided, anti-worldliness is of the essence of their contribution. It belongs partly to a Manichean, world-denying strain that entered Christian mysticism through Plotinus and Pseudo-Dionysius. It belongs also to a pre-scientific, pre-humanist, pre-industrial age in which if one cannot master the world, the only thing to do is to foresake it or try to forget it. No mystic writing today in fact uses *that* language.

We need to reclaim the more authentic, universal power of mysticism with its innate cosmological and ecological orientations. Firstly, we need to confront the frequently-expressed fear that creation-centred mysticism is a form of pantheism. On this topic we quote the Russian theologian, Nicholas Berdyaev (1935, p. 242):

> Mystics are always suspected of pantheistic leanings and, indeed, when an attempt is made to understand them rationally and to translate their experience into the terms of theology or metaphysics, they certainly come very close to pantheism. Yet, while pantheism is in reality a highly rationalistic doctrine, mysticism uses paradoxical and apparently contradictory expressions, because for the mystics both the identity between the creature and the Creator, and the gulf which separates them, are equally facts of existence.

Mysticism is a *practical*, not a *theoretical* wisdom. It articulates a divine-human relationship on the basis of *experience*, touching the depths of encounter but also the depths of estrangement. Just as Jesus, in his hour of agony, could address his Father in words of childlike trust: 'Father into your hands I commend my spirit', with equal, if not greater intensity, he shouted out: 'My God, my God, why have you forsaken me?' In the genuine mystic both aspects are held together; divinity is perceived to be at work in both. Modern writers use the term *panentheism* to describe this quality of godliness which the mystics perceive to be inherent in all living reality.

At first sight, Eastern mysticism seems far more global and ecological than its Western counterpart; that is a misconception as Fr Matthew Fox OP demonstrates in his books on creation-centred spirituality. Fox however, does concur with Capra's view that:

> The difference between Eastern and Western mysticism is that mystical schools have always played a marginal role in the West, whereas they constitute the main stream of Eastern philosophical and religious thought. (Capra, 1976, p. 24.)

Western spirituality has been heavily influenced by an 'otherworldly' outlook, generating an antipathy towards, or at best a suspicion of, any trend towards acknowledging the sacredness of human and earthly life. For a religion whose main focus is that of *incarnation*, Christian spirituality has been disappointingly dismissive of the created order.

Today, we experience a new spring of mystical zeal. Meister Eckhart, one of the great Christian mystics (condemned in the fourteenth century, for supporting the women's liberation (Beguines) and peasants movements of his day) is read and studied by Taoists, Hindus, Buddhists and some Christians. Meanwhile, writings of the Buddhist and Hindu tradition flood the Western market (cf. Ferguson, 1982, p. 400). Western scholars (notably students of comparative religion, psychology, physics and religion) move Eastwards in the footsteps of Teilhard de Chardin, Carl Jung and Thomas Merton, seeking the 'missing dimension' of the Western world-view. A strange and powerful global ecumenism encompasses our universe. It is not entering our lives through churches or formal religious systems; it seems to be transcending official structures, declaring them unsuitable, if not totally inappropriate, channels for this new force. Of course, mystics have never been favourably received, especially in the Christian churches, and not a small number of 'heretics' might well be mystics in a more favourable spiritual climate.

Today's mystical arena is a point of convergence for friend and foe of earlier times. Scientists dialogue with mystics, theologians consult psychologists, ecologists study the lives of the saints. Strange things are happening! The Spirit of God is at work where we least expect him (her), but where, perhaps, he always operates most creatively – on the fringes, in the marginal spaces of our lives and institutions. The marriage of modern science and Eastern mysticism is among the best documented of these new and inspiring moves:

> . . . the basic elements of the Eastern world view are also those of the world view emerging from modern physics. They are intended to

suggest that Eastern thought and, more generally, mystical thought provide a consistent and relevant philosophical background to the theories of contemporary science; a conception of the world in which scientific discoveries can be in perfect harmony with spiritual aims and religious beliefs. The two basic themes of this conception are the unity and interrelation of all phenomena and the intrinsically dynamic nature of the universe. The further we penetrate into the submicroscopic world, the more we shall realise how the modern physicist, like the Eastern mystic, has come to see the world as a system of inseparable, interacting and ever-moving components with the observer being an integral part of this system.

The organic, 'ecological' world view of the Eastern philosophies is no doubt one of the main reasons for the immense popularity they have recently gained in the West, especially among young people. In our Western culture, which is still dominated by the mechanistic, fragmented view of the world, an increasing number of people have seen this as the underlying reason for the widespread dissatisfaction in our society, and many have turned to Eastern ways of liberation. It is interesting, and perhaps not too surprising, that those who are attracted by Eastern mysticism, who consult the *I Ching* and practice yoga or other forms of meditation, in general have a marked anti-scientific attitude. They tend to see science, and physics in particular, as an unimaginative, narrow-minded discipline which is responsible for all the evils of modern technology. (Capra, 1976, pp. 30-31.)

In his more recent work, *The Turning Point*, Capra outlines the complementary nature of these two approaches:

The fact that modern physics, the manifestation of an extreme specialisation of the *rational* mind, is now making contact with mysticism, the essence of religion and manifestation of an extreme specialisation of the *intuitive* mind, shows very beautifully the unity and complementary nature of the rational and intuitive modes of consciousness. (Capra, 1982, p. 32.)

Creativity, intuition and imagination have been held suspect by religion and science alike. Religion popularly understood, is perceived to be a doctrinal package of moral codes and legal imperatives. It is seen as something external, with observance based on rules and practice, on ritual and ceremony. It has become excessively cerebral and institutional. Religion of the heart (the spiritual centre) has been neglected, even driven underground. Its retrieval is a matter of urgency, not alone for a

KEY NAMES IN THE NEW GLOBAL/ECOLOGICAL VISION

Name	Major Work	Leading Theory
Thomas Kuhn	*The Structure of Scientific Revolutions*, Chicago University Press, 1980	One of the best known exponents on scientific paradigms and on the characteristics of paradigm shifts, a theorist who provides valuable insights on the shifting values of our age of transition.
James Lovelock	*Gaia: A New Look at Life on Earth*, Oxford University Press, 1979.	One of the original creators of the Gaia hypothesis which claims that the earth is an organism in its own right, sustained and animated by a sophisticated and delicate balance of physical, chemical and biological elements.
Ilya Prigogine	*From Being to Becoming*, San Francisco: Freeman, 1980	Nobel prize winner for his theory of *Dissipative Structures* which claims that living systems thrive on an irreversible process, moving towards higher orders of existence, a movement of self-renewal and reorganisation made possible by the interaction of the open-system with its environment. Instead of eventual breakdown, there is progressive breakthrough.
Erich Jantsch	*The Self-Organising Universe*, Pergamon Press, 1981	A work which applies Prigogine's theory of *Dissipative Structures* to the evolution of life at all levels, creating a new unifying paradigm of *self-organisation*. This new world view emphasises process over structure, fluctuation over equilibrium and individual creativity over collective stabilisation.
James Miller	*Living Systems*, McGraw-Hill, 1978	A leading exponent on the general theory of living systems, indicating the mutual interdependence of all life-forms, from the single cell to the ecosystem itself.
Rupert Sheldrake	*A New Science of Life: The Hypothesis of Formative Causation*, Paladin Books, 1981	Biological systems are regulated by invisible organising blueprints (morphogenetic fields), facilitating the transference of behaviours across large distances, without a mediating physical/observable link.
Fritjof Capra	*The Turning Point* Flamingo/Fontana, 1982.	Provides one of the clearest and most thorough expositions of the contemporary paradigm-shift from a predominantly mechanistic culture (based on the world view of Newtonian science and Cartesian philosophy) to a holistic one.

better quality of religion but indeed for the survival of civilisation.

Our world today does not need profound doctrine, moral imperatives or impermeable institutions. It can survive without all these as it did for millions of years before formal religions arose. But it cannot survive without the mystical vision which is at the core of human aspiration, connecting mankind in an unique way with the Spirit of God at the heart of creation.

In 1976, the theologian, Anthony Padovano remarked: 'Faith is not dying in the West, it is merely moving inside' (quoted in Ferguson, 1982, p. 405). The evolutionary leap generates a new depth of consciousness. External performance and observance no longer satisfy our human thirst; our hearts are hungry for fresh food; meanwhile, our 'heads' linger for the goodies which are running out. Almost in spite of ourselves, the Spirit is leading us where we would rather not go, although deep inside we know it's the right course to follow.

And this inner, spiritual turmoil creates all types of confusion. Some abandon the faith; others cling ever more rigidly hoping that renewed fervour will dispel their fear and anguish. The more enlightened pick and choose. Spiritually, humanly, religiously, it is not a comfortable time to be alive. However, it has its advantages for those who know what's happening.

For those who can identify with the mystical vision, and enter into its flow, new spiritual possibilities begin to unfold. According to Marilyn Ferguson (1982, p. 417):

> Two key principles seem to emerge in all mystical experience. We might call them 'flow' and 'wholeness'. The ancient Tibetan teacher referred to them as 'the principle of the non-abiding' and 'the principle of non-distinction', and he warned against harming them. Our culture has indeed harmed these principles. We try to freeze the non-abiding, we try to imprison that which exists only in movement, freedom, relationship. And we betray wholeness, non-distinction, by breaking apart everything in sight so that we miss the underlying connection of everything in the universe.

Amid the pain and confusion of our declining culture, the seeds of resurrection are beginning to sprout, a new global consciousness is in the making and humans are reconnecting with the Centre. In many ways, the upsurge is unprecedented; we can neither comprehend nor appreciate its impact without a radically new wisdom, namely the *mystical* mode of perception. Today, more than ever, we stand to benefit from a revival of mysticism: eyes to see, ears to hear and reawakened hearts to comprehend the transformation taking place in our universe.

To the 'unenlightened' the contemporary world is dominated by pain, misery, destruction and death. We are inundated with sensationalism and violence. We continue to exploit universal life: blindly, brutally, and feverishly holding on to whatever power and control we can engineer. Meanwhile, a new reality is being born. It is happening all around us. It is subtle, gentle, unassuming, but pervasive and enduring. Alvin Toffler (1980) calls it *Third Wave Civilisation* (the former two being those of the *agricultural* and *industrial* revolutions).

The emphasis in the present chapter has been on the *perceived* necessity for all life-forms to work in a new and unprecedented harmony. The word *perceived* is used in a double sense:

a) Our evolutionary breakthrough, with special focus on the psychic and spiritual, is imbued with a deep desire to transcend the barriers, dichotomies and divisions of our dwindling materialistic and mechanistic culture;

b) Even those who do not subscribe to cultural evolution (possibly, 90% of mankind) acknowledge (however tacitly) the need for a greater ecological consciousness, closer economic and political co-operation and a shared responsibility for earth's life and resources. The concept of man as *master* of creation is fast losing ground. It is clear that on our own we, humans, cannot and do not seem destined to achieve mastery of all life's forces. Our vocation is one of *stewardship*, not mastery. (Cf. Rifkin, 1985, pp. 254-258.)

The biggest change facing the citizens of the Third Wave is the readiness to subdue the human urge to control, manipulate and exploit. The future of our planet is in the hands of those who are prepared to 'let go' of past securities and embark on a new and risky endeavour, based on freedom, trust, mutual enrichment and, above all, on a profound awareness that, under God, the earth is ours as our birthright. It is also home to the birds of the air, the fish of the sea, the plants and animals alike. Only when we begin to live in the awareness of our mutual interdependence, profoundly respecting and fostering the common good, have we regained our freedom and our birthright as children of Mother Earth. Then, and only then, have we really changed.

4: The Emerging Scientific Consciousness

The aims of scientific thought are to see the general in the particular and the eternal in the transitory. – A. N. WHITEHEAD

Sooner or later, nuclear physics and the psychology of the unconscious will draw closer together as both of them, independently of one another and from opposite directions, push forward into transcendental territory. – C. G. JUNG

All things are interdependent. – MEISTER ECKHART

Contemporary Western society considers the scientist to be the connoisseur of certitude and immutability. What science has declared to be definitive is considered to be the final word on any subject. There is no room for question or doubt, for speculation or alternative possibilities. The so-called *scientific attitude* with its aura of certitude and supremacy and its tendency to project rational science as the apex of truth is, in fact, quite alien to the spirit and pursuit of some of the great scientists of our age.

Albert Einstein, who needs little introduction to the contemporary reader, once wrote: 'As far as the laws of mathematics refer to reality, they are not certain and in so far as they are certain, they do not refer to reality' (Einstein, 1954, p. 233). Einstein went even further to suggest that *mystery* is a necessary aspect of reality in its deepest meaning; his words are frequently quoted:

> The finest thing we can experience is mystery. It is the fundamental emotion that is at the roots of true science. Those who cannot know it, those who cannot admire, those who are no longer capable of experiencing a sense of wonder, might as well be dead. (From 'My Credo', a recording made in Berlin, Autumn, 1932 and published in *Naturwissenschafter*, 1 (1965), p. 98.)

Already in the latter half of the nineteenth century, Louis Pasteur, a pioneer in modern science wrote: 'Science advances through tentative answers to a series of more and more subtle questions which reach deeper and deeper into the essence of natural phenomena' (quoted in Capra, 1982, p. 93). And the Danish physicist, Neils Bohr, writing in 1934, states: 'The great extension of our experience. . . has brought to light the insufficiency of our simple, mechanical conceptions and, as a consequence, has shaken the foundation on which the customary interpretation of observation was based.'

Finally, Werner Heisenberg, who introduced the concept of the *Uncertainty Principle*, a mathematical formula to explain the relation between the uncertainties of *position* and *momentum* of a particle in motion, once wrote these words:

> (In modern physics), one has now divided the world, not into different groups of objects but into different groups of connections. . . What can be distinguished is the kind of connection which is primarily important in a certain phenomenon. . . The world thus appears as a complicated tissue of events, in which connections of different kinds alternate or overlap or combine and thereby determine the texture of the whole. (Heisenberg, 1963. p. 96.)

This random sample of quotations depicts an image not popularly associated with the rigorous scientific attitude of our times. In fact, the history of science exhibits a degree of openness and flexibility, quite at variance with the type of dogmatism we attribute to scientists. This latter view may be more the product of the late nineteenth and early twentieth centuries when science, as a tool of technology, became a powerful implement in apparently *controlling* and *explaining* aspects of life previously posing a threat to human survival.

The Scientific Transition: From Breakdown to Breakthrough

The second Law of Thermodynamics is one of the great dogmas of science and one of the last strongholds of technological imperialism; even Einstein himself concurred with the perceived supremacy of the Second Law.

The *First Law of Thermodynamics* states that all matter and energy in the universe is constant; it cannot be created or destroyed. Only its form can change, but never its essence. We cannot create *more* energy; the only thing we can do is transform it from one state to another. And according to the *Second Law*, the transformation can only be in one direction, from usable to

ARCHITECTS OF THE NEW SCIENTIFIC PARADIGM

Name	*Contribution*
Albert Einstein	Published his theory of special relativity in 1905 and the general theory in 1916, the first major challenge to the objectivity of the space/time categories. The motion of the observer partly determines how reality is perceived. Our perception of life is *relative* rather than objective or permanent – at all levels of existence.
Max Planck	Originator of the Quantum theory (in 1911) when he discovered that the energy of heat radiation is not emitted continously (in 'logical', mechanical sequence) but appears in the form of 'energy packets' which Einstein called *quanta* and recognised them as fundamental aspects of nature.
Erwin Schrodinger	Discoverer of *wave mechanics*, winner of the Nobel prize (with Paul Dirac) in 1933. Atoms are not merely solitary existents, but behave in a manner requiring the use of a wave field; hence his oft-quoted phrase: 'The device by which an organism maintains itself stationary at a fairly high level of orderliness. . . really consists in continually sucking orderliness from its environment.'
Neils Bohr	The Danish physicist who introduced the principle of *complementarity*, proposing that the newly-discovered dual aspects of the microcosm (particle and wave) are analagous to the long-known dual aspects of the macrocosm (mind and matter) and function not in isolation but in complementary fashion.
Werner Heisenberg	German physicist who formulated the *uncertainty* principle, according to which an accurate measure of a particle's position and its speed could not be obtained simultaneously. This theory proved to be a major challenge to the 'scientific certitude' of science, philosophy and religion.
Linus Pauling	Nobel prize winner and founder of modern chemistry; the first to apply the principles of quantum mechanics to molecular structure. He has explored new quality 'relationships' (resonance or wave-like patterns) between chemical structures.
David Bohm	The universe functions like a *hologram*, whose essential nature is that of its implicate, enfolded order, which is manifest in the explicate, unfolded state.

unusable, from available to unavailable and from ordered to disordered. Consequently, the amount of useful energy in the universe is being absorbed continually through heat, friction, etc., and the process of depleting energy will continue until the universe burns itself out.

Both laws have several applicatons in everyday life. For example, if we burn a piece of coal, the energy remains but is transformed into sulphur dioxide and other gases, then dispersed into space. While no energy has been lost in the process, we know that we can never use that piece of coal again. Therefore, every time energy is transformed from one state to another there is a net loss of the amount of energy available for useful work. This accumulation of 'unavailable energy' we call *entropy*. Even when energy is absorbed in creating 'order', it is usually at the expense of greater disorder in the surrounding environment; the available energy continues to deplete.

The Entropy Law held sway, dominantly and powerfully, until the early 1970s, when a number of scientists, especially biochemists and biologists called attention to the fact that life, instead of moving towards more random and less ordered states, appears to be moving through *apparently disordered fluctuations* towards increasing order and harmony. One of the leading proponents of this theory is Ilya Prigogine, a Belgian physical chemist, working in Brussels and at the University of Austin in Texas and winner of the Nobel prize in chemistry in 1977.

Prigogine and his colleagues claim that the Second Law is applicable *only in closed systems*. If the process of depleting energy is taking place in an *open* system, energy and matter are taken in while entropy and the end-products are expelled. The incoming energy not merely replaces the losses but replenishes anew the entire system. How does this happen?

The continuous flow of energy in a living, *open* system causes fluctuations; if they are minor, the system dampens them and they do not alter its structural integrity. But if the fluctuations reach a critical size, they 'perturb' the system. They increase the number of novel interactions within it. They shake it up. The elements of the old pattern come into contact with each other in new ways and make new connections. The parts reorganise into a new whole. The system escapes into a higher order.

What is unique in Prigogine's theory is not so much its challenge to the Second Law, as to the presumptions on which that law is based. For long, scientists have acknowledged (however, tacitly) that the Second Law applies only to closed systems, i.e., physical, material reality in which energy but not matter can be exchanged with the outside surroundings. Another branch of science, called *Nonequilibrium Thermo-dynamics* relates to living (open) systems in which both matter and energy are exchanged with the environment, thus replenishing the energy-losses and ensuring new growth and development. Open systems include human beings, organisations, factories and nations.

The Second Law claims pride of place on the assumption that closed systems dominate and control open systems. The universe itself is considered to be a closed system, a law unto itself. But this latter view is no longer widely held, even in the scientific world. Once we assume that our universe is a *living organism*, then we have seriously undermined the Second Law. Energy-consumption is no longer a matter of depleting *material* stocks because now we are beginning to realise that *matter* itself is conscious and consequently an *open* rather than a *closed* system. And within the material universe are continual *fluctuations* which, if allowed to 'flow' according to the 'innate wisdom' of our planet, create new order rather than more entropy. Therefore, the ironclad dictates of Entropy Law no longer provide an appropriate frame of reference for our evolving universe.

However, we cannot and must not dismiss the Second Law as being outdated and irrelevant. Many of our major institutions operate out of this law (often unknowingly) and are likely to continue doing so as the present transition expands and becomes more pronounced. Indeed, a great deal of planetary destruction, e.g., pollution, is the fruit of those people and institutions who unreflectively operate out of the Second Law, frequently in complete ignorance of that fact. Before ever transcending the Entropy Law, many people have to grow into a holistic self-awareness; hopefully, then they can understand and acknowledge the laws that govern their limited perceptions and destructive actions (cf. Rifkin, 1985).

Two corrolaries follow from these observations:

a) All living systems, interacting with a favourable and supportive environment, have an inherent propensity for self renewal, what Jantsch calls autopoiesis (see pp. 10, 29-35). Initially, such regeneration is felt as a threat, a disruption of the equilibrium, deranging the stability of the person or organisation. Collective resistance will tend to be more pronounced since institutions are, by nature, self-perpetuating; consequently, the initial response to change tends to be one of suspicion and self-defence. In fact, 'innovators' may be purged out, or blocked out, even before the task has begun.

Even when change is strongly resisted, a level of mutation, no matter how insignificant, takes place. The very suggestion of re-organisation creates ripples. A sense of restlessness begins to pervade. Dissenting voices gain prominence, especially if espousing a cause for more equity and justice within what is perceived to be an unjust or corrupt system. If and when a feeling of disintegration predominates (everything seems to be falling apart) then, change is well under way and the outcome will tend to be that of *breakdown* or *breakthrough*. A third option is possible, what one cultural historian calls, 'a low level of minimal survival', which can last for decades in the case of social institutions and for centuries in the case of civilisations.

b) Regarding the ecosystem itself, the process of renewal is much more predictable. Created reality as a whole functions in a holistic fashion for the benefit of the whole and the parts that comprise it. In traditional language, one can say that there exists within creation a creative life-force, whether we consider it to be divine or otherwise. Alternatively, we can assume that God has entrusted creation to its life and purpose, in which case, God is not likely to interfere for the maintenance and nurturance of the natural process. Rather, we may, with an increasing number of scientists suggest that there subsists within all reality, at a very subtle level, an unified field of consciousness, a substratum of 'awareness', creating interconnecting links between all aspects of creation, humans included. With this vision, perhaps, we can grasp what Jantsch means when he claims that 'God is the mind of the universe'. Globally, we may suggest, that this level of consciousness is represented by the ozone layer in the upper atmosphere without which all life-forms would rapidly evaporate.

We therefore detect a consciousness from within each human being, but also a global, universal consciousness at the 'heart' of creation itself. This new discovery has led to one of the most promising links of all time, that of Western physics and Eastern mysticism, as exemplified in the work of scientists such as Werner Heisenberg, Fritjof Capra, Peter Russell, Brian D. Josephenson and David Bohm.

The Vision of Fritjof Capra

Few contemporary scientists seem to have grasped and explained the new paradigm as succinctly as Fritjof Capra. Professor of Physics at Berkeley, California, Capra published *The Tao of Physics* in 1976 and *The Turning Point* in 1982. In *The Tao. . .* , his main focus is outlined in the subtitle: *An Exploration of Parallels between Modern Physics and Eastern Mysticism*, and the thrust of this fascinating work can be gleaned from the following passage:

> We see that the ways of the modern physicist and the Eastern mystic, which seem at first totally unrelated, have, in fact, much in common. It should not be too surprising, therefore, that there are striking parallels in their descriptions of the world. Once these parallels. . . are accepted, a number of questions will arise concerning their implications. Is modern science with all its sophisticated machinery, merely rediscovering ancient wisdom, known to the Eastern sages for thousands of years? Should physicists, therefore, abandon the scientific method and begin to meditate? Or can there be a mutual influence between science and mysticism, perhaps, even a synthesis?
>
> I think all these questions have to be answered in the negative. I see science and mysticism as two complementary manifestations of the human mind; of its rational and intuitive faculties. The modern physicist experiences the world through an extreme specialisation of the rational mind; the mystic through an extreme specialisation of the intuitive mind. The two approaches are entirely different and involve far more than a certain view of the world. However, they are complementary. . . neither is comprehended in the other, but both of them are necessary, supplementing one another for a fuller understanding of the world. To paraphrase an old Chinese saying, mystics understand the roots of the Tao but not its branches; scientists understand its branches but not its roots. Science does not need mysticism and mysticism does not need science; but men and women need both. Mystical experience is necessary to understand the deeper nature of things, and science is essential for modern life. What we need, therefore, is not a synthesis but a dynamic interplay between mystical intuition and scientific analysis. (Capra, 1976, pp. 338-339.)

In his subsequent work, *The Turning Point* (subtitled, *Science,*

Society and the Rising Culture), Capra sets the new vision, outlined in his first book, in its historical and evolutionary context.
The new scientific attitude merely reflects a current of change
passing through all dimensions of contemporary life. The traditional world view seems unable to generate the energy and
enthusiasm to sustain us meaningfully on this earth. According
to Capra, it is predominantly *mechanistic*: reality tends to be perceived in terms of *machines*, operating according to the law of
cause and effect and presumed to function effectively as long as
each individual part performs according to plan. This orientation
owes its origins to a combination of Newtonian science and
Cartesian philosophy. It is not interested in the *whole*, but in the
parts, subconsciously assuming that if all the parts function effectively then the whole will be fruitful and productive.

The logic is perfect and the rationale seems compelling, but *it
is not true to life*. Humans are not machines, neither is the
universe. Indeed, even machines themselves deviate from the
simplistic logic of this model. Capra's primary concern is not with
the inappropriate nature of the model; it *has* served society well
but it has *outgrown* its usefulness.

As a species we are rapidly discarding, even abandoning, the
mechanistic paradigm. It falls short of our deepest hopes and
aspirations; it is losing respect and credibility. Subtly, but powerfully, a new perceptual mode is arising, making its impact in a
variety of human and cultural disciplines and this, Capra calls the
holistic, from the Greek, 'holos' (whole) to conceptualise reality
in terms of wholes, whose properties cannot be reduced to those
of smaller units.

The transition from the old to the new is taking place all round
us. Like many previous evolutionary changes it is not sudden or
dramatic but its impact is irresistible and its repercussions profoundly affect the society in which we live. Most people today are
aware of this change but are poorly informed on its origin or
outcome; to quote Capra:

> (Our crisis) is essentially a crisis of perception. . . It derives from the
> fact that we are trying to apply the concepts of an outdated world
> view – the mechanistic world view of Cartesian-Newtonian science –
> to a reality that can no longer be understood in terms of these concepts.
> We live today in a globally interconnected world, in which biological,

psychological, social and environmental phenomena are all inter-dependent. . . The beginnings of this change from the mechanistic to the holistic conception of reality, are already visible in all fields and are likely to dominate the present decade. (Capra, 1982, p. xviii.)

The new vision poses a particularly strong challenge to the science which has produced both the Industrial Revolution and the information-technology and computerisation of our time. Traditional science cannot be faulted for its immense contribution to human and earthly progress, but *it has fulfilled its purpose*, and is incapable of serving the needs and aspirations of humanity entering a new phase of evolution. As with the other aspects of latterday culture, science must let-go, it must *die*. Meanwhile, a new scientific vision begins to unfold:

> This is how modern physics reveals the basic oneness of the universe. It shows we cannot decompose the world into independently existing smallest units. As we penetrate into matter, nature does not show us any isolated, basic building blocks, but rather appears as a compli-cated web of relations between the various parts of an unified whole. As Heisenberg expresses it: 'The world thus appears as a complicated tissue of events, in which connections of different kinds alternate or overlap or combine and thereby determine the texture of the whole.' . . . The shift from *objects to relationships* has far-reaching implications for science as a whole. (Capra, 1982, p. 70 – emphasis mine.)

Traditional science could be characterised by words like *mechanistic, quantifiable, verifiable, objective, uniform, certain.* The new paradigm uses a very different type of vocabulary, which initially may seem uncongenial: *holistic, global, interconnected, interdependent, uncertain, complex, complementary, relative.* The differences are quite pronounced and apparent even to the unscientific reader. For science to veer towards a flexible, in-definite, fluid, open-ended universe is considered by many to be a betrayal of the orderly, certain, quantifiable 'world', the product of a rigorous scientific pursuit. Amid confusion and bewilderment, people wonder whether we (society, nations, churches, culture) are progressing or regressing. Words like randomness, complex-ity, uncertainty, probability, connote chaos and disorganisation where as simplicity and order are deemed more conducive to personal growth and universal progress. (On modern, scientific terminology, see Suppes, 1984.) This, too, is what the major religions tend to propound, although this line of emphasis is quite contrary to the *spirit* of the great Eastern religions.

In fact, the new paradigm is not about chaos and disorganisation. It does disown the traditional attitude, which sought to reduce everything to 'basic building blocks'. According to Capra and his colleagues, we cannot do this without grossly interfering in the natural, spontaneous evolution of life, personally and globally. Apart from the inappropriateness of such interference, a substantial body of modern scientists (especially those of an ecological slant) claims that we do not have the right to intervene in this way. Now that we cannot identify or classify data in a precise and certain manner we are more reluctant to offer a solution to match the problem. The new paradigm encourages us to tolerate disorganisation, fluidity and flexibility (even chaos, perhaps), not to rush in with quick solutions, but instead allow the innate regenerative process to surface from the death of the old reality; once more, we touch on the Death-Resurrection experience.

Our manipulative urge, with a compulsion to prevent or inhibit the negative, really has been a cultural unwillingness to confront death. We have been living under an universal delusion, denying one of life's most essential realities. We have been running away from one of the most creative forces in nature. We have succeeded in trivialising death to such a degree that we now inflict it widely and savagely. We need a thorough reawakening on what it means to die, and this is the supreme challenge of change involved in the new scientific paradigm.

Einstein's Theory of Relativity

Albert Einstein was once asked by reporters in New York to explain the essence of relativity in simple language. He replied:

> If you will not take the answer too seriously and consider it only as a kind of a joke, then I can explain it as follows. It was formerly believed that if all material things disappeared out of the universe, time and space would be left. According to relativity theory, however, time and space disappear together with things. (Quoted in McKenzie, 1960, p. 310.)

Einstein's special theory of relativity was published in 1905. It

CHARACTERISTICS OF TWO PARADIGMS

Present paradigm of the physical sciences	*Complementary paradigm*
Essentially an ordering of sense experience; validation through repeatable observations and experiments	Includes intuitive, noetic experience; no consensus yet on how public validation to be achieved
Reductionistic explanations (e.g. physiological processes in terms of elemental physical and chemical interactions)	Holistic explanations (e.g. physiological processes in terms of their function in the life pattern of the whole organism)
Deterministic models (both causal and stochastic)	Teleological models (e.g. goal-impelled systems)
Measuring; quantitative	Deals largely with the non-quantitative, and with subjective reports
Value-inattentive (e.g. physics, astronomy, biochemistry)	Value-focused (e.g. health sciences, psychotherapy, extension of human capabilities)
Consciousness is essentially an epiphenomenon; meaning is irrelevant or arbitrary	Consciousness and its contents are primary data; meaning is of central concern

Source Michael Cazenave (1984), p. 368.

is called the special theory because it is confined to systems moving in relative uniform motion; it was later (c. 1916) extended in the general theory of relativity to cover all types of motion.

According to Einstein, all movement is relative; time, mass, speed, momentum and energy may be different for all observers. To cite one of Einstein's own examples, a passenger in a moving train and a person sitting on the station platform will observe the speed and distance (time and space) of an object relative to their individual experiences. Space and time are human constructs and not realities with an absolute and permanent existence (as Newton had postulated).

As observers we may all share similar information about an object. Our observations, however, will vary according to individual perceptions relative to our state of being and to our experience of the process of observation. Even if both observers are sitting on the station platform attending to the same object, their perceptions may vary considerably relative to their state of *consciousness*. Strictly speaking, there is no such thing as an objective opinion. *Relativity* rather than *objectivity* becomes the norm of 'truth'. (On Einstein's theories, especially those of Relativity, the person with little or no scientific background is referred to the simple and lucid rendition provided by Pelletier (1978, pp. 56-59, 241-242, 251-252).

When Albert Einstein outlined his special theory of relativity in 1905, to be supplemented subsequently by the principles of complementarity (Bohr) and uncertainty (Heisenberg), he was effectively saying that nothing in life is *absolute* (other than the absolute itself, which we christians call God). This does not mean that everything is *relative*, in the sense of being trivial or unimportant; quite the opposite, in fact. It means that everything is relatively important compared with everything else. The Western value-system is mediated through terms like absolute, definitive, immutable, etc., a conceptual framework, based on Aristotelian philosophy, which tends to perceive some aspects of life as being important and others quite insignificant. Arbitrarily, the negative dimensions tended to be dismissed and forgotten, except by the major religions whose fortune it was to espouse the cause of that which rational science wished to discard.

Einstein's theory of relativity, contrary to popular opinion, is a profoundly positive, life-giving and holistic principle. *Everything* in life has a relative importance, negativity included. Moreover, everything is in complementary relationship with a 'partner' (often considered its 'opposite' in Western dualistic thought). Heisenberg's principle of uncertainty is an important stepping-stone in the expanding scientific elasticity. 'Uncertainty' to the average person connotes vagueness, indefiniteness, restlessness and confusion, but for Heisenberg it essentially means that we cannot apply to anything in life a certain, dogmatic, once-and-for-all explanation. In doing that we inhibit all new understanding; we confine and restrict creative energy to our limited perception; we strip life of its mystery and deepest meaning; we deny the significance (indeed, the very actuality) of death.

Relativity, uncertainty, complementarity and other key words referred to above, mark the breakthrough from the mechanistic to the holistic. And the story is only beginning; once we open-up the possibility and power of mystery, we begin to discover that it is a very creative ambiance to work within. It nurtures and nourishes untold possibilities. Science enters a new, global arena.

In less than a decade there has been a distinctive swing from the attempt to 'boil down' everything to the essential building blocks, to the global possibility of 'supersymmetry' (*New Scientist*, 15/3/84, p. 28) and 'Superstrings' (a theory of everything) recently named the TOE theory (*New Scientist*, 29/8/1985, pp. 34-35 and 31/10/1985, pp. 45-47). Finally, Einstein's unfulfilled dream to account for all the forces of life and matter in a single unified scheme may be nearing realisation as theorists energetically pursue the *Grand Unification Theory* (GUT) (cf. *The Economist*, 18/1/1986, pp. 69-72.)

The British physicist, David Bohm, suggests that there are two types of cosmic life, that of *explicate order* governed by the law of cause and effect and perceptible in the world around us, and *implicate order* (not accessible to the external senses), whereby every part of the universe contains the whole enfolded within it. Therefore, the manifest world is only a reflection of the 'unbroken wholeness' in the unmanifest. To describe the *implicate* order Bohm uses the analogy of the *hologram*, a three-dimensional image which, when illuminated at any point, will show up the entire image* (cf. Wilber, 1982, pp. 6, 18, 126-128).

* Holography is a method of lensless photography in which the wave field of light scattered by an object is recorded on a plate as an interference pattern. When

To understand the implicate order, Bohm has found it necessary to regard consciousness as an innate and essential feature of
universal life. Even the 'lifeless' stones have a 'mind'. In fact,
mind and *matter* are categories we invent in order to name the
manifest forms of a higher reality which reveals itself not as *mind*
or *matter*, or mind *causing* matter, but as *both* mind and matter;
the two are mutually unfolding projections of a higher universal
power.

A number of important corollaries follow from this theory:

a) There is actually no such thing as pure energy or pure
matter. Every aspect of creation is neither a thing nor no-thing;
instead it exists as a kind of vibrational or energetic expression.
Energy is the essence of life but always expressed through the
relationship and interaction of its different aspects.

b) Everything in the universe (living and non-living alike) exists
as a whole unto itself, containing a complete store of information
about itself. One is not suggesting that a stone knows about itself
in a manner similar to a human being's self-awareness. The
vibrational information is unique to each 'species' and presumably can be shared creatively at some future stage of evolutionary progress.

c) Every aspect of the universe seems to be part of some larger
whole: a more elaborate being or a more comprehensive system.
The whole is greater than the sum of the parts, yet is not possible
for the whole to swallow up individual parts. Every single part is
essential to the diversity of the whole. In fact, it would be more
accurate to say: each part complements the whole in a mutually
interdependent relationship.

d) In a holographic universe, *time* and *space* are not simply
linear or localised, nor can they be exclusively identified. Neither
do they function independently, but rather in a space/time continuum. This new orientation, probably one of the most radical
tenets of Einstein's theory of relativity, needs some elaboration.

---

the photographic record – the hologram – is placed in a coherent light beam like
a laser, the original wave pattern is regenerated. A three-dimensional image
appears.
   Because there is no focusing lens, the plate appears as a meaningless pattern
of swirls. *Any piece of the hologram will reconstruct the entire image.* (Wilber,
1982, p. 6.)

Time and Space: Categories of Meaning

In our everyday lives, we think of *time* as linear and segmented, extending forward into the future and backward to the past. We think in terms of taking one thing at a time. We speak of time being saved, wasted, lost, made up for, accelerated, slowed down and running out. Similarly with *space*: it is the distance we perceive between objects, measurable and quantifiable. According to the Greeks, geometry is inherent in nature and therefore the categories of space and time could easily be invented from the 'mechanics' already at work in the universe. Einstein's relativity theory seriously undermines this approach:

> The central recognition of the theory of relativity is that geometry. . . is a construct of the intellect. Only when this discovery is accepted can the mind feel free to tamper with the time-honoured notions of space and time. (Capra, 1976, pp. 178-179.)

Space and time, therefore are categories we humans invent in order to make sense out of our existence. In some cases we use the same object to measure both, e.g., the clock.

We tend to take space and time for granted. The very notion that they might be imperfect and inhibit rather than augment our progress, sounds preposterous to many. Consequently, to grasp these notions as *inter-related* and capable of being understood differently from our present awareness, is extremely difficult for many people. It is as if we have been brainwashed into linear, structural, unalterable thought patterns. We are in cultural danger of being enslaved by our inherited perceptions. Consequently, if people are to have some measure of freedom and choice regarding our future evolution as a species, it is important that we try to communicate the major ideas of our age in language and concepts that people can comprehend. Frequently, this process is hampered by the fact that new ideas, of their very nature, often demand a new vocabulary. Even language is relative!

Let us therefore attempt to recast the notions of space and time as perceived by contemporary science and culture. Let us imagine a situation in which I am standing on a mountain slope, looking down on a valley. I see a variety of objects, colours, contours; some things may be moving, but much of the landscape seems stationary. If I were to come back in a few days, nothing would seem to have changed. Externally, at what David Bohm calls the unfolded order, we seem to be surrounded by permanence.

At the *unmanifest* level, what the human senses cannot perceive (what only the *heart* can *intuit*), the landscape is one massive, restless flow of energy. Everything I see in that countryside consists of minute particles, forever changing and fluctuating in wavelike patterns. And according to Quantum theory, we cannot say when one particular particle ceases to exist and another comes into being; we can only speak of the *virtual* existence of such 'beings', which are operative not in isolation but in relationship with associate particles and in co-operation with the environment.

What I perceive, therefore, is not a landscape of *facts* or objects, but one of *events*, of process, movement and energy. In this creative flow, past, present and future are indistinguishable; every creation of matter, influenced as it is by consciousness, is a recapitulation of all past creation and carries an inherent propensity to *become* something more than it is at any moment of its being. For this continuous, creative movement, David Bohm coined the term *holomovement*.

Space denotes a great deal more than the distance between two points. According to Tiller, 'Space is embedded in the domain of Spirit' (quoted in Wilber, 1982, p. 140), in other words it is an 'instrument' we use to differentiate objects from each other in order that we may be able more effectively to control our environment (the mechanistic approach). But that very process can be counterproductive, because in a holographic universe, a vibration in one area, no matter how small, affects the life quality in all other areas.

Distance is a relative term, even at an external, physical level. My perception of the space and distance between objects becomes more vague and imprecise as I look across the valley. In fact, I can only perceive space or distance when I take a global view, that is, when I sense the object in the total context of its environment. So, the field in the distance only makes spatial sense in terms of the surrounding landscape. Unknown to myself I have always been operating out of a holographic brain, that is *primarily* tuned to perceive and understand in a holistic way and not in the fragmented, utilitarian manner we have inherited from our culture and education.

One is not heralding the end of the space and time categories. Rather, one is proclaiming a new way of understanding, appropriate for new evolutionary growth. As dimensions of our perceptual awareness, space and time are not static, objective and unrelated entities; quite the contrary as Capra suggests:

> In relativity theory, one of the most important developments has been the unification of space and time. Einstein recognised that space and time are not separate, that they are connected intimately and inseparably to form a four-dimensional continuum: space/time. A direct consequence of this recognition is the equivalence of mass and energy and the intrinsically dynamic nature of all subatomic phenomena. The fact that space and time are related so intimately implies that subatomic particles are dynamic patterns, that they are events rather than objects. So the role of space and time and the dynamic nature of the object studied are very closely related. (Quoted in Wilber, 1982, p. 219.)

There is a sense, therefore, in which my daily sensory perception is an illusion; my life is based on a lie; my senses continually deceive me. That is a rather negative way of putting it and fails to do justice to my human and global reality. My sensory repertoire has served me appropriately for my evolutionary development up to this time, but thenceforth is neither an adequate nor appropriate frame of reference. I must become a new person, born anew, as many religions proclaim, if I am to participate meaningfully in the approaching new age. And no external agent, divine or otherwise, is going to bring this change about – not until I am prepared to forgo and abandon my earlier way of looking at reality and open my being to new possibilities.

Most people find this invitation unattractive, even scary. We have been so conditioned to one way of being, so docile to the influence of others, so subservient to higher authorities, so subdued in terms of our own inner potentialities, that we are loath to take initiatives about our own evolutionary growth. We have not taken ownership of, nor responsibility for, our creative power, for the many and varied God-given resources which often go unused throughout an entire lifetime.

Darwin was not far wrong in suggesting that it is the fittest who survive. What he did not realise is that it is we ourselves who set our own limitations by allowing ourselves to be caged and stultified in institutions and structures which seek to make permanent mores and customs, perceptions of reality which evolution had intended to be merely partial and temporary.

Our traditional views of space and time are the remnants of the fragmented, piecemeal, mechanistic mind-set which is no longer capable of serving either our deepest needs or our noblest aspirations. Nor is this traditional understanding even in accord with our own basic nature as human beings, as indicated in the work of Karl Pribram, a neurophysiologist at Stanford, who has developed a holographic model of the brain. Pribram's initial work was on *memory storage*. How does the human brain store memories? For a number of years, neuroscientists speculated that memory was both recorded and stored in higher brain centres. Pribram decided to test a new hypothesis: memory is not encoded in any *one* centre but distributed throughout the brain. Using intricate mathematics, he speculated that the brain functions as a *hologram*, interpreting bioelectric frequencies, not at individual centres but throughout the brain. Information is not localised, but spread throughout in wave-like, frequency patterns, along a network of fine fibres on the nerve cells. Only such a model could interpret a holographic universe.

Equipped with holographic brains essentially means that we, humans, are capable of adjusting, accommodating and integrating vast varieties of information, even of a paradoxical nature. At a perceptual/learning level, *no change is beyond our comprehension*. It is not lack of intelligence that will inhibit our ability to perceive anew, to change our understanding. The 'lack' is not one of intelligence but of courage, will-power and appropriate motivation. We have within ourselves all the resources needed to enter the new evolutionary era.

What we have not yet achieved is an appropriate wisdom to release and utilise our inner capabilities. We are all the products of a managerial, mechanistic culture, concerned with the effective management of the parts so that they all work to capacity for the benefit of the whole. But we now realise that the whole is greater than the sum of the parts; the totality, whether it refers to the universe, the nation, or the human personality, renews and regenerates itself not on the basis of managerial skills or mechanical principles but by virtue of an innate regenerative propensity.

New Age Science and Holistic Health

Scientific discovery has always complemented medical progress, especially in recent centuries. Accompanying the new wave of science, outlined above, we are rediscovering a sense of health-care which, in time, may profoundly affect standard medical practice. Some obervations on this newly emerging model, popularly known as *holistic health*, remind us that the contemporary scientific revolution has immense potential not merely for a more enlightened world but also for a healthier lifestyle. The contrast with the older scientific and medical models becomes apparent as we review the approach in the new paradigm.

Consider for example, the patient complaining of severe headache; no longer can she be considered as an object with a particular anatomical or physiological problem which traditional medicine would seek to rectify at what it considers the source and location of the illness. In holistic medicine, the headache is considered to be a symptom of a more profound personality disorder associated, perhaps, with pressure, tension, wrong diet, inadequate rest, other malfunctions in the organism or maybe a combination of all. The symptoms may be cured with an appropriate drug just as a part of the machine can be repaired by designated technology, but the underlying cause may still prevail, eventually causing long-term illness and, perhaps, death.

Instead of the quick and efficient prescription for valium, librium or any of the other pep-pills which cost the British economy an estimated £50 million (i.e. 74 million US dollars) per year (while the USA has an annual production of 20,000 tons of aspirin) our 'patient' seriously needs to review her lifestyle in terms of values, attitudes and behaviours; she may need to consider a more balanced diet, regular exercise, appropriate rest and the ability to think positively and creatively. The *whole* rather than the *part* may need to be healed, in which case, remedial action in piecemeal fashion, no matter how effective, will not compensate for the weaknesses in the total personality.

Nobody denies that the medical progress of the twentieth century procured the vastly improved quality of health which many people enjoy today. It would be naive, however, to turn a blind eye to the illness and disease we induce by a Western way of life, clearly out of tune with man's basic nature: coronaries, cancer,

CHARACTERISTICS OF THE HOLISTIC HEALTH MOVEMENT

1. Sickness is a symptom which occurs when the person is off-centre; illness indicates disharmony with the cosmic order.

2. Healing is a matter of rebalancing vital energies and re-establishing life-giving relationships with people and with the cosmos.

3. Holistic health concerns the whole person in body, mind and spirit and acknowledges that we have within ourselves and/or within the universe all the resources to live happy, healthy and fulfilled lives.

4. Attitudes play a (*the*?) dominant role in personal well-being.

5. A healthy life ensues from an integrated personality where *all* dimensions: physical, social, psychic, spiritual, aesthetic, emotional, etc., are expressed and experienced appropriately.

6. Achieving a sense of complementarity between the *Yin* and the *Yang* polarities (e.g., the balance between rest and activity) makes for a balanced, healthy person.

7. *We* are responsible for our health; medical personnel are intended to facilitate that sense of self-responsibility and thus empower us to *prevent* rather than merely *cure* disease.

8. Healing comes from within (the person and nature); drugs and medicines may *help*, but will not, of themselves, *heal*. New age therapies seek to activate the inner powers for self-healing.

9. Healthy people and a healthy environment are complementary; one without the other is a contradiction.

10. Nature heals and enhances growth through many media, including plant-power, music, art, diet, exercise and the appropriate activation of our energy-fields (massage).

alcoholism, anorexia nervosa, a variety of stress-related ailments, increasing dependency on coping drugs whether of the tranquillising or stimulating types. Much of our illness is induced and a great deal more is self-inflicted through destructive behaviour/ lifestyle patterns and our abusive (often, ravaging) treatment of the earth.

How can we expect to be healthy people when so much of what we consume comes either from (a) slaughtering other species; (b) torturing birds and animals so that they can produce at a rate that accrues maximum financial gain; (c) pumping fertilisers into the earth with little or no recognition of the earth's own productive cycles and potentialities; (d) packing and canning foods which lose much of their nutritious value and often contain preservatives of dubious import? If earth and nature are meant to be our friends for survival we would need to treat them a little more gently and lovingly. Our barbaric attitudes to Mother Earth may well be the major cause of an advanced society still heavily inflicted with sickness and suffering. It is surely ironic that the USA, which banned the use of DDT as long ago as 1972, still manufactures over 18 million kilograms a year for export, mainly to the Third World.

The holistic health movement, therefore, is not merely a different way of treating illness. It is another dimension of the unfolding global vision. Healthy people need a healthy environment and a healthy world; one is meaningless without the other. Alternative health movements advocate a return to nature's own capacity for healthy living by (a) adopting a lifestyle, moderate and balanced, which utilises most effectively our inner, personal resources (attitudes and values) to be *naturally* healthy; (b) using nature's own healing powers, available in the air we breathe, the food we consume and the fascinating array of plants, herbs, juices, even crystals, with healing potential. Today, three-quarters of the world's children who have recently suffered from leukaemia are now alive due to properties discovered in a tropical forest plant called Rosy Periwinkle; (c) relating with each other in a more loving and caring way; our competitive, aggressive and envious attitudes cause untold pain both to ourselves and to our world.

If we humans chose to do it, we could make the entire medical profession redundant.[6] In primitive times, religion and medicine were understood to complement one another. Both sought to explore and utilise the mysterious powers of nature and those of the human personality. Prehistoric medics (often *Shamans*) worked on the basis of intuition rather than on factual knowledge. Illness was considered to be a disruption in one's relationship with God, with nature, with fellow men or women or with one's own inner self. Healing and restoration of health were inconceivable without reconciliation with God, nature, the community and the self. This was made possible by special rituals in which the sick person entered a kind of trance and emerged healed and whole again. The application of one or more natural remedies during or after the ritual frequently took place. Such ancient ceremonies used in religion and medicine alike, tend to be classified as the product of a primitive, uncultured and, therefore, underdeveloped mind. The anthropologist, Lucien Levy-Bruhl initially propounded this theory in 1923, but subsequently reformulated it in the light of substantial evidence to the contrary.

People in every age and culture consider the prevalent wisdom to be normative and superior to that of prehistoric times. Comparatively speaking this may be so, but the intensity and integrity of lived values may be more coherent and life-giving at other times than they necessarily are today.

Our prehistoric ancestors were richly endowed with an *unified* world view which is sadly lacking in contemporary culture. Unencumbered by the dichotomies and divisions which presently fragment our lives, personally and culturally, our ancestors felt a strong sense of the oneness of God, man , nature and the universe. Their ecological sensitivities were highly developed. Occasional evidence for cannibalism and child-murder undoubtedly exists, cumulatively no more savage than the mass murder of our age exemplified in abortions, wars, torture and criminal activity. Our roots as a species are very sacred and in a time of cultural transition it can be a salutary experience to reconnect with our origins.

Returning to contemporary medicine: every nation, both developed and underdeveloped, spends millions of pounds on health care. For the medical profession itself it is lucrative business with an accompanying power and status in the community generally. Our medics will not part easily with these privileges and hence the inevitable resistance to the alternative approach, with its emphasis on self-help, better relationships and a greater

DIMENSIONS OF HOLISTIC HEALTH AND HEALTH CARE

Strata of Life Process	Self-care Practices	'Natural' Therapeutic Interventions	Orthodox or Radical Therapeutic Interventions
Spiritual	Medication, Spiritual practices, Prayer	Spiritual counseling, Pastoral counseling, Group religious practice	Psychiatric drugs, Cults
Environmental	Awareness of toxins, Detoxification	Environmental clean-up, Allergy presensitisation	Chemotherapy
Societal/Cultural	Social/Political involvement, Productive work	General political process	Institutionalisation
Community/Family	Communication skills, Committed relationships	Family or group therapy, Community activity	Institutionalisation
Psychological	Stress reduction, Coping skills	Counseling	Tranquilisers, etc
Mental (attitudes, values)	Self-awareness, Self-responsibility, Planning, Commitment to goals, Learning	Psychotherapy	Cults, Institutionalisation
Lifestyle	Awareness of negative addictions, Learning, General health practices	Group therapy, Counseling	General illness care
Anatomical	Aerobic exercise, Dance, Yoga, Martial arts	Physical therapy, Spinal manipulation, Massage, Bodywork, Metabolic therapies	Surgery
Genetic/Cellular	Detoxification, Visualisation	Metabolic therapies, Meganutrition	Chemotherapy, Radiation therapy
Biochemical	Improved nutrition balance, Awareness	Meganutrition, Acupuncture	Chemotherapy
Energetic	Energy practices	Reflexology, Homeopathy	

Source: Bliss (1985), p. 17.

appreciation of nature's healing gifts. The change envisaged for both patient and practitioner is revolutionary. In spite of its common sense and profound innate wisdom, it will be a long time yet before it is widely recognised or accepted. Old models, despite all their limitations, die slowly.

As indicated in Chapter Two, change includes a death experience: old ways, established models, inadequate perceptions, must be left behind and abandoned. We tend to forget that change also involves 'resurrection', embracing new possibilities with fresh responsibilities and novel challenges. Without this second dimension, the first phase of abandoning the old only culminates in a lifeless resignation, characterised by feelings of loneliness,uselessness, depression, despair and in extreme cases, suicide. To take on a meaningful alternative demands courage, vision, support and, above all, appropriate knowledge and information.

To effect change in contemporary medical practice, both the givers and receivers of medical aid need to abandon the model of the body as a machine, and appropriate the new vision provided by the contemporary scientific and social enlightenment. According to the holistic model of health care, the human being has within herself and within the environment, *all* the resources to live a fulfilled and healthy life. On the part of the patient/client, that recognition can only be translated into an appropriate lifestyle and behaviour on the basis of strong conviction, new vision and a revitalised quality of human relationships. In the new model the practitioner becomes something of a 'systems' servant' (something of a doctor, psychologist, religious minister and sociologist all combined) functioning *primarily* as a catalyst for life-giving change, a role somewhat akin to that of the *shaman* in prehistoric times. Instead of dishing out pep-pills, or seeking to replace or rectify parts of the biological machine, he becomes the facilitator who seeks to unleash the inner healing powers of person and nature, so that these can function (i.e. inter-relate) more effectively. It is not a diminished role, but it is a *transformed* one.

Transformation is a more encompassing name for change. It does not denote change for the sake of change, nor is it primarily concerned with the alteration or modification of *external* structures. The focus is *internal* in a double sense:
— activating the potential for change (i.e. for growth and self-

renewal) that is inherent in every living system, whether it be the human body or the universe itself;
— allowing life to unfold with the evolutionary flow of cultural change in such a way that we become its beneficiaries rather than its victims.

With these observations we return to the spiritual realm; we move inside. Already, we noted the revival of mystical consciousness and its dialogue with contemporary science and ecology. Mysticism serves the unfolding of godliness at the heart of creation, but it is also a powerfully transforming radiance in *human* life, and to that personal quest and its modern expression, we now turn our attention.

5: Spiritual Revitalisation

Humanity has reached the biological point where it must either lose all belief in the universe or quite resolutely worship it. . .
　　　　　　　　　　　　　　　　　　　　　　　　　　– TEILHARD DE CHARDIN

The explorer of inner spaces cannot afford the baggage of fixed beliefs.
　　　　　　　　　　　　　　　　　　　　　　　　　　– JOHN LILLY

Strategic planning is worthless – unless there is first a strategic vision.
　　　　　　　　　　　　　　　　　　　　　　　　　　– JOHN NAISBITT

Debate about the existence of God and accompanying religious belief features in every age and culture of man. Since the initiation of formal religion some 4,000 years ago no less than nine major religious systems have flourished on earth.* Commitment to religious belief has never been quite as widespread as people tend to assume; every age has had its agnostics and atheists along with a substantial number of nominal believers.

Formal religion is a very recent visitor to our planet. Beginning with Hinduism, about 2,000 BC, it covers a mere 7% of the human evolutionary time-scale. Prior to 2,000 BC we tend to assume that people were pagans. That very assumption is not merely erroneous but underpins one of the most prevalent misconceptions of our time.

Our prehistoric ancestors were not *religious*, but they were definitely *spiritual*. Their lives were marked by a deep inner urge, connecting them with another 'reality' (we call, 'God') which endowed their life and existence with meaning and purpose. The ancients articulated their spiritual convictions in a vast variety of custom and ritual – often complex and elaborate – for an estimated 70,000 years before formal religions transpired. Humanity has a long and rich spiritual history.

Probing Our Spiritual Depth

The all important distinction between the *spiritual* and the

---

* Also referred to as the 'great religions', namely, Hinduism, Judaism, Zoroastrianism, Taoism, Confucianism, Buddhism, Christianity, Islam and Sikhism.

religious is frequently overlooked or ignored. All humans are spiritual: we enter life endowed with an *inner capacity for transcendence*. We are equipped with an openness to the 'divine', with an inner space which 'mystery' alone can fill. In articulating this 'power' (or in answering this 'need') the human species has created a vast array of rites and rituals, and eventually a set of formal religions, most of which are still extant. The *religious* structure, therefore, serves the articulation of the *spiritual* capacity. Humans are religious in so far as they profess allegiance to one or other religious system, but their felt need to belong to a formal religion is not *religious*; instead, it springs from their spiritual depth.

Whether or not we humans belong to a formal religion, we still remain *spiritual*. We cannot disown our spiritual identity. We may wish to forget it – that leaves us restless; we may try to disown it – that usually creates guilt-feelings which in turn we may bury deep in the unconscious. *Inadvertently*, we sublimate the spiritual in a variety of socially acceptable outlets, e.g. the popular escape-mechanisms we use to transcend the serious side of life: drugs, drink, prestige, power, etc. *Unknowingly,* we may pervert it by a blind allegiance to one or other religious system. Finally, we may spend a whole lifetime seeking appropriate expressions for our belief; this, in fact, *may* be the most mature response of all.

Formal religion in today's world has become heavily and excessively institutionalised, to such a degree that it poses a serious threat to the spiritual unfolding of humanity and the universe. The spiritual has become so fossilised in antiquated structures and liturgies that it is no longer easily identifiable for many people both inside and outside our churches. To reawaken humanity from its spiritual torpor and indifference, to enable the species to reconnect with its spiritual roots, is one of the supreme challenges of our time.

It is difficult to imagine a revival coming from within the churches, nor does one wish to suggest that a new world religion would bring about the spiritual revolution. The spiritual survived without formal religion for so long, it is conceivable that it may thrive without it again. The rise of basic christian communities and house groups in the various christian churches may signal a new spiritual hunger for intimacy, spontaneity and community in fluid and flexible structures, clearly at variance with the anonymity and formality of institutional religion.

Erich Jantsch (1980) writes of the complementary evolutionary forces at both the *macro* and *micro* levels. The contemporary religious revival exemplifies such development. At the *micro* level, we have the basic christian communities and the house-group churches, enabling spiritual and human growth at the personal and communal levels of existence. At the *macro* level, we experience the upsurge of *mysticism*, often camouflaged in the variety of Eastern meditation and relaxation techniques, in ecological and anti-nuclear movements and in the pursuit of alternative lifestyles.

In Chapter Three we explored the meaning of *mysticism,* especially in its connection with earthliness and materiality. Mysticism is the supreme and most integrated expression of spiritual growth: ·

> (It is) the art of becoming fully conscious. It is the way of removing the filters. It is the path to getting fully in tune with reality. Mysticism is a new way of being that transforms everything it touches. It puts me in touch with my deepest self, my hidden powers. So profoundly does it transform me that the mystic state is described as touching the divine. (Edward Stevens, 1973, pp. 15-16.)

At heart, we are all mystics. We operate out of a spiritual depth, a primordial restlessness, a primal eagerness for a fuller, richer and more integrated life. In the formal religions, we associate this fulfilment with the after-life, considered to be acosmic, unearthly, high above this vale of tears. But in the christian vision, the 'fullness of life' embodies itself in the fabric of human flesh and within the web of earthly materiality. Even in his resurrected, glorified state, Jesus communicated with his earthly friends and followers. After-life may not be *acosmic* (cut off from the cosmos), but *pancosmic* (entering a new spiritual relationship with the cosmos). Heaven and hell may not be *physical* states outside the world but *spiritual* states within it.

In our spiritual/mystical depth we don't try to escape the body; we forever try to *transcend* it and that very transcending may be possible only through the *transformation* of our bodies. What this means we don't really know but all the major religions formulate this conviction in one way or another: in the Far East by the process of transmigration; in christianity, by the resurrection of the dead on the last day, when we shall be reunited with our bodies. Both theories are attempts to retain and redesign our fundamental connection with the universe.

Cut off from the world, our lives seem to be totally meaningless. In other words, it is the permanent task of spirituality to rediscover our rootedness and bond with creation (humanly and spiritually) in each new era of global and evolutionary growth. Spirituality is earthly and global at its very core, something the great mystics of East and West have always proclaimed, and thankfully we are rediscovering this long-lost wisdom in the contemporary development of *Creation-centred Spirituality* (cf. p. 97).

Without something of that vision and vitality of the mystic, we cannot hope to share in the spiritual revival of our age. The 'conversion' required for entry to the Aquarian Age makes heavier demands than most other changes envisaged in the transformation. We are so out of touch with our spiritual depth, alienated because of brainwashing or conditioning, so routinised by institutional religion, lured by the false gods of power, pleasure and prestige, that the pilgrim journey may just be too much for most people. One is not wishing to cast aspersions or make judgements. We live in an age of mass agnosticism and widespread religious indifference, vantage points that do not lead easily to spiritual awakening. Nonetheless, the spiritual seeds are in each person's heart, and even our hardened hearts may begin to soften when touched by the Spirit who also fills our universe and enlivens everything in it.

Carl Jung and Modern Spirituality

So far in this chapter we have reviewed our human tendency to transcend, to express our spiritual yearnings and enter into meaningful relationships with God, humanity and our earth as exemplified in the lives of the mystics. These reflections are based on claims, which, to many readers, may seem fantastic, even outlandish. I now propose to examine this vision from another angle, that of Jungian psychology and its concepts of the *Collective Unconscious* and the *Archetypes*.

Carl G. Jung, son of a minister of the Swiss Reformed Church, was born in Switzerland in 1875. He soon broke with his father's devotion to Christianity, rejecting Calvinism as so much 'fancy drivel' and oppressive 'mumbo-jumbo'. His early religious disenchantment became the driving force for a life-long spiritual

MAIN TENENTS OF CREATION-CENTRED SPIRITUALITY

1. Creation is the supreme expression of God's creative energy (dabhar).

2. On entering this world, we are marked with an 'original blessing' rather than with an 'original sin'.

3. The earth is a place of warmth, welcome and goodness; we need to savour its pleasure.

4. Trust is the basis for a renewed relationship with the God of creation.

5. Our trust is expressed as an *aesthetic* rather than an *ascetic* spirituality.

6. We transform creation by embracing our earthiness, not by rejecting it.

7. Holiness is cosmic hospitality, rather than a quest for personal perfection.

8. There is a creative *dialectic* (both/and) between God and creation, not a divisive dualism (either/or).

9. Compassion and the pursuit of justice form the new contemplative attitude; the Church becomes the servant of the Kingdom.

10. The call to duty becomes a call to beauty.

11. The political will-to-power becomes the prophetic call to abandon exploitation and manipulation.

12. Rationality and intellectualism give way to feeling and imagination.

Source: Based on Matthew Fox (1983)

exploration which brought him into conflict with many of his psychiatric colleagues.

Associating himself with Freud from 1907 to 1913, he accepted the latter's view of religion as a projection of our childhood fears and fantasies. Amid great bitterness he broke from his mentor, especially on the issue of sexuality, which Freud considered to be the focal point of human instinctual drive, but which Jung regarded as a dimension of human life concerned more with meaning, purpose and integration rather than with destructive tendencies. From 1921 on, and especially in the final period of his life (1952-1961), Jung developed his own distinctive approach to psychological well-being, unique in many ways, but especially in its recognition of spirituality as a powerful, integrating and healing force in human life.

Carl Jung was a parent-figure for today's global consciousness. Whereas Freud postulated three possible states of awarness: *conscious* (what I am *now* aware of); *preconscious* (what I become aware of when I recall a past experience); and *subconscious* (a form of psychic energy which governs most of my behaviour although I am totally unaware of its origin or influence) – all centred in the *individual* person, Jung assumed a radically different approach.

With something of a mystical vision, Jung postulates a *collective unconscious*. He called it a *Grenzbegriff*, a concept used to describe something that feels very real but somehow beyond analysis or even description. (Kant used the same term to designate the concept of *God*.) For Jung, the *collective unconscious* is a vital force permeating all creation; it contains both past and future, light and shadow, presently active in humans and in all created reality. It may be described as a type of etheral energy, containing all the thoughts, feelings, dreams of the past and all the hopes and aspirations of the future, even the evolutionary 'aspirations' of the universe itself. It contains both good and bad, more as complementary rather than opposite poles and its attraction or magnetism is towards growth and integration.

What proof have we for the existence of the *collective unconscious*? *None*, in terms of rational thought or scientific verification. According to Jung, the reality of the unconscious represents the mysterious, suprarational within humanity and within creation and this, for Jung, is as real, and merits as much attention, as the rational and observable. It is at this juncture that many colleagues of orthodox psychiatry and academic psychology part company with Jung, considering his taste for the spiritual and mystical to be unscientific, misleading and even dangerous.

Jung continues to elaborate his concept of the *collective uncon-scious*, claiming that it consists of *archetypes:* inherent predispos-itions, reflecting symbolically the entire history of man:

> There are many symbols that are not individual but collective in their nature and origin. These are chiefly religious images; their origin is so far buried in the mystery of the past that they seem to have no human source. But they are, in fact, 'collective representations' emanating from primeval dreams and creative fantasies. As such these images are involuntary spontaneous manifestations and by no means intentional inventions. (Jung, 1968, pp. 41-42.)

In other words, we as a species, share inherited, primordial beliefs, images, values, many of which are common to all human-ity, irrespective of time, creed or culture, and this shared wisdom is what is expressed in the *archetypes*. According to Jung, this cumulative wisdom forms the common ground of human belief, variably expressed in the different religious systems of mankind.

According to Paul F. Knitter (1985, p. 57), archetypes are:

> . . . predispositions towards the formation of images, *a priori* powers of representation, inbuilt stirrings or lures that, if we can feel and follow them, will lead us into the depths of what we are and where we are going. They might be called messages-in-code, which we must decode and bring to our conscious awarness.
>
> It is difficult to speak about what these messages contain. Their general contents, Jung tells us, have to do with light and darkness, death and rebirth, wholeness, sacrifice and redemption. He saw such archetypes as the common seedbed of all religions.

Ray L. Hart (1968, p. 298) makes the following list of prominent archetypal themes:

> . . . wrestling power from the Gods – fate and freedom, questions of danger, vengeance, retribution; of change, rebirth, old age, death; the passage of time, the revolutions of the seasons; origin and con-tinuity – of man and the earth; food supply and the earth's fertility; the contest of the sexes and its derivatives – masculine concept and feminine intuition; good and evil, innocence, justice; the relations of family and the struggle between generations; ordeal and trial, the test

by outrageous onslaught.

What we have in such lists are timeless questions and timeless answers. It belongs to the archetype to run in this direction.

Finally, to keep our exploration connected with the central purpose of this book, we note the following observations made by Daryush Shayegan (quoted in Cazenave, 1984, p. 392):

> Jung and Neumann tell us that when cultural canons become exhausted, and when symbols decline, dying their beautiful deaths, the collective unconscious becomes volcanic once more, throwing up new archetypes.

Myth and Symbolism

To decode the archetypes, Jung employed *myth* and *symbols*, two means of constructing reality, used by humans since the dawn of civilisation. Our prehistoric ancestors grappled with the great mysteries of life and articulated their fascination in folklore and mythic tales. These narrations are no mere flight of fancy, nor can they be evaluated in the light of today's rational and logical thought-patterns. What we have in folklore is a story, imbued with human feeling, emotion, intuition and an articulation of the human will-to-meaning:

> In order for life to be creatively negotiated, a person must live out of a narrative infrastructure. Even philosophers like Sartre, who proclaim a meaningless existence where each moment is alien to every other, are secretly supported by a narrative pattern which enables them to courageously accept that existence. Narrative is an inherent quality of experience and so a primal form of human discourse. . . The very act of storytelling is an implicit affirmation of ultimate meaning. (John Shea, 1980, p. 88.)

The power of mythic stories is not in their veracity or accuracy of historical fact, but in their ability to awaken *archetypal* values, feelings and emotions, and give them a form of expression that enables the narrator and listener to connect with new levels of meaning and purpose. This connecting takes place primarily at a *psychic* and *spiritual* level and in spiritual literature is explained by the term *transcendence* (see Ó Murchú, 1986, pp. 32-37). Transcendence is not a form of escape; quite the opposite. It is essentially a new way of perceiving reality, of relating to life with a motivating force to become more involved in one's world.

Myth has a derogatory connotation in our society. It denotes a fable or legendary tale, which the rational mind of the twentieth century quickly and irrationally dismisses. Myth and folklore are powerful, cultural expressions (indeed, living proof) of the human need and capacity for a relationship with divinity. There is no age without myth and folklore. In today's society they tend to be camouflaged in socially acceptable modes of expression, e.g., the self-induced 'high' of psychedelic drugs, the social release of tension in the consumption of alcohol, the wild ecstatic behaviour of rock-and-roll or punk music, the extensive and varied exploration of sex, the widespread use of violent movies which help to articulate 'out there' the pent-up emotions we hold within, or finally, Merleau-Ponty's observation that psychoanalysis is the witchcraft of contemporary Western society. In time, all these *avenues-seeking-transcendence,* will collapse, and up out of the subconscious will arise a new story with many of the symbolic images of traditional folklore – living proof of the persistence of the archetypes.

It is difficult for contemporary Westerners to grasp the significance of *symbolism.* A symbolic gesture such as a handshake can be explained away (rather than explained) by describing it as a *sign* of friendship. It is a great deal more. When experienced appropriately, it evokes a variety of human feeling, awakens psychic energy, initiates communication and establishes a bond of friendship. Symbolic objects are also taken for granted. We stand to attention before a national flag, but, perhaps, never stop to think that this is a mere piece of cloth on which we have conferred meaning, because, somehow, the ensuing behaviour enhances the meaningfulness of our lives. We are in dire need of an education in symbolism; we need to be enlightened on the very forces which motivate our daily action and give meaning and purpose to our daily lives. (More on this topic in J. C. Cooper, 1982.)

The Jungian archetypes are envisaged as 'embodiments' of symbolic images and values which have universal significance. Commenting on the Jungian perspective Roger Schmidt (1980, p. 137) writes:

> . . . the similarity of myths is indicative of inborn tendencies or permanent features of the human psyche; thus recurrent symbols such as water, the earth-mother, the hero, the number four and the divine

child are manifested in myths and dreams. In this light myths are terribly important because they are public dreams that bring us in touch with the unconscious depths of human existence. Myths express the inner or psychic life of man.

In a similar vein, William J. Bausch (1975, pp. 70-71) writes:

That is why certain basic myths called 'archetypal' keep popping up. Some are the sharing of food. . . denoting the sharing of the very substance that keeps one alive; hence, the supreme hospitality, brotherhood, fellowship; the shedding of blood as a loss of vitality and drinking it as drinking the source of life. There are gods who died and rose again to explain the seasons. Miracles were used as proof of divine power. Virgin births were spoken of. The point is that these symbols are not unique to christianity nor should they be. They are basic myths that explain man's eternal hopes, his answers to the meaning of life, birth, death, tragedy and suffering.

The progression from the unconscious to the archetypes to myth and symbolism culminates in acting out, giving concrete social exprssion to, one's spiritual aspirations and this behaviour we formally call *ritual*. Every major religious system has its sacraments and sacred rites. Even people who are not affiliated to one or other Church partake in ritual behaviour, usually in a social or recreational capacity. Although the context is secular rather than sacred (as these words are popularly understood), *subsconsciously*, if not consciously, the ritualistic behaviour also serves a spiritual purpose. It supplies an outlet for transcendence, if only at a very mundane level. In fact, one may expect that 'secular' ritual becomes significantly more important for the 'non-practising' than for the practising who partake in 'sacred ritual'. Of course, the latter may be so fossilised and institutionalised, as it is in many churches today, that the believer and non-believer alike may be equally starved of meaningful spiritual nourishment.

Mircea Eliade (quoted in Hart, 1968, p. 295) suggests that in the absence of appropriate religious ritual, 'archetypal organisation' now takes place primarily '. . . in the imagination of the inner man'. However, humans are also *social* beings and, consequently, one assumes that all 'inner states' seek complementary external expression. Whether at a sacred or secular level (terms that become quite meaningless in this context) ritual serves to embody, objectify, make tangible the inner spiritual life with

JUNGIAN CULTURAL SYNTHESIS

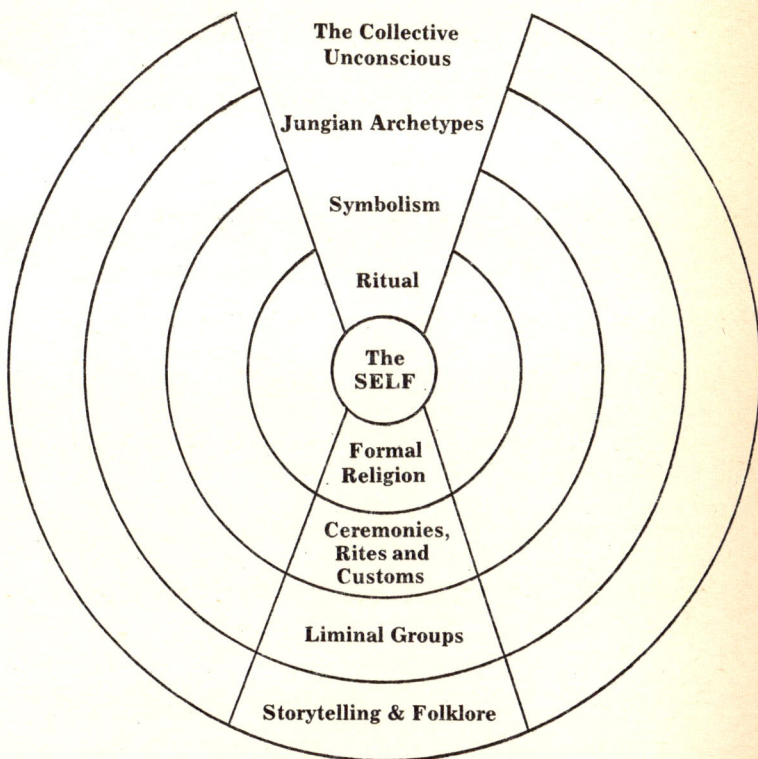

The Collective
Unconscious

Jungian Archetypes

Symbolism

Ritual

The
SELF

Formal
Religion

Ceremonies,
Rites and
Customs

Liminal Groups

Storytelling & Folklore

Explanation: The circular lines, named on the top half, represent the Jungian stages leading to *individuation* (realisation of the Self). The circular spaces, named in the lower half, represent the 'media' and structures humans have created (and continue to create) to articulate, in word and action, our internalisation of the stages. *Individuation* involves, among other things, the ongoing reappropriation of the stages and their articulation in relevant and meaningful 'media'.

external, earthly existence. Ritual is not an exercise in privatised, devotional practice, but a public social act striving to hold together in a creative way the different polarities of human existence. It has to do with the serious side of life, with survival in its deepest and most holistic sense.

For Jung, the final stage in the human, spiritual journey is that of *individuation*, whereby the conscious and unconscious selves are experienced in the oneness and wholeness of the personality. It has been described as the moment when one really connects with the God-within or fully experiences the archetype of the Self. It is also characterised by a sense of unity with all created life, with inorganic matter and even with the cosmos itself. In expounding the theory of individuation, Jung is at one with the mystics. In his experience as a practising psychiatrist, Jung notes that it was mainly people in the latter half of life who achieved individuation, and not infrequently after some form of psychiatric illness, an observation which has many parallels with the spirituality of different creeds and cultures.

Towards a Global Spirituality

This excursus into Jungian thought serves a number of important purposes for a deeper understanding of global and cultural change. In conjunction with modern science, mysticism and ecology, psychology, too, facilitates a deeper understanding of the forthcoming evolutionary transformation.

It casts the relation of the individual and the universe in radically new terms without the destruction or diminution of either. Jung does not deny the existence of individual consciousness in both its positive and negative elements. Like Freud, he acknowledges the instinctual drives and egotistic tendencies, but enunciates a very different understanding of psychic life:

> The self is not only the centre but also the whole circumference which embraces both conscious and unconscious; it is the centre of this totality, just as the ego is the centre of the conscious mind. (*Psychology and Alchemy*, par. 44.)

Despite this declaration, individual consciousness, as Jung construes it, is subject to and governed by the *collective unconscious*. The consciousness of the universe overrides, even controls, personal consciousness. We cannot modify the collective unconscious in terms of inherited wisdom, nor can we ward off its influence. However, we have the choice of being either its *victims* (when we are unaware of, or resistant towards, its powerful influence), or *beneficiaries* (when we acknowledge its influence and dispose our lives to its energy and power). However, we can influence and modify the collective unconscious in terms of its *future*; in other words, the cumulative global wisdom which we each inherit takes on new potential (positive or negative) as it assumes our contribution to life and to the world.

We refer to our relationship with the collective unconscious in terms of *influencing* and being *influenced by*, solely for reasons of clarification. Immediately, we need to add the inadequacy, even the inappropriateness, of such terminology. The Jungian vision is essentially *holistic*; it seeks to transcend the categories of cause and effect. Mutual interdependence among the different aspects, rather than one influencing the other, is the norm. In our mechanistic world view we are engrossed in manipulative influence, consciously or subconsciously emulating the engineer who 'influences' the machine by switching around or replacing the parts, or the doctor 'influencing' the health pattern by medical interference. Subconsciously, we project a need to be in charge, in control; we have built a whole philosophy and theology on this concept of the uniqueness of man as master of creation. It is a human vision riddled with cosmic contradictions.

We are not the masters of creation. Life is not about mastery; it's about creativity, unfolding, 'letting-be'. We are participants in the divine, cosmic drama, unique in our own right, but no more sacred than the birds of the air, the fishes in the sea or the stars in the sky. Our call is not to control (still less, destroy) the elements, but to relate with them in a creative interdependence. We need all other life-forms for growth and survival; they don't necessarily need us (as evolution clearly demonstrates); their existence is obviously enhanced by our caring and nurturing presence, but not by our mechanical, technological manipulation.

The integration of spirituality with cosmic human life is one of Jung's finest contributions to the current debate. Even before the present transition came to light, Jung (1966) wrote in a strangely prophetic strain:

These archetypal images belong to humanity at large and can crop up autochthonously in anybody's head at any time or place, only needing favourable circumstances for their reappearence. The suitable moment for this is always when a particular view of the world is collapsing, sweeping away all the formulas that purported to offer final answers to the great problems of life. It is, as a matter of fact, quite in accord with psychological law that. . . when a religion glorifying the spirit disappears, there should rise up in its stead a primordial image of creative matter.

Since 1970 in particular, Jungian psychology has earned a formidible role in current trends of spirituality. We are indebted to Jung for the rediscovery and fresh formulation of the spiritual as a powerfully integrating force; setting this new vision in a global, universal context enhances its depth and credibility.

Jung was also keenly aware of the distinction and frequent disparity between the *spiritual* and the *religious*, an awareness which evoked in him some harsh words for the official churches:

Christian civilisation has proved hollow to a terrifying degree; it is all veneer, but the inner man has remained untouched and therefore unchanged. His soul is out of key with his external beliefs. . . Too few people have experienced the divine image as the innermost possession of their own souls. Christ only meets them from without, never from within the soul; that is why dark paganism still reigns there, a paganism, which now in a form so blatant that it can no longer be denied and now in all too threadbare a disguise, is swamping the world of so called Christian culture. (Jung, 1966, par. 12.)

Because of stereotyped, formalised liturgies and a commitment too exclusively based on legal rectitude and moral imperative, Western christianity has evoked some measure of external conformity but little if any spiritual awakening. One consequence, perhaps the main one, is the decline of Western christianity. Formal religion has contributed, in no small measure to its own downfall; inadvertently, it has sheltered humans from their own spiritual quest and thus hindered them from being a more effective leaven for society at large. In fact, all formal religious systems have, to varying degrees, arrested or at least hindered, the reactivation of spiritual vitality.

Although his criticisms are aimed mainly at the churches, Jung's interest in religion and spirituality is not as a church force but as a *global, universal reality.* Spirituality is inherent to all forms of life – even at the level of inanimate matter. Without a spiritual perspective, our comprehension of the world is not merely inadequate; it is grossly superficial and leads to inappropriate and exploitative action.

Of course, this has been and continues to be, the message of all the great religions. The difference is that, for Jung, spirituality is more profound and comprehensive than any of its attempted expressions. The normal mode of expression will be that of formal religion; it may also be the primary medium of mediocrity and stagnation. In this observation, Jung shares a fear and apprehension held by many people today, inside and outside the formal religious systems.

A New Wave of Consciousness

Jungian psychology and classical mysticism are remarkably similar in their global vision, one they share today with an increasing number of scientific disciplines. From all sides we hear prophetic voices, announcing a new paradigm, an emerging world view, radically different from the present state of affairs. Are the visionaries of the different disciplines working in isolation (as we usually perceive them) or are they united by an unseen harmony and synchronisation, a new evolutionary consciousness for which they are merely the first envoys? The increasing interest in *consciousness* may in itself be the most pertinent clue and therefore we must explore the possibility (some would say *probability)* that we are the first generation of a new wave of consciousness!

What is *consciousness?* In the West we use the word *consciousness* to describe a number of mental states ranging from subjective awareness to self-awareness (i.e. being aware that I am aware) to attention (focused awareness), all in the *awake* state; there are also 'internal' states of awareness such as sleeping, dreaming, coma or anesthesia. In the ancient Indian language of Sanskrit, some twenty different words are employed: for example, *chitta* is the mindstuff or experiencing medium of the individual; *chit* is the eternal consciousness of which individual awareness is a manifestation; *dhyana* is consciousness focused on an idea; *purusha* is the essence of consciousness and *turiyh* is the experience of pure consciousness without an object.

We no longer simply identify consciousness with human 'awareness' in the awake or asleep states, nor can we easily and naively dismiss other forms, e.g., trance, the mystical state, extrasensory perception or consciousness as a dimension of inanimate life, simply because they cannot be accommodated within our scientific parameters of measurement and verification. The cumulative wisdom and experience of mankind *intuitively perceives new levels of awareness:*

> Our normal waking consciousness, rational consciousness as we call it, is but one special type of consciousness, while all about it, parted from it by the filmiest of screens, there lie potential forms of consciousness entirely different.
>
> We may go through life without suspecting their existence, but apply the requisite stimulus, and at a touch they are there in all their completeness. . .
>
> No account of the universe in its totality can be final which leaves these other forms of consciousness quite disregarded. (William James, quoted in Ferguson, 1982, pp. 74-75.)

These may not be recent discoveries; all indications are that they have always existed in the primordial psychic recesses of mankind and of the universe itself. But the time was not ripe for their expression and utilisation. One is not suggesting the moment of truth has arrived, but the variety of developments, outlined in this book, unambiguously point to a profound cultural transformation which is about to affect, if not already affecting, the contemporary world.

In Chapter One, reference is made to the rapid growth in knowledge and information, and the accompanying trend to 'store' knowledge in physical units becomes progressively smaller to the point of being almost invisible to the human eye. This progression not merely reflects technological skill but augurs for something a great deal more powerful about the 'mind' behind the skill. It may serve as an example of *mind* declaring its supremacy, consciousness taking over.

Peter Russell (1982) suggests that consciousness in its current usage should be understood as a *field of influence*, within which all experience takes place. It is therefore the *context* in which all experience happens, whether in an awake, sleeping, dreaming or coma state. And it is not restricted to humans, but shared by birds, fish, animals, and reptiles. We are becoming increasingly

DIFFERENT FORMS OF CONSCIOUSNESS

State	*Description*
1. Dreamless Sleep	
2. Dreaming	'Relative' states of ordinary consciousness
3. Waking	
4. Transcendental consciousness	This is a state of pure awareness marked by inner peace and harmony. The gross levels of reality are transcended and things begin to appear as they really are. Normally achieved in and confined to ecstatic, mystical or meditative experience.
5. Cosmic consciousness	This is understood to be a permanent state in which pure awareness and relative, ordinary awareness are experienced simultaneously. The absolute is experienced even at a subjective level.
6. God Consciousness	(*Not* the consciousness *of* God). Everything is perceived as being filled with the divine. The laws of nature remain intact but their operations are comprehended in an universe come alive with godliness.
7. Unity Consciousness	This is the highest state which the human being is capable of reaching, one of perfect harmony and mystical union between the person and divinity. The absolute/relative paradox is resolved.

Source: Based on Anthony Campbell (1976)

aware of a quality of consciousness in plants (see especially, Watson, 1973) and the debate about matter and consciousness is currently gathering momentum.

Traditionally, two positions have been purported, one which argues that consciousness is the product of matter once the latter has reached a certain complexity and the other which claims that consciousness is the basis of all reality of which the material is merely a manifestation. Today, physicists and mystics alike veer towards the position of regarding matter and consciousness as two aspects of all reality, animate and inanimate. At the inanimate level, they draw primary evidence from their discoveries that subatomic particles, the basic ingredients of matter, are not stable, objective entities but wave-like patterns of energy, whose existence can be mapped in probable sequences or resonances (cf. Capra, 1975, pp. 274, 297f.) rather than in static categories of time and place. All life, even in its rudimentary expression, seems to be governed by a flow of energy, which in its dynamic activity is beyond the comprehension of our external senses.

Many of these observations underlie Bohm's theory of the un-folded and enfolded states of being, the former being the outward expression while the latter remains invisible and internal but equally 'real'. If I correctly understand Bohm, he would consider conscious-ness to be the underlying 'energy' of both states. I am not sure if Bohm would concur with the viewpoint which considers con-sciousness to be the organising, ordering, 'meaning-conferring' energy of the universe. R. Mattuck (cf. Cazenave, 1984, p. 109) argues that the transforming agent, creating order and purpose out of the randomness of life (the fluctuations), is consciousness. Yet, consciousness is not about extrapolating simplicity from com-plexity; it seeks simplicity, not through *simplification,* but through *integration.* To quote Peter Russell (1982, p. 37):

> An important attribute of conscious beings is the ability to form internal models of the world they experience; the greater the consciousness the more complex the models.

In other words, the more profoundly and holistically we can per-ceive and understand, the more we grasp reality in its variegated and diverse nature, including its consistencies and contradictions.

Consciousness, as used above, is not confined to the human mind. Here we draw on an important distinction made by Capra, who in agreement with Gregory Bateson (1979), claims that *mind* is a necessary and inevitable consequence of a certain complexity which begins long before organisms develop a brain and a higher nervous system. For Bateson, *mind is the essence of being alive,* yet it is not an entity in itself but rather a process activated by the organisation and interaction of multiple parts. (Bateson, p. 103). Human mental activity is one manifestation of mind, but a limited one in so far as the brain, the centre of such activity, is still evolving. Consequently, the human brain in itself is not capable of linking humanity with the universal mind; we need to utilise other dimensions of our personalities – psychic and spiritual – to tune-in appropriately with the evolutionary consciousness of the universe. We need to use both *head* and *heart* simultaneously if we are to relate holistically with global reality.

The mechanistic world view of Newtonian science and Cartesian philosophy has strongly endorsed the perception of man as *master* of creation. The mastery we have experienced and still subscribe to, in large measure, is almost exclusively external and therefore predominantly functional, utilitarian, materialistic and consumerist. Because of this orientation, many aspects of technology have proved to be precariously harmful to human growth and to cultural progress.

With the industrial era in decline and the information age emerging, our concept of *external mastery* reveals many limitations. In contrast to the industrial revolution, *we* have not invented the information upsurge. It has happened almost in spite of us and, as already indicated, we seem to be running out of technological skills to control it (the microchip being one of our last resources). In other words, the thinking behind our latest evolution as a species is not confined to our brains, to our heads, even to human beings. Our only hope of tuning into the new reality (de Chardin's psychic evolution) is to shed our compulsive need to master and control – especially with our brains – and explore new ways of *knowing* and *listening* to the higher intelligence governing our universe.

Meditation: Technology of the Heart

How do we do that? Where do we begin? Our universal, religious heritage contains the basic wisdom we need for this time – if we are sufficiently open, flexible and unbiased to seek it out. The

means we call *meditation*, a word with many contemporary con-
notations. In the West, we have turned meditation almost exclusively into a *thinking* exercise, with the head playing the major
role. We have further jeopardised its usefulness by making it a
specialised feature of life in a monastery or convent. In more
recent times, we tend to set it in a context of reflection on Sacred
Scripture. Meritorious though all these approaches are, they
deviate from the real meaning of the word, which properly
belongs to *mystical* experience and today survives in its true form
in the East rather than in the West.

Many people describe meditation as the technology (the 'know-
how') for an age of consciousness (i.e. the era of psychic evolution). Each scientific breakthrough has a corresponding set of
technological skills to articulate and apply the new information.
For the electronic age, we invented televisons, videos, etc. For
the information age, we invented computers. For the forthcoming
age in which we are asked to participate in the experience of
being part of the 'unified field of consciousness', we need a new
global, supra-material technology, namely meditation.

Meditation has been described as the art of *centering*: gathering
together the diverse energies of attention so that I become
grounded in the centre of my being. It is a process that facilitates
inward movement (*interiority* rather than *introspection*), a calm-
ing-down of sensations and feelings, a mental alertness, and an
overall disposition of openness and receptivity. Walter Starcke's
description is worth quoting at length:

> Technically, this is what meditation accomplishes. We are starting a
> journey with our conscious mind. That conscious mind is like the one-
> eighth of an iceberg which appears above the ocean. The seven-
> eighths not apparent to the naked eye is the subconscious. Beyond
> the subconscious is the collective unconscious, the noosphere, univer-
> sal consciousness, or the total Godhead. This collective unconscious
> is like the ocean in which all the icebergs float. This ocean is not only
> the means of communication between all the icebergs, but it is the
> collection of total truth to which we, as individual icebergs, have
> access. Through meditation we contact that total truth, we transcend
> our finite limitations and we communicate with each other.
>
> Meditation is simply the name we put on whatever means we use
> in order to turn within and go from our conscious, through our uncon-
> scious, into the experience of pure truth or God. (Starcke, 1974, p. 33.)

Meditation is a type of tuning-up process, facilitating a communication between my being and the 'being' of life in the world around me (*God*, if you wish). In this way it becomes a transformative, rather than a passive experience. I begin to see, feel, know, intuit in a different, more sensitive way and this colours my attitudes and values along with the *quality* of my action. Meditation is neither *action* nor *non-action*; it is a different state of being which includes both, like the Yin-Yang polarities of Taoist philosophy (see J. C. Cooper, 1981). It includes everything that is religious, yet transcends all our religious categories. Its arena is that of pure mystery and the experience is one of reassurance that, in the final analysis, our relationship with mystery is benevolent. Meditation may be (in all probability, *is*) the most appropriate means for releasing the information (wisdom) encoded in our holographic brains:

> Through meditation one quiets the brain so that it can become sympathetically in tune with (entrained to) this universal frequency pattern. When this occurs, the encoded information about the universe becomes holographically decoded, and the individual experiences a state of unitive consciousness with the entire universe. I find this model appealing for three reasons. First, the common experience of meditators having a deeper meditation with a group of experienced meditators is compatible with this model, because such a group could set up a more powerful, localised field with which to become entrained. Second, the EEG findings of a number of investigators (Banquet, 1973; Gellhorn & Kiely, 1972; Domash, 1976), showing the synchronisation of the entire cerebral cortex during such states lends support to the idea of a holographic mechanism involving the entire brain. Third, such a model could explain the experience of knowing everything at once in such unitive states. (John R. Battista, quoted in Wilber, 1982, p. 148.)

There are several methods or techniques of meditation. In line with the great spiritual masters, we could say that it is not we who meditate; rather, the Spirit of God meditates in us. Meditation is very much a matter of 'letting-go', releasing the props, the attachments, the will to power and control, which has been so much part of our Western conditioning. The matter of letting-go is quite unique to each person although there are a number of accepted modes (see p. 114).

The mystical mode of meditation is that of disposing oneself, in

SOME WELL-KNOWN MEDITATION FORMS

W E S T E R N

Discursive

Traditional, Western (Christian) form of mental prayer, in which the practitioner seeks to calm, concentrate and focus the mind, using texts and images from the Scriptures. Spiritual Masters speak of three stages – purgative, affective and illuminative – leading the practitioner to union with divinity, i.e., *contemplation*, the highest possible state attainable at a human level.

Centering Prayer

The goal in this practice is to become more fully attuned with the 'God-within'. A mantric phrase or word tends to be employed, calming down sensations and feelings, leading to greater mental alertness and an overall disposition of openness and receptivity. In the christian tradition, the 'Jesus Prayer' is one of the better known versions.

Meditation Through Art

Activating rather than *calming* the senses is basic to this form. A variety of expressions are used – visual, audible, kinetic, tactile – with a deliberate focus on natural and cosmic life. The goal of this practice is attunement between the outer and inner creative processes as experienced in the practitioner's life.

E A S T E R N

Transcendental Meditation

One official, structured form of the Indian/Hindu tradition. It is a mantric form, similar to the Centering Prayer tradition, but differing from the latter in seeking to transcend (by means of an image-less mantra) mental imagery and accompanying emotions in an effort after pure transcendence.

Buddhist Meditation

The goal of this form is the attainment of enlightenment (Nirvana), that state of complete release from suffering. The practice seeks to cultivate *mindfulness*, initially through *concentration* using the breathing rhythm as the focus of attention. The underlying assumption is that enlightenment is achieved primarily (if not solely) through the medium of the purified, ordered, concentrated mind.

Zen Meditation

This is a derivative of the Buddhist form, employing the use of *koans* (paradoxical phrases which are 'felt' rather than 'thought'), designed to stop the thought process, thus making the student ready for a non-verbal experience of reality.

Body Movement

This is a variant of the 'Meditation through Art' described above. The Taoist, T'ai Chi Ch'uan serves as an example. It consists of a set of rhythmical 'yogic' movements, performed spontaneously without interference of any thought. A variety of martial arts come under this category. The goal is that of attunement with one's universe, a transcendence of daily experience in its fragmented nature to one of undifferentiated union.

Eastern forms tend to be less explicitly religious than Western forms. It is clear, however, that they serve a similar *spiritual* purpose, and the approach best suited to individual needs largely depends on each practitioner's level of spiritual growth and development.

quietness and solitude, to the vibrations of inner power, especially the spiritual energy we call *grace*. In the East and West alike, there is a well founded tradition of *Centering Prayer* (cf. Basil Pennington, 1982), more widely known today as *Mantric Meditation*, the *Jesus Prayer* of the West and *Transcendental Meditation* of the East being the better known versions. In this approach, the focus is on gathering together our scattered energies so that we may utilise them in a more unified and holistic way. In the Buddhist tradition there is a strong emphasis on *concentration* (especially in the breathing), in an effort to bring the mind to the 'still point', thus entering the process of *enlightenment*.

Matthew Fox (1983, pp. 188-200) devotes considerable attention to the idea of *meditation through art*, a creative medium that unleashes repressed and unintegrated energies, expressing them in a novel way, open to new perceptions and creative possibilities. In Fox's outline, *art* may be that of music, sculpture, poetry or a variety of other media. Finally, contemporary science seeks to open-up unprecedented avenues for tuning into the mystery of life (see Chapter Four above).

There are many approaches to meditation, whether in a spiritual or secular context, categories which tend to become superfluous in the contemporary understanding of meditation (and indeed, in the *mystical* understanding also). Meditation is, first and foremost, *a natural birthright,* a potency within every human being. There is a danger today that we perceive meditation as a highly specialised skill (especially for religious freaks) that we can buy with money or learn from a textbook. We are in danger of trivialising this precious commodity which, although innate to the human psyche, needs tender and careful nurturing by experienced meditators, whether spiritual gurus, creative artists, mystics or spiritual directors.

Our cultural formation and education has been so rationalistic, so left-brain-centred, that the intuitive, meditative capacity, although innate, is not easily cultivated. The collective environmental consciousness, being still dominantly rational and mechanistic (especially in the West), makes the transition to the holistic, inner realm slow and even difficult to attain. Learning to meditate means learning to live anew, out of a novel set of perceptions and a radically altered way of interacting with life. Such a transition can be negotiated successfully only in a very supportive environment with sensitive and appropriate guidance.

One does not wish to suggest that the new age would commence if everybody began meditating. In fact, it is unlikely that big numbers will begin, because there exists in people generally a deep resistance to meditation. In the West, at least, we still seem to be operating out of an institutional, religious paradigm where ultimate responsibility is attributed to the Gods and their earthly representatives, rather than to people themselves.

Initially, many Westerners experience meditation as 'hard work', and because it doesn't produce immediate and quantifiable results, is quickly discarded. Others rush in, seeking and often finding a 'high' which, of course, tends to be short-lived. What makes meditation so difficult and also so illusive is its combination of sheer simplicity and absolute profundity. As Capra has succinctly observed, it is well nigh impossible for us in the West to grasp the notion that opposites can act in a complementary way, and this is particularly true in our failure to enter and appreciate the mystical, meditative state.

Many people today dabble in meditation; some continue and begin to realise its immense potential, personally and culturally. Not a few of these same people participate in other new-age movements, e.g., holistic health, alternative technologies, ecological conservation, etc. As the meditation experience deepens, the change in consciousness, with consequent action of a global orientation, becomes quite consistent. One is not suggesting that it is an easy transition. For a small but expanding network of people it seems to be the only evolutionary-enhancing option. One hopes that in time the number swells to sufficient size to activate the *morphic resonance* that spills over for the benefit of the lethargic masses, 'stuck' in their mechanistic, functional world view.

The present chapter has taken us over a wide and variegated territory. We began with the mystical vision, which seems to be a basic articulation and expression of the human capacity/need to believe and to live out of a transcendent world-view. We drew particular attention to the mystical 'oneness' with creation, an aspect more dominant in Eastern than in Western forms.

Turning, then to the Jungian *collective unconscious*, we pointed out that the mystical heritage itself is also a cosmic heritage. Underpinning all life-forms is what today we call *an unified field of consciousness*, which we experience in a superficial way through traditional thought and logic, but is capable of being experienced in a more holistic and integrated way through meditation.

Through these reflections on mysticism and the Jungian unconscious, we wish to explore the thesis that there can be no evolutionary leap, especially one inaugurating new psychic and global possibilities, without an accompanying spiritual awakening. Nor can we assume that formal religion connects people with this new transcendence; it is becoming abundantly clear that it doesn't. In our rapidly changing world, with its risk of disarray and dislocation, we need a new religious framework to hold together the psychic and spiritual forces impinging on our lives and on our world.

Without the spiritual revitalisation, we will try to fit an expanded vision into the stifling recesses of an old static model, an approach which is likely to exacerbate the confusion, frustration, despair and suicide already rampant in our world. Without a radically new spiritual vision many will lose out on a breakthrough which occurs perhaps, only every 50,000 years in the course of evolution.

Thankfully, we humans cannot stop the breakthrough; regretfully, it is likely to happen without millions being even aware of its occurrence. Once again, we become either the *victims* or *beneficiaries* of change; which one we do become very much depends on the depth and integration of our spiritual faith.

6: The Enigma of Polarisation

Opposites are abstract concepts belonging to the world of thought and as such they are relative. – FRITJOF CAPRA

The climax of every tragedy lies in the deafness of its heroes. – ALBERT CAMUS

An infinitesimal amount of energy is required to perturb the equilibrium when any system approaches extreme stability. – KENNETH R. PELLETIER

In the course of an extensive study on the rise and fall of different civilisations, sociologist, Pitrim A. Sorokin (1950, p. 297) wrote:

> My studies led to the generalisation that in the great crisis of transition from the declining old to the new emerging supersystem, the polarisation of human souls, groups and values regularly occurs. Most persons and groups, who under normal conditions are neither too saintly nor too sinful, who render to Caesar what is Caesar's and to God what is God's, tend in the conditions of catastrophe and crisis to polarise. Some become more saintly, more religious, more ethical; others more sinful, more atheistic, more cynical than before. The positive, religious-ethical polarisation appears as a renaissance of religion and ethics, noted by Spengler and others. Factually, in the period of transition the full picture is growth, not only of religiosity and morality but also of irreligiosity and demoralisation. Only later on, when the new cultural supersystem emerges, does the positive polarisation prevail and make the first phase of an emerging civilisation ethically strong and noble.

In a time of transition change takes place at all the different levels of society. As we noted in Chapter Two, people in general *resist* change. Others, however, welcome it, feel quite at home in its flow and tend to foster and promote its growth. For the greater part, however, humans like to hold on to the 'familiar', even in the face of its obvious limitations and contradictions.

In the face of change, we can become so immersed in safeguarding the status quo, or alternatively in seeking its demolition, that we may lose sight of the *process* of change itself, which is a great deal more subtle and complex. In a time of change, the most compelling and intricate dynamic at work is that of the 'in-between tension', generated by the promotors and resisters of change. Awareness of this phenomenon can provide many beneficial insights for people on both sides of the divide; without such an awareness there can never be that mutual encounter necessary for a meaningful dialogue.

In the present context, therefore, the word *polarisation* refers to that experience of expanding distance between two sets (poles) of perceptions, one which regards the rising culture as threatening and dangerous and, therefore, something to be resisted and the other seeing it as a necessary stage of progress to be welcomed and supported. Polarisation is no mere intellectual construct; it is not a well-thought-out analysis of what is happening. Rather, it consists in strong, emotional feelings, deep-rooted in the psyche, often blind to reason or logic and frequently quite irrational in both formulation and application. It tends to be the product of the Western mind set with its often assumed irreconcilable differences between opposites, rarely perceived as *complementary* as in the East.

Synergy-Levels in Contemporary Society

Change is a great deal easier to cope with once we recognise and accept *polarised* positions. Then we attain a new freedom based on fresh perceptions, an interpretation of greater depth and the possibility of responding in a more sensitive and dynamic way. Firstly, let us note that polarisation is related initially to the decline of the old supersystem; the former culture is dying and the first reaction is: 'Let's try and rescue it'. Secondly, decline and decay in any living system tends to be marked by a low level of *synergy*, an anthropological concept that will enable us to understand polarisation in greater depth.

Synergy from the Greek *syn-ergos*, meaning to 'work together' refers to natural and spontaneous functioning of each organism for the benefit of the whole. Anthropologists studying primitive, tribal systems, have found that groups high in synergy spontaneously tend to work out of social and psychological structures in such a way that the activity of the individual is naturally in tune with the needs of others and the needs of the group as a whole. Conflict and aggression tends to be low, respect for public property and the environment is generally of high quality; people tend to live out of a communal bond where the well-being of each unit impinges on every other aspect for the benefit of the entire system.

In societies marked by low-level synergy, the picture is quite different and, alas, much more easily identified in terms of contemporary life. *Exploitation* is the key feature of a low-synergy society: we use the world to feed the self; we exploit our surroundings, other people, even our own bodies. Peter Russell (1982, p. 110) outlines some of the familiar features of today's low-synergy society:

> People vie with each other to stay top-dog; scientists keep their work secret so that they can be the first to publish; high-rise housing goes empty while people go homeless because the situation is in the interest of the owner; Catholics and Protestants blow each other up because they cannot live together; nations fight over resources because they cannot share them; the rich countries hoard grain while others fight famine, because its in their own economic and political interests.

Conflict, aggression, self-aggrandisement become rampant; crime and violence tend to escalate; moral decay and corruption become widespread. To arrest the decline, new infra-structures are created, e.g. drug-squads, fraud-squads, new punitive measures, restrictions on media coverage, subversive tactics. The new consciousness, with its focus on bringing some order into the chaos, can swing public opinion in the direction of right-wing movements, e.g. the National Front in Britain, 'born again' movements in the white suburbia of the USA and the current tendencies towards a new fascism (noted by Kenneth Leech, 1981, pp. 97-126):

> The right tries to retrieve an authoritarian, patriarchal, militaristic society tied this time to powerful modern technology. It appeals to a divine image, but that divine image is no longer the living God of justice and peace. It is rather a war-god, a god of oppression, an idol. The idol in turn provides religious legitimation for demonic destruction. (Holland & Henriot, 1983, p. xiv)

A political swing to the right has been evident in the Thatcherism of Britain and the Reaganism of the USA. The political strategy tends to be one of curbing violence, arresting dissent and suppressing pluralism, a subtle pursuit of uniformity which can never be achieved while the underlying ills are either being ignored or denied. In the face of change the tendency for right-wing movements is to 'dig-in-the-heels' and hold their ground. Maintain the status-quo and especially the power and privilege accompanying the system:

> One aspect of synergy. . . is what it does to power structures. Low synergy societies are those where power tends to be jealously guarded, where power attracts more power, where authority is kept at the central offices that represent the peak of the hierarchical pyramid. In a synergistic community, on the other hand, power is something to be given away. (William Hague, 1969, p. 156.)

On a global scale the low-synergy polarisation is nowhere more obvious than in the field of economics. 'The toughest element in all the changes that will need to be made,' writes Raymond Williams (1983, p. 253) 'is the economy.' Productivity and profit dominate all our thinking; monetary institutions have become excessively introverted, to such a degree that finance has become divorced from life, productivity from production and capital from people. Capital is no longer at the service of the economy; it is merely a weapon of power and influence in the hands of ruthless entrepreneurs (e.g. the multi-nationals) who exploit the resources of creation for a form of economic prowess, alien to human, cultural and even material progress. Inflation, mass unemployment, world starvation and the arms race are all dimensions of our cold-blooded inhuman, monetary structures. They are the festering sores of a corrupt capitalistic system which, although rotten at the core, could dominate our lives for yet another fifty to one-hundred years. With good reason, Clarke & Hendley (1975, p. 166) can declare: '*Homo economicus* is the roughest diamond of the lot, cutting through subtlties with ease and profit.'

Defenders and Explorers

Against this background of economic corruption, flanked by right-wing politics (even Russian has its power-elite) and military paraphernalia, the high-synergy polarisation takes shape. It goes something like this: the rank and file of society feel hopeless and helpless in the face of the monetary and political powers; often they feel they cannot even challenge their values never mind change them. They see no future in confrontation. This leaves them with either of two options: become a slave of the system and live as nobly as possible within it, almost impossible to do without becoming absorbed into the system and governed by its values *or* opt out and explore alternative ways of living. This latter course of action is the one adopted by a small but increasing, worldwide network of individuals, and movements belonging to what we call 'new age movements', or to what Marilyn Ferguson calls the *Aquarian Conspiracy*.

Initially, the latter group tend to be perceived as 'drop-outs', often accused of being reactionaries, acting on their feelings rather than from rational judgement:

> It is understandable that people still trapped in the old consciousness really do see the new movements of our time – peace, ecology, feminism – as primarily 'emotional'. Those who have most to lose exaggerate this to 'hysterical'. (Raymond Williams, 1983, p. 266.)

The accusations against the supporters of the status quo can be equally vociferous, using terms such as 'conservative', 'traditional', 'archaic', etc. Labelling people, movements or groups only serves to harden attitudes and inhibit creative dialogue. Both poles express something of the Yin and Yang of all life-forms, the need for what Erich Jantsch calls 'novelty and confirmation', the former to maintain a freshness and vibrancy conducive to growth, and the latter to allow new information to be absorbed and integrated.

The respective positions (i.e. attitudes) may be described as *defensive* and *exploratory*. By striving to maintain the status quo, adherents of old institutions wish to *defend* what they perceive to be permanent, unchanging, fundamental values. They further perceive themselves as the guardians of those sacred values, people who feel they must be continually on the defensive against the attacks of those who seek to undermine the establishment. Truthfully, a great deal of defensiveness is *subconscious* rather than conscious, determined by the 'social mentality' of the institution. Institutions tend to be self-perpetuating, a condition they acquire through the combined consciousness of vested interests. Over a period of years or centuries, the interests slide out of focus and give pride of place to the preservation and maintenance of the institution itself, which at this stage may no longer serve the best interests of its members, a fact to which the official leadership (and sometimes, the entire membership) can be largely or totally

FEATURES AND CONSEQUENCES OF POLARISATION

Symptoms of Polarisation

1. Overestimation of the Institition
2. Illusion of Invulnerability
3. Belief in Inherent Morality of the Group
4. Collective Rationalisations
5. Stereotypes of Out-groups
6. Closed-Mindedness
7. Pressures Towards Uniformity
8. Self-Censorship
9. Illusion of Unanimity
10. Direct Pressure on Dissenters
11. Self-Appointed Mindguards

Symptoms of Defective Decision-Making

1. Incomplete Survey of Alternatives
2. Incomplete Survey of Objectives
3. Failure to Examine Risks of Preferred Choice
4. Failure to Reappraise Initially Rejected Alternatives
5. Poor Information Search
6. Selective Bias in Processing Information at hand
7. Failure to Work Out Contingency Plans
8. Dissenters are Alienated or Driven Underground

Source: Based on Janis (1982), especially p. 244

blind. In this case, the maintenance of the institution is not just a matter for serious concern; it has become an ideology of blind, fanatical allegiance.

The *explorers*, on the other hand, have lost faith in the system or, at least, are in the process of losing it. They perceive the system as faulty, perhaps, corrupt. Rarely, do they *consciously* opt for abandoning the system; *intuitively*, it seems to be the appropriate thing to do. Often the option to abandon arises from apprehension at the thought of trying to reform from within: 'will it be worth it?', 'have we really got a hope', 'change is impossible here'. There is a mixture of helplessness and hopelessness and the sheer size of an enterprise can be so daunting as to make reform seem well nigh impossible.

There is no way out except to explore *alternatives*. What the system sets out to achieve may be attainable in other ways, by other means. It is a creative, imaginative approach which says: 'Let's explore other possibilities'. In many ways, it seems more true to the human condition and, undoubtedly, institutions do stifle creativity. Moreover, it may be the only appropriate response in this age of psychic evolution with the focus on mind, spirit and the inner flow of life.

Fritjof Capra captivates something of the tension between the defenders and the explorers in the final paragraphs of his book, *The Turning Point*:

> During the process of decline and disintegration the dominant social institutions are still imposing their outdated views but are gradually disintegrating, while new creative minorities face the new challenges with ingenuity and rising confidence.
>
> . . . While the transformation is taking place, the declining culture refuses to change, clinging ever more rigidly to its outdated ideas; nor will the dominant social institutions hand over their leading roles to the new cultural forces. But they will inevitably go on to decline and disintegrate while the rising culture will continue to rise, and eventually will assume its leading role. As the turning point approaches, the realisation that evolutionary changes of this magnitude cannot be prevented by short-term political activities provides our strongest hope for the future. (Capra, 1982, p. 466.)

Evolutionary Consciousness

The above passage aptly describes the emotional tensions opera-

tive in a transition phase. Particularly worthy of note is the subconscious driving force behind this process. It seems as if some
'third party' is engineering the entire plot and were it not for the
fact that this process has occurred previously in the decline and
disintegration of institutions and civilisations alike, it would be
baffling in the extreme.

The 'third party' seems to be a new quality of evolutionary
consciousness operating at the level of the Jungian collective
unconscious. It seems to affect human thought and feeling right
across the world, eliciting a variety of responses: a yearning for
liberty and dignity among peoples of the African and Latin American continents; a drive towards self-assertion, often masqueraded
in ruthless power-seeking, among the peoples of the Islamic
world; a desire for new technological skill among many Eastern
nations; a swing to the political right, a feature of Western governments shared by many rank-and-file supporters; finally, a vast
array of minority groups: CND, feminist associations, new age
movements, alternative lifestyles, etc., operating in different
parts of the world.

Although the new consciousness has a wide variety of expression in global terms, it is most pronounced in the Western world
in the polarisation of the *defenders* and *explorers*. The dynamic
at work goes something like this: a new evolutionary consciousness has entered our world, marking the onset of psychic evolution, a process that may take another few hundred years to unfold,
although all indications are that it will be a few decades rather
than a few centuries. Our contemporary Western world, operating largely out of a mechanistic set of perceptions, with the accompanying technology to keep the machine functioning through
pyramid-like leadership structures, capital-intensive economies,
functionally-structured institutions and a body of cerebral knowledge ultimately geared to controlling all aspects of the mechanical
operation, is impervious to the new wave of consciousness. Western civilisation is based, almost exclusively, on *closed* systems,
the ultimate goals of which are profit and power; even our
churches, at subtle levels, operate out of such models.

It's not that we in the West do not want to know; many of our
people, being quite well educated, know about evolutionary
growth and progress, intellectually endorse and fully support the
idea, but this is largely an intellectual, academic exercise that

leaves large numbers unable to transfer the vision from their heads to their hearts. In fact those who wish to make the transition tend to step outside the system. Whether they do this for convenience or because it is the only real option, is debatable; the *fact* seems to be that those who do step outside seem to espouse the new vision with greater facility than those who remain inside.

Prophets on the Margins

The new wave, therefore, being unable to blossom within the official structures where most of the people are most of the time, veers towards the margins (what the anthropologists call the 'liminal spaces') to find an appropriate niche. Segments of society considered to be drop-outs, the rejects, the misfits, become the beneficiaries of new wisdom, the pioneers of new possibilities and the prophets of new hope. The rebels become the real revolutionaries.

Anthropologically and spiritually, every society has sought to accommodate this group in a liminal space, through the medium of hermits, monks and members of religious orders. Historically and anthropologically, these groups, which society wishes to call its own, are set apart and endowed with values (expressed in the *vows*: celibacy, simplicity, poverty, obedience, asceticism, etc.) which jolt and even contradict the cherished values of the populus. They are primarily intended to be mirror-like centres, which reflect back to society its deepest (archetypal) values and challenge the populus not to become too immersed in, or conformed to, the systemic values and structures of the status quo.

Of course, when the Monastic and Religous Life itself becomes part of the 'machine', which it is today (because it has been absorbed by it – in the West, at least), then it can no longer serve this liminal purpose. In fact, it needs only a little imagination to realise that many hippie-like groups and cults of recent years embody monastic/religious life values in a much more explicit and profound manner than do the established Orders or Congregations (on *cults*, see Bryan Wilson, 1982, pp. 89-98).

The fact that every culture and society has attempted to accommodate this element (referred to invariably as the *prophetic*, the *liminal*, the *archetypal*, the *marginalised*), means that we are not dealing with irreconcilable opposites. There is a meeting point and, deep in the hearts of each one of us, is a desire to reach that point. Unfortunately, the desire itself can also be irretrievably destroyed (except, perhaps, for the grace of God) by mechanical conditioning.

The first and greatest conversion must be on the part of those who seek to uphold the status quo. From a self-righteous position we can often prejudge and thus inhibit dialogue, because the other party is unshaven or shabbily dressed; defenders of the status quo judge much by externals; it is a feature of the mechanical mind-set and often this jeopardises even the *possibility* of a fruitful exchange. Behind the shabby dress, the street protest and perhaps the 'foul' language can be a depth of feeling and awareness, much more in tune with reality than any of the orthodox analyses of officialdom. Wisdom works in strange ways!

Dialogue: The Way Forward

The polarisation, if appropriately negotiated, can be the seed-bed for real progress. The dialogue is risky and demands great openness and courage, especially for those on the defensive; when it happens it becomes a boost to our hope and optimism. In November, 1985 a group of lawyers and other specialists gathered in London to act as a conscious-raising tribunal, seeking to establish the international legality of nuclear warfare. A television coverage of the event synthesised the imminent dangers of such an attack along with the gross infringement by the superpowers of all major international agreements, negotiated during the twentieth century. To many viewers it was a new and stark revelation.

In fact, the Campaign for Nuclear Disarmament (CND) had been saying the same thing and a great deal more for the previous ten years. Nobody listened because CND is not an official organ of the status quo, and their methods of protest are considered inappropriate. But they have been telling the truth and had they not occasionally used unorthodox methods, perhaps, they would never have evoked the global consciousness that led to the London convention. In fact, history may yet record that it was CND consciousness that saved the world from nuclear holocaust!

It is becoming progressively and painfully obvious that our national and international institutions are unable to respond to the new consciousness. Even the social institutions that impinge on our daily lives are singularly out of tune with a new quality of awareness, as yet somewhat confused and ambivalent in its coming to maturity. Whatever the differences in these strands, and let us not under-estimate their magnitude and complexity, we must strive to transcend them in the pursuit of dialogue. The survivors of today's polarisation will be neither the defenders nor the explorers: the *defenders* are likely to stifle and choke in the smothering confinement of dying institutions; the *explorers* run the risk of disillusionment, exhaustion and burn-out in the lack of appropriate supportive structures.

We need a *network*, a converging point that will accommodate a divergence and diversity of experience and expertise. We need to sit down, not at one, but at several conference tables. And in our dialogue, there is no superior wisdom; both Pope and Emperor belong to the old order. In dialogue, we are united in our poverty, the little we know about the future that unites us. Relying on the wealth of what we know from the past will not carry us over the threshold into the new future. The future brings the past with it, but in such a transformed state as to be virtually unrecognisable.

In our poverty in the dialogue experience, we come not so much to give as to *receive*. And we receive not merely from each other but also from the creative God who spearheads the new evolutionary breakthrough. We are the privileged recipients of this creative energy which we are called to mediate for each other and for the universe entrusted to our stewardship. In this attitude of receptivity lies our greatest hope and the most daunting challenge of change. We must learn to yield to the creative energies of life; we are not masters of creation; we do not own the universe; we have no rights over Mother Nature; we have duties to cultivate, to care and to love. In this lies our uniqueness and our greatest strength.

The change from a culture of mastery to one of stewardship and receptivity may well be the supreme challenge facing mankind as we approach the end of the twentieth century. To trust the creative process and trust one another as mediators of creative goodness is not an easy attitude to cultivate in a culture perverted by competition, distrust, suspicion and exploitation, not to mention the bitterness and hatred that divide peoples and nations alike.

The wounds of the past will not be healed by managerial skills no matter how sophisticated. Talks between the superpowers to *control* nuclear weapons deployed for use *in case of war*, is a devious and pernicious rationalisation of dictators who think they own the earth and unconsciously consider all the rest of us to be passive robots. The build-up of nuclear armaments, in a world where over half its people live in daily contact with death and destruction because of hunger and poverty, is a chilling reminder of how insensitive we, in the West, have become to the plight of our fellow-human beings in other parts of the globe. And the institutions we create and maintain only exacerbate the problem. We, Westerners, are rapidly approaching the point, where, in contradistinction to our past, we have nothing to offer humanity except pain, misery and destruction.

The way out and the way forward must be different. But governments and churches will not make things different. The rank-and-file of our world must reclaim its power as stewards of creation. We must rise up and make our voices heard. And let us take courage in the fact that we are not alone on our journey; increasingly the protagonists of the institutions are waking up to their inherent powerlessness; there *are* sympathetic confreres in high places!

The truth is beginning to penetrate: *there is a future* – for those who can *change* and participate in the network of dialogue. It will be a rocky road and a turbulent journey, but those among us already on it know only too well that there is no looking back. The only future is the one *we* choose to make for each other as we journey to the promised land of a new tomorrow.

Part Two

Social Change

7: Models of Social Change

Things derive their being and nature by mutual dependence and are nothing in themselves. – WERNER HEISENBERG

Any philosophy that can be put 'in a nutshell' belongs there.
— SYDNEY J. HARRIS

When we change our level of awareness, we start attracting a different reality.
— GASTON SAINT-PIERRE

Changes taking place at a global level affect the social fabric of human life. The structures and instititions within which we operate – home, school, work, recreational opportunities, worship – are all influenced by cosmic mutations. What seems to be falling to pieces, breaking at the seams all round us, is just another manifestation of the pervasiveness of change in contemporary life.

Even our most sacred institutions – the family and the church – seem to be under attack. Traditional customs and mores are eroded; traditional bonds of social cohesion fragment. Chaos, and disorganisation reign supreme. And, worst of all, we seem totally unable to do anything about it.

Governments meddle around with 'patchwork' legislation. Many western governments have legislated for abortion, divorce, a wide range of contraceptives (often used for casual sex rather than for responsible family planning). Western powers continue to promise full employment, when it is blatantly clear that 'working for a wage' is an outdated construct that cannot be salvaged. Administrations spend much time addressing *symptoms*, and fail

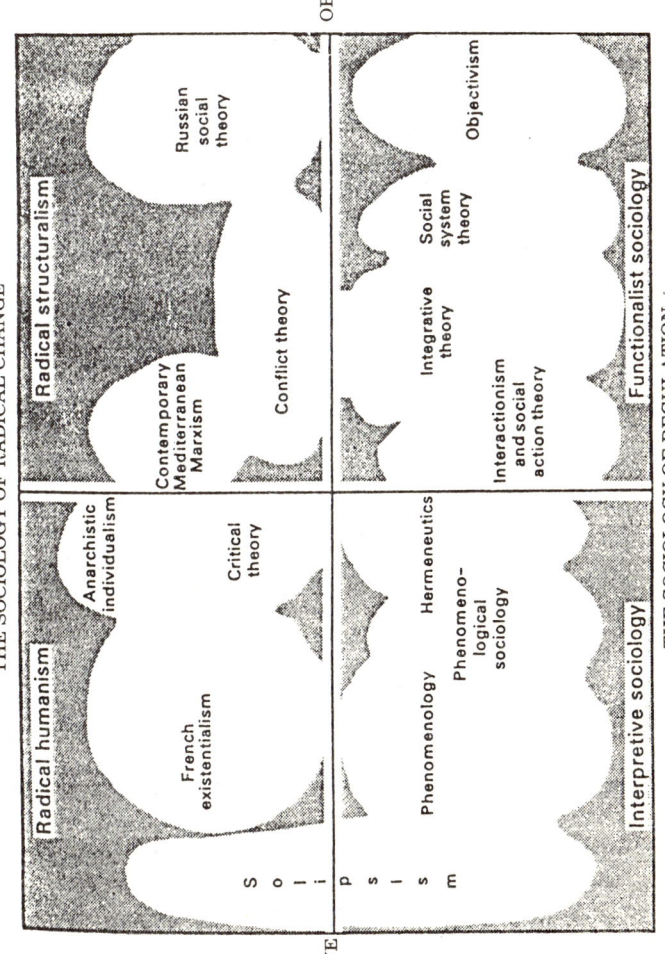

MODELS OF SOCIAL CHANGE

THE SOCIOLOGY OF RADICAL CHANGE

Radical humanism | Radical structuralism

Anarchistic individualism

French existentialism

Critical theory

Contemporary Mediterranean Marxism

Conflict theory

Russian social theory

Interactionism and social action theory

Integrative theory

Social system theory

Objectivism

Phenomenology Hermeneutics

Phenomenological sociology

Interpretive sociology | Functionalist sociology

SUBJECTIVE — OBJECTIVE

Sociology

THE SOCIOLOGY OF REGULATION

Source: Burrell & Morgan, 1979, p. 29

to perceive the underlying *causes*. We work out of a compulsive need to right the wrongs of society; we fail to employ our reflective capacities and perceive what the 'wrongs' symbolise. Like the cultural matrix, the social context is also in decline. *It is dying*, but its official institutions, primarily set on retaining the status quo, are desperately resisting that death.

The process is identical, globally and socially. The difference is that we can disaffiliate ourselves from the global scene – an irresponsible escape – but we cannot bypass the social context which comprises a large portion of our daily existence. Humans are social animals. Our need for filiation, companionship, intimacy is deeply ingrained in our being. Our individual existence is meaningless outside the social context. We exist for each other. Our deepest meaning as humans is not to be found in asserting our individual identity (and we do not wish to deny human uniqueness) but in the relationships and interdependence that binds us to one another.

Operating in a Social System

Ever since the agricultural revolution (c. 10,000 years ago), humans have followed a course of personal manipulation and control of the land and, consequently, of other people in appropriating material goods. With this new evolutionary 'power' came many undesirable side-effects, not at all different from the negative consequences of the Industrial Revolution. With the division and portioning of land there arose class-distinction, warfare, new forms of human aggression and, above all, a false superiority of man over nature. An accompanying perception of humans as individually unique in prowess and competence, rather than socially responsible to and dependent on one another, came to the fore; it reached its fullest expression in the 'one dimensional man' of the industrial and technological revolution of our own time.

Sociologists confirm this view in their studies of social change. Burrell & Morgan (1979) summarise the sociological tradition from its earliest days when mechanical and biological models were used to understand the structure and function of the social system. (Cf. diagram on p. 131.) *Regulation* was the key word, while *order, equilibrium* and *stability* were the cherished qualities for the effective functioning of the system. Parallel to the strictly *functionalist* approach was the *interpretative* slant, which sought to prioritise *people* within the system and, in a sense, initiated the manipulative and exploitative orientation which has produced today's multinationals.

The functionalist and interpretative schools, which include many of the founding fathers of modern sociology, accepted the status quo and sought meaning from within its established structures and norms. Under the influence of German idealism, existentialism, and especially Marxism, another school of thought emerged, namely that of *radical change*. In its humanistic form it suggests that we need to modify human *consciousness* and this, in time, will facilitate structural reform. Mainline Marxist thought, however, opts for reform at a more explicit structural level: it is not enough to change *thought*, the institutions themselves must be changed and for the radical structuralists this means *overthrown*, by violent means, if necessary.

Burrell & Morgan (p. 28) claim that the functionalist paradigm still dominates the social fabric of Western society and that most organisational theorists and industrial sociologists operate out of this model.

It is difficult to evaluate the impact of Marxist theory today. De Beus (1985) attributes much importance to the fact that one-third of mankind is under the direct political influence of Marxism. Negatively, the emphasis on violent revolution with the accompanying suppression of human rights, especially freedom of speech, seem to be the main issues causing worry and concern. Yet, we know only too well that the so-called democratic nations often perpetuate similar and even worse injustices. Economically, the free and equal sharing of resources seems to be a grandiose ideal to which neither Communism nor Marxism has ever subscribed *in practice*. Consequently, it rarely succeeds in producing the economic or political 'paradise' which it proclaims so vociferously.

Where internal developments in communist-controlled nations are concerned. . . State-enforced conformity makes it impossible to produce from inner resources the energy to maintain a vigorous life. Stagnation is likely to set in. . . If non-communist nations can hold their own for another generation or so, they may well be faced at the beginning of the twenty-first century by a communism that has lost much of its present dynamic energy, whose institutions are becoming empty and brittle shells, and whose leaders and followers have become mere bureaucrats instead of being crusaders. (Salvadori, 1975, p. 171; On Soviet Marxism see Lane, 1985, pp. 83-97.)

The impact of social change and features of the different change models, have been neatly conceptualised by Holland and Henriot (1983) under the headings of *traditional, liberal* and *radical* (see diagram, p. 135). The emphasis in the *traditional* model is on the innate, biological, functioning of a system that never changes fundamentally, but repeats a similar process over and over again. The role of leadership is strictly that of guarding the internal order so that the system continues to function as it always did.

The *liberal* model corresponds to Burrell & Morgan's *interpretative* paradigm. People begin to play a more important role and perceive themselves as 'managers of the machine'. Parts of the system grow old and may be no longer useful; consequently, the *nature* of the process will change as new models evolve or are developed. However, the process must be carefully *managed* by keeping all the parts in *balance* and deflecting conflict which, at all times, must be considered secondary and superficial.

In the *radical* model we have the qualities and characteristics of change which includes the ideals of the radical humanist and that of the radical structuralist but also *transcends both*: what does this mean?

Model of Radical Change

All four models outlined by Burrell & Morgan envisage humans as the agents of change, in terms either of *consciousness* or *action*. The models do not acknowledge that change can influence us without we necessarily activating the process or influencing it in its effects and impact. And this is the unique feature of the *radical* model, as yet a conceptual ideal rather than a lived reality.

The underlying metaphor is that our world, and every living system in it, is a work of art, the product of a transcendent, 'external' power, whether we call it *God, Life*, the *Collective Unconscious* or whatever. Within this artistic design is an interplay of interdependence and participation: everything and everybody need each other. It is meaningless to attempt a modification of the whole because that is beyond our reach; it is equally inappropriate to change any part *in isolation* because the whole is greater than the sum of the parts. And within that 'totality' (at both macro

INTERPRETATIVE MODELS OF CHANGE

Issue	*Traditional*	*Liberal*	*Radical*
View of TIME	Cyclic	Evolutionary	Transformative
View of SPACE	Organic	Pluralistic	Interdependent
Governing Principle	Authoritarian (Order)	Managerial (Balance)	Participative (Community)
Underlying Metaphor	Biological (Human Body)	Mechanistic (Machine)	Artistic (Work of Art)
View of Conflict	Deviant	'Manage it'	Creative
Basic Social Virtue	Order and harmony	Moderation and management	Imagination and initiative
Focus for Work	Agrarian	Industrial	'Holistic'
Politics	Stability	Aid	Mobilisation
Health	More Technology	Better Distribution of Services	Alternative Health Systems
Spirituality	Legalistic and Devotional	Liturgical	Charismatic
Focus of Ministry	Sacramental System	Parallel Structures	Basic Christian Communities
Church allied with	Aristocracy	Middle Classes	The Poor

Source: Based on Holland & Henriot, 1983.

and microcosmic levels) everything is potentially good and useful; even conflict can be creative.

The end result of the interactive process is one of transformation. We humans are transformed by the creative powers at work in our world. Of course, we can resist that process, even to the point of destroying ourselves and, sadly, others too. In responding positively, we help to transform the creative process itself, leaving the imprint of our personal uniqueness upon it. As agents of transformation our influence has more import on the future than on the past. We cannot modify the past we inherit – we can only graciously and gratefully accept it.

Our past – individually and collectively – is important; it lights up the path we have traversed, the good we have achieved and the mistakes we have made. By ignoring the past we are condemned to repeat it in a meaningless and destructive way. Sadly, many people who live out of the past ('we always did it this way'; 'the old way is the best') have an ideological fidelity to the past which condemns their sacred history to a lifeless repetition of verbal formulae and insipid action.

Ray L. Hart (1968, p. 11) reminds us that we *understand* out of the past, but *live* out of the future. In other words, everything we do in life, no matter how explicitly we relate it to the *past*, is essentially aimed at creating a better *future*. Almost in spite of ourselves we live for the future. We need to grasp this fact if we are to appreciate the full impact of the model of *radical* change. Change which aims at equilibrium with a focus on the present, or at restoration with a focus on the past, is not *change* but *stagnation*. The *radical* model seeks neither to balance nor restore, but to rediscover continually the 'forward-moving life-force' which creates each new *present* out of the experience of the *past* in order to move towards the *future*. In the *radical* model, past, present and future are interrelated and interconnected, but the power for transformation comes from the future-orientation rather than from the established past.

No other aspect of our christian faith has been so misunderstood as its future orientation. Christianity is, first and foremost, a religion of the future. The risen Christ is the embodiment of that final stage of life and growth to which we all aspire, while the 'new Jerusalem' (Rev. 3:12, 21:2) and the 'new creation' (Rom 8:22ff, 2 Pt 21:5) are the ultimate landmarks that give purpose and direction to the christian people on their pilgrim journey. Occasionally, christians have used the *future* motif as an *escape* from the call to be human, but for the christian family in general, the 'eschatological vision', epitomised and realised in the resurrected Christ, is the kernel of the christian Gospel, without which christianity would long ago have become extinct.

The models outlined by Burrell and Morgan (p. 131) are piecemeal expressions of a global and holistic phenomenon which no one model, not even all four together, can adequately express. Nor can we any longer think of change simply as a past-present-future continuum. Real change, holistic change *happens* to us (as distinct from *caused* by us) and is motivated by the *future* (rather than by past). It is a provocatively new way of interpreting change, demanding a radically new quality of consciousness, already referred to in Chapter Six. But old models and perceptions die hard and the letting-go is painful. It may be helpful to realise that what we are asked to let-go of is not that basic either to our origins or our evolution as a species and what we are asked to take on, original though it seems, is not entirely new to humankind. A consoling thought and also a reassuring message, one worth pursuing in further depth!

Recapitulating our Tribal Roots

Prior to the agricultural revolution a much more profound social consciousness prevailed, noted among many contemporary tribal peoples. And this was no mere instinctual response necessary for physical survival. Rather it touches a primordial experience of what being human means. Like our animal forebearers we humans are endowed with an innate sense of sociability; we need each other, not primarily for protection or nourishment, but for intimacy, support, companionship, affirmation and love.

We are most genuinely human in our capacity to 'connect' with the emotional, psychic and spiritual levels of our being. We need each other to bring out the best in one another and without this quality of intimacy, we atrophy and stagnate; we simply fail to become the vibrant, creative people that life (*God*, if you wish) has destined us to become. Deprived of such human bonding, we lose our sanity and, eventually, die.

For our prehistoric ancestors, the social fabric (which was by no means perfect) also contained a strong, ecological slant. It was fashionable among anthropologists of earlier times (and still is among a diminishing number) to portray our early ancestors as crude, cannibalistic, savage and ruthless. Against this background, the renowned ethnologist, Lucien Levy-Bruhl (1975) described our prehistoric ancestors as prelogical in their mode of thought, an allegation he withdrew towards the end of his life, under the pressure of accumulating evidence to the contrary. Our derogatory image of early peoples often arises from a rationalisation of contemporary behaviour: 'if we are so depraved, they must been much worse!' We then gather some fragmentary and dubious evidence to substantiate our viewpoint. It is worthy of note that most of this evidence comes from the post-agricultural epoch. Modern warfare (humans killing fellow humans) can be traced to guerrilla skirmishes which became widespread as people fought over land and its aquisition.

Prior to 10,000 BC, we have little evidence to suggest that humans behaved in the irrational and savage manner, with each person compulsively set on procuring her own welfare and status. Recent anthropological research points much more insistently towards a co-operative, socialised, caring and co-responsible mode of existence. Joseph Campbell (1959) cites many examples of the social customs of our hunting ancestors, noting that killing was neither ruthless nor random, but highly ritualised and often supervised by the Shaman, the spiritual chief of the tribe. The respect and love for nature features strongly in food-gathering tribes; Margaret Mead (1937) cites many examples from both contemporary and ancient tribal peoples. The social bond, uniting humans in fellowship, also forged links with nature and with universal life.

This social/ecological consciousness is portrayed in vivid fashion by Clarke & Hendley (1975 p. 71) in this quote attributed to an old Wintu woman from a tribe in California:

The White people never cared for land or deer or bear. When we Indians kill meat, we eat it all up. When we dig roots we make little holes. When we build houses we make little holes. When we burn grass for grasshoppers, we don't ruin things. We shake down acorns and pinenuts. We don't chop down trees. We use only dead wood. But the White people plough up the ground, pull up the trees, kill everything. The tree says 'Don't, I am sore. Don't hurt me.' But they chop it down and cut it up. The spirit of the land hates them. They blast out trees and stir it up to its depths. They saw up the trees. That hurts them. The Indians never hurt anything, but the White people destroy all. They blast rocks and scatter them on the ground. The rock says, 'Don't. You are hurting me.' But the White people pay no attention. When the Indians use rocks they take little round ones for their cooking. . . How can the spirit of the Earth like the White man? . . . Everywhere the White man has touched it, it is sore.

Above and beyond the bond with nature was the integrating force of primitive religion, for which Joachim Wach and Mircea Eliade are probably the best contemporary exponents. What today, we derogatorily call *paganism* was, in fact, a highly refined, integrated set of beliefs and rituals, elaborately celebrated and powerfully cohesive for human and social life.

> For once, a broad and sweeping generalisation about the primitive can be made which is strictly true: the primitive encounters the sacred many times during the course of his ordinary day. For him the sacred is in the fabric of his life, and instead of being set apart for brief display once a week its presence is felt during those occasions which are most important and occur most frequently during daily routine. (Clarke & Hendley, 1975, p. 170.)

The religion of prehistoric people had a strong social undercurrent. It helped to create and sustain a strong sense of community, which people today experience in 'house churches', otherwise known as Basic Christian Communities.

Within the group, and by means of it, the individual attained and maintained her personal uniqueness in primitive societies. Ken Wilber (1983) has written extensively on the *pre/trans fallacy* (PTF), whereby we tend to give transpersonal value to prepersonal experiences. What Wilber calls the *prepersonal* is the equivalent of the natural 'prelogical' stage of our prehistoric ancestors, destined thereafter to move through *personal* and *transpersonal* (divine) stages to experience the fullness of growth and development. Wilber is justifiably concerned that modern anthropology may be overlooking the nature and dynamic of evolution attributing to early humans qualities which he perceives to belong to the transpersonal state of cultural and human development.

His concern is built on a misconception (I think!). Modern anthropologists, as I understand them, do not wish to portray our prehistoric ancestors as being more highly developed – humanly, spiritually, socially – than our contemporaries. That would make nonsense of our evolutionary unfolding. What they do wish to assert are *two challenging observations*:

a) Primitive behaviour and lifestyle, because of its spontaneity and purity in terms of cultural conditioning, portrays, in clearer relief, basic, primordial, characteristics of human nature, e.g. a bond with Mother Earth, an innate spiritual yearning, a will towards meaning, a natural tendency towards fellowship, integration of individual and group concerns.

b) Prehistoric peoples, because of the absence of cultural conditioning, seem to have enjoyed a capacity to integrate diverse aspects of life with a facility *comparatively* greater and more integrated than contemporary peoples.

Our diversion into anthropology serves to remind us of the innate nature and capacity of our social identity. Our need to relate, communicate and filiate with each other, with our environment (especially, nature), and with God (consciously or unconsciously) is deeply imprinted in our nature and essential for our survival. Consequently, we invent structures and institutions for the expression and articulation of that need. Primary among those institutions are the *family* and the *workplace*, both of which are changing rapidly today; we'll return to these important topics in subsequent chapters.

Individual and Group

Already the nature of our thesis may seem confusing and unclear. One is not asserting that the *individual* is *less* important than the *group* to which she belongs, but neither is she *more* important than the group. She is unique within the group; so is every other human being; so too, are all the elements of life and nature but obviously in a different sense. This is particularly true of our ancestors of old:

> Most people in most societies have been born into communities in which the subordination of the individual to the welfare of the group was taken for granted, while the aggrandisement of the individual at the expense of his fellows was simply a crime. (Words of Slater, quoted in Clarke & Hendley, 1975, p. 84.)

Our urge to situate humanity over and above nature, and to perceive individual beings as being more important than human-

ity (in its various groupings), is the product of a particular historical consciousness which has become most pronounced in
colonialism and in the Western, capitalistic, economic system. It
receives further credibility from the mechanistic perception of
life, dominating the West since the seventeenth century, whereby
we view the world, the nation, the institution, even the body as
being no more than the sum of many different parts. Our need
to uphold personal autonomy is both a way of subscribing to this
mechanical model (the person is both operator and controller of
the machine) but also a reaction to the sheer impersonalisation
of modern technology.

At this stage, readers begin to see *red*: 'this is communism or
socialism in a new guise'. Certainly not the former, because in a
communist state people are perceived merely as production units
in the state conveyor belt; they are devoid of both dignity and
uniqueness. Moreover, significant social groupings are also suppressed, or at best tolerated to bolster state manipulation. In other
words, the system militates against personal freedom by exploiting or suppressing the social vehicles and institutions that are
created in the first place to facilitate the exercise of such freedom
in a climate of fellowship, friendship, support and affirmation.

The changing nature of contemporary life, as it affects the
individual and her social context, cannot be understood in any or
even all our inherited categories. We live at a time of new evolutionary breakthrough. Old systems and structures are not *wrong*
or *right*; they are simply *inadequate* to express the dreams and
aspirations of *homo novus*. A process of transformation is under-
way; old systems are in decline, some are already crumbling.
New social structures are emerging, but they are so different from
the neat, easily-identifiable, machine-like models of former times
as to be virtually unrecognisable. And they transgress so many
accepted moral and cultural norms as to be virtually perverse, a
judgement which tends to ignore the subtle but corrosive evils
that permeate many of our standard institutions.

We sometimes get the impression that people are swept along
in the flow of social change, with little reflection on their values
and little commitment to ideals. To a point, this is a valid criticism,
but we cannot easily encompass everybody in its range, because
many people in the matrix of change do not feel engulfed by it;
in fact, they experience it as profoundly liberating. Their

individual loss of control is not felt as a deficiency; people often rejoice in the fact that their individual limitations will be compensated for by the strengths of others. Nor do they feel threatened by an impersonal system; they acknowledge that they *are* the system. It will work to their advantage to the degree that they acknowledge and respect its complex and enriching diversity.

The focus has moved away from entities in isolation to the global reality, rich and diverse in what it has to bestow on all members. The climate of this new reality is well epitomised in the religious traditions of our race, all of which in one form or another, express the christian sentiment: 'He who loses his life will find it and keep it until life eternal' (Mk 8:35, Mt 10:39, 16:25). Our impending cultural transformation and its implication for human and social life, is succinctly expressed in that biblical phrase.

Attitudinal Change

Finally, we review briefly the formation of attitudes and their social impact. The mechanistic view of the universe owes its origin to a combination of Newtonian science and Cartesian philosophy. According to Descartes, thinking precedes and governs action; hence, his famous dictum: 'I think therefore I am.' The West in particular has espoused this philosophy to the extent that *thinking* has dominated our life and behaviour in an exclusively imbalanced way. Our entire educational system has been heavily weighted in favour of rational and linear thought, cerebral perception and the consequent impoverishment of feeling, emotion, imagination and creativity. Attitudinally, we also assume that our perceptions and values are primarily cerebral, i.e., that we change attitudes under the impact of new thought, new information or new ideas.

New *action*, rather than new *thought* (ideas) is much more likely to modify our attitudes along with consequent behaviour and activity. Probably, the best-known study on this subject is Leon Festinger's *Cognitive Dissonance Theory*, which indicates that people are influenced to think and act in a new way as a result of exposure to, or involvement in, new behaviour. This discovery has important bearings on our response to social change. New information may enable us to be more adaptable to and receptive of change, but is not likely to be as influential as the *experience* of enountering change in action. Conversely, if we are being influenced 'in spite of ourselves', drawn into a web of change over which we seem to have very little control, we can become extremely irritated and confused, particularly if we subconsciously operate out of a cerebral (thinking) model, as many people do in today's world.

The impact of contemporary, attitudinal change may be discerned by recalling the role of the christian churches in the past, exerting a strong influence through the power of 'mental' processes, namely preaching and writing. With the upsurge of media and its influence on human personality at more profound and holistic levels (*holistic* in the sense of the *total* person), the power of the spoken and written word has dwindled considerably and the churches today, in fostering value-formation fail dismally to influence thought and activity. Television brings *action* right into our homes; projects *real* life in a sensational and impressive (if often exaggerated and false) way. The media, more than any other facet of contemporary culture, has profoundly modified our value system and our range of attitudes.

In a rapidly changing world, initiated and sustained by a new phase of evolutionary growth, we are 'at the mercy' of change. Three options are open to us:

a) *Deny that it's happening;* pretend not to notice; keep oneself in the dark. It is an immediate instinctual response, born out of ignorance, fear and mistrust. But it *works*, and it can be a powerful means of coping. Sooner or later, the reality catches up and the defences grow weak. The individual may have survived well in the *defensive* state; the chances are that one has caused much pain and anguish both to oneself and to others.

b) *Adopt a negative, begrudging attitude;* in other words, play the martyr! It wins you notice and attention and the consoling but superficial impression that you are supporting others who feel exactly the same as you do. This stance is the one adopted by people who become the *victims* rather than the *beneficiaries* of change.

c) *Accept change;* learn to adopt in a positive and informed way. Link up with people interested in change and align yourself to supportive networks. Create an environment where change works to your benefit and to the benefit of those around you. Make yourself aware of the origin of change, the dynamic at work in the changing process (positively and negatively), the direction which change is taking and the role you can play to enhance its course, positively and constructively.

The third option is not one to attempt alone. Of its very nature it demands both a spiritual and social context: *spiritual* – to comprehend and appreciate the evolutionary undercurrents, the unifying and creative force, rather than the superficial appearances; *social* – to maximise the potential benefit for everybody, in a climate of deliberation and discernment, shared action and a supportive environment. In this way, we become the *beneficiaries* of change rather than its *victims*.

Many people today operate out of a restrictive and debilitating perception of reality. Our education system, at least in Western nations, has survived on and reinforced this perception. We have an inherited body of wisdom which served us well up to the 1960s and, in ways, is still useful but clearly limited as a working model. It is becoming increasingly clear that the stability desirable for growth and progress, has become, in many cases, a *static*, stifling conformity. It seeks to shelter us from real life, adorning our world with cages and masks which choke our individual uniqueness and camouflage our social and spiritual identity.

Our neat, functional model has served us well, producing the great discoveries of the technological age. It is becoming apparent, however, that this model does not benefit our civilisation even when it produces 'the goods'. There is more to life than mundane achievement; the variety of creation can only blossom in an *open system*, where structures serve the growth process rather than absorbing the process itself. Despite the achievements of the past, we have left our universe in something of a mess. And if today, evolution is carrying us forward at a rapid rate (as seems to be the case) could it be that we are experiencing an outburst of freedom-energy, long repressed by our manipulative technology? Let us recall the observations made in Chapter Three: Our universe is a self-organising, self-renewing organism; we may arrest its growth *temporarily*, but, in the end, the creative hand of Life (God, if you wish) can neither be thwarted nor suppressed.

We humans have always known change; it forms the fabric of human and universal life. Nonetheless, contemporary change, because of its evolutionary context, brings with it a novel impact. Because of its global nature and accelerated pace it is difficult to accommodate; nor can we easily identify with the recapitulation of our past which features in every evolutionary shift. Trends in neotribalism, with the accompanying breakdown of traditional social and moral mores (exemplified especially in the lifestyle of rebellious youth), are not easy to stomach and, viewed out of context, seem bizarre and purposeless.

Yet, these are the signs and symptoms of a change that can be neither thwarted nor arrested. Evolution is winning out, as it always does. We can consider ourselves the fortunate beneficiaries of this special moment and embark on a new venture, assuming both its pain and its pleasure. We can opt out or try to withstand the flow; our freedom allows both options; in either case we end up being losers.

Because of the universal impact of social change, all contemporary institutions are enduring something of a crisis. Church, government, education, industry, marriage, the family are not just 'under attack', as we are often led to believe. They are crumbling under the impact of an internal malaise. In their apparent inadequacy, they can neither assume nor assimilate the new-age adventure. They are stuck in old ways of being and cannot respond to new vision.

This fragmentation touches our individual lives in a variety of forms, but is likely to affect us all, to a lesser or greater degree, in two key areas: the *family* and *work*. We examine both topics in the chapters that follow.

8: Family, Relationships and Sexuality

In social network intervention, we are experimenting with the idea of setting in motion the forces of healing within the living social fabric of people whose distress has led society, and themselves, to label their behaviour pathological.

— SPECK & ATTNEAVE

The family is moving into a new phase in its long history. The resistance is great and the passage is rough. — McGINNIS & AYERS

Humanity's recapitulation is renewed growth. — ST IRANAEUS

The family is one of the most sacred and enduring institutions of society. Its existence predates historical records (Goode, 1963; Robb & Rotberg, 1971). Initially, it appears that the family centred around the mother, with the father serving mainly in the capacity of fertilisation. Progressively, the father spent more time with the family, until, as in European civilisations, a child inherited his or her father's name.

The family also serves as the basic, social unit of society and many primitive, hunting and kingship groups would have originated through the interaction of different family groups. The family has served civilisation as a *primary socialising* agent, with accompanying charges of nurturance and education. Its unique and special role has been unquestioned for millenia. Theoretically, it still holds a place of honour, but there is an expanding gulf between the theory and the practice.

Symptoms of Fragmentation

Because our culture has had a long investment in family life, one expects a strong reaction to the contemporary crisis. In this area, too, one notes a polarisation: those committed to restoring the traditional, stable image of the 'happy and united family', which they perceive to be *under attack* from a variety of angles; and the other pole, which considers the nuclear family (father, mother plus one–three children) to be the epitome of a closed-in, almost incestuous, system which breeds greed and selfishness, a bourgeois superiority and independence, a degree of social isolation and, not too often, a breeding ground for neurosis and psychosis.

The meeting point for both extremes may be that of a more recent school of thought (epitomised in 'New Age' movements and alternative lifestyles) which claims that the family is an *inadequate* social and cultural context for those who wish to espouse the more expansive and dynamic relationships made possible by the emerging, holistic world-view. Accordingly, it may be more appropriate to consider the family as an *agent* rather than a victim of social change (cf. Savells & Cross, pp. 32-43). This third option merits further elaboration.

Acknowledging once more the basic thrust of this book, that contemporary change is a global phenomenon impinging on all social and personal reality, including the family, then no system or institution no matter how unique or sacred, can escape this influence. The family is *changing and will continue to change.* We can be the *victims* or *beneficiaries* of that change, depending on how we perceive and understand the process at work. One is not suggesting that the change is *good*, but it is *inevitable.* Whether it brings good or bad very much depends on how we, humans, acknowledge its inevitability, anticipate its impact and cope with its ramifications.

On the grounds of simple observation, the following changes are detectible in family-life today:

1. Marital discord is rampant, frequently culminating in divorce or permanent separation.

2. Increasing numbers of women are employed in the formal economy and/or find fulfilment in roles other than that of the homebound housewife and mother; this development has altered the nature of family-life; consequently, the family-setting is no longer the primary locus of socialisation.

3. The concept of family has broadened to include unions based on cohabitation, one-parent families, homosexual unions. This means greater fluidity and an extension of the traditional concepts of stability and permanence.

4. The family as a centre for moral-growth and value-formation is a largely outdated myth. At this level, perhaps more than any other, the traditional family has become increasingly ineffective as young people in particular acquire morals and values from

peer-group and media-influence. Nor should we ignore the fact that many parents themselves operate out of a confusedly ambiguous moral and social set of values.

5. Frequently, today's homes (family-units) are described as *lodging-houses*, where the family gathers for rest and food and occasionally for recreation. Their 'real life' in terms of work-satisfaction, fruitful relationships, value-formation, recreation and perhaps, worship, takes place outside the home rather than within. By locating the educational system outside the family abode, society has unconsciously paved the way for this development.

6. In towns and cities in particular – where large percentages of the population live – social mobility has become a way of life. Some families move frequently from one place to another and within more stable units individual members come and go a lot. For an increasing percentage of people, a whole lifetime goes by without ever striking roots or forming deep bonds of love and friendship.

7. Traditional values of friendliness, generosity, hospitality, etc., seem to have declined in the transition from the extended to the nuclear family, particularly in the West.

8. Unemployment and poverty have created tension and hardship for family life, leading to the break-up of marriages, with painful consequences for many households.

The Crisis Within

One can find a variety of *external* causes for the fragmentation and disintegration of family life. These would include unemployment, poverty, marital infidelity, women's liberation, social mobility, liberal attitudes with an anti-family bias. What remains somewhat obscure, but nonetheless real, are the *internal* causes. Something seems to be at work within the family institution itself bringing about its own demise. Very few people *denounce* family life, at least outrightly, and when this happens it is frequently more of a self-disclosure than an objective statement with a factual foundation. Something is happening to the family; it is changing rapidly. The old model seems to be falling apart. Why?

Could it be that the traditional closed family unit is no longer capable of containing the new consciousness, which today is influencing our lives and activities? Like other institutions of earlier times, the family was perceived to function with *mechanical simplicity*: father was the breadwinner; mother the nurturer; children were reared according to a set of universally shared mores, norms and expectations; on completion of education family members moved into employment (then easily available) and thence to the formation of their own lifestyle. But all that has changed; we never set out to change it; it simply happened.

Today, father is frequently the 'home-minder' (because of unemployment or redundancy); mother the wage-earner; rearing standards and home values vary greatly from one place to another, even from one family to another; expectations are vague and frequently ambivalent. A teenage daughter is likely to come home and announce she is pregnant – with a simple explanation: 'Well, at least, I can produce a child, which means I am worth something to somebody'. A statement of desperation, not at all uncommon in today's world.

There are tremendous personal and social pressures on the modern family. In some households anything up to six adults may be unemployed, all living under the one roof. The family was never intended to host the frustration and apathy which this situation generates. As a social unit the family is not capable of containing the quality and quantity of interaction, generated by adults, all sharing the same plight. This institution needs a bigger and broader context to negotiate successfully both the hopes and fears inherent to this predicament. It needs a communal context, a national one, even a global one. Resources and imagination of a quality superseding that of the family are needed to resolve this dilemma.

In many cases, unemployment benefit may be perceived as a great 'cop-out'. We assume that if a breadwinner has enough money to support spouse and family, then he can continue to function as a 'normal' member of the family; this is a fallacy. Unemployment and long-term redundancy changes our perceptions and value-systems. People tend to cultivate such a depth of 'being useless' that even the care and concern for spouse and family begins to deteriorate. For the greater part, the family is incapable of coping with this dilemma.

Nor does it seem appropriate to suggest that we can *train* the family to cope better – in itself, that demands yet another structure. The way forward seems to be an extended range of relationships (networks) above and beyond the limits of the traditional family. In other words, the 'community' has to care for its citizens and not merely for the unemployed. Indeed, the community in today's world, may have to assume many functions traditionally maintained by the family.

Brigitte & Peter Berger (1984) argue that the family unit is still essential to society for the nurturing and development of children, since it is the only environment conducive to that quality of warmth and trust which fosters a mature and integrated personality. This conviction has a two-pronged perception: (a) Despite its limitations, the family has served society well for thousands of years; we cannot and must not quickly discard our past; (b) One of the few viable alternatives is the *commune* movement; judging from the USA experience, this has been a disaster, especially for child-rearing. The Bergers go on to assert that *the family will definitely continue* – history alone verifies this. Consequently, we must aim at 'capturing the middle ground' by a more concerted effort (by government, the public and families themselves) to re-establish the primacy of the family while addressing the limitations and problems currently undermining familial values: 'The meaningful question is not *whether* there will be an institution of the family in future but, rather, *what kind* of institution is likely or desirable' (p. 160).

Extending the Family Network

That the family will continue is indisputable, nor does one wish to deny the primacy of traditional family values and aspirations, especially those of warmth, trust, love, security. However, the *structure* and *format* of family life is changing and in all probability will alter even further. The Bergers seem to acknowledge this phenomenon, but because of their conviction about the *historical pervasiveness* of the family, fail to recognise fully the implication of more recent cultural and historical developments. For example, they suggest that today's family needs *mediating structures*: '. . . institutions that stand between and meaningfully link the isolated individual and the mega-institutions of modernity' (p. 197). In other words, familial values can only be fostered and sustained by an extension of the traditional family concept. The family institution in itself cannot cope (perhaps, was never intended to) with the challenges and pressures of modern life.

MARITAL LIFE-STYLES: CLOSED v. OPEN

Areas of Functioning	Closed Style	Open Style
1. Basic patterns of marital interaction	Rigid patterns centred around roles, duties, oughts and ought-nots, penalties, status, appearances, etc. (i.e., around the *mechanics* of the relationship). Partners may be locked together in a tight twosome, or fighting and undermining each other, or too busy to pay to pay attention to each other.	Flexible patterns fostering personal growth and the *quality* of the marital relationship. They are nurturing and and freedom-granting. Partners enjoy and feel close to each other without putting 'hooks' on each other.
2. Marital communication patterns	Tend often to be blocked or distorted by with-drawal, overbusyness, indifference, diversions, meaningless chatter, judgmental remarks, argument, blame, suppression, etc. Feelings poorly communicated, rarely listened to.	Open, clear, effective, meaningful. Partners share freely their thoughts, feelings, wishes, dreams, expectations, hopes, victories and disappointments. Listen to each other and check each other out.
3. Marital roles	Roles tend to dominate the relationship as if fulfilling roles were the main purpose of marriage. Rigidity of roles either stifles growth or results in endless friction and dispute.	Roles are subordinate to the human and nurturing goals of the marriage. They are flexible and negotiable to meet preferences, abilities and changing needs and circumstances.
4. Conflicts and decision-making in marriage	Tendency to competitiveness, jealousy, rivalry, blame. Conflicts simmer or flare without resolution. Decisions imposed by one partner, or avoided until forced by a crisis, or reached by unsatisfactory compromise.	Conflict kept nondestructive by partners' sensitivity and mutual respect. Decisions reached by negotiation, taking needs and feelings of both partners into account.
5. Expressing affection or love in marriage	Tendency to take partner for granted, not express affection or love (except very infrequently). Love may take distorted forms; be possessive, restrictive of freedom, conditional on behaviour, perhaps poisoned by distrust.	Free, unrestrained, expression of warmth, affection and love by both partners. Love is accepting and trusting, non-possessive, not restrictive, not conditional on behaviour.
6. Sexual functioning in marriage	Routine, sporadic, or no sex at all. Often separated from love and affection. May be dysfunctional (i.e., impotence). Often used coercively (i.e., imposed by one partner as a 'right' or withheld).	Natural, spontaneous, mutually enjoyed. Associated with feelings of affection, love, comfort, reassurance, happiness, celebration of an event, etc. Not used coercively.
7. Reaction of of partners to outside relationships.	Unless shared by both partners, they violate the closed system and pressure is brought to end them.	Freedom to cultivate outside friendships; but care is taken not to hurt a spouse. Part-ners are responsible, sensible and trusting.

Source: McGinnis & Ayers (1976), pp. 115-116.

Many commentators, especially those who argue for the preservation of the traditional family, consider these *challenges and pressures* to be essentially negative and destructive and often they perceive them as deliberately intent on undermining traditional family values. The thesis I wish to submit is that the factors necessitating change (as distinct from *undermining*) in today's family are *primarily positive and hopeful* and serve to remind us that the family is capable of adapting to change. What this change implies is a broadening horizon of interaction, co-operation and interdependence, an option for an *open* rather than a *closed* value system (cf. p. 151).

It may be a question of complementing the family with new befriending and supportive structures, but it may also mean – and this is what creates the fear and panic – that the fabric of family life itself will change significantly to accommodate the changing values of the emerging culture. In a time of evolutionary change the latter rather than the former is a more likely outcome.

What is vanishing therefore is the traditional, privatised, closely-knit, self-sufficient, nuclear family. What's beginning to emerge is a more open-ended, extended, network (cf. Speck & Attneave, 1973; Savella & Cross, 1978, pp. 190-206), significantly linked with a local, supportive community:

> Like the transformative adult relationship, the transformative family is an open system, rich in friends and resources, giving and hospitable. It is flexible, adaptive to the realities of a changing world. It gives its members freedom and autonomy as well as a sense of group unity. (Marilyn Ferguson, 1982, p. 441.)

The transition from one model to the other will not be smooth or easy (it is a death/resurrection process) and the initial experimental stages, that we now seem to be experiencing, will exhibit many fragmented and disturbing features.

Firstly, we review the nature of emerging familial relationships. In the traditional family, *fidelity* rather than *love* often kept a couple and family together; in not a few cases, love had virtually ceased and no real growth in intimacy or understanding had taken place for many years. Sometimes, the fidelity prevailed 'for the sake of the children', whose psychic and emotional growth had also suffered because of the parental problems.

Today, we experience a very different reality: if relationships within the home do not satisfy basic emotional needs, people veer towards relationships outside the family. It may be the local pub or women's club; it may be into new relationships, normal healthy friendships, but sometimes, illicit and even adulterous unions. Teenagers and young adults tend to go through a number of temporary relationships, often considered enriching depending on the quality (perhaps, quantity) of eroticism and genitality. Cohabitation, unwanted pregnancies, abortion may ensue. It is no longer a marginal practice for a person to have two, three or more spouses in a life time.

The average, contemporary couple, promising 'until death do us part' must often feel confused and bewildered, knowing only too well that the odds are stacked against them in realising this ideal. And when problems arise in the marriage, the tendency today is to opt out rather than seek professional help and work through the problem. It is a chaotic scene, potentially destructive and bound to cause much pain and suffering for society at large. In the face of such fragmentation, one can appreciate the loud, clarion call for the restoration of traditional family values.

But can we be sure that this is the solution? If we assume that the features outlined above are *symptoms* of an underlying malaise, or the chaos engendered by a civilsation in transition, are we not in danger of addressing symptoms while ignoring the main issue? In that case, we end up with a more devastating travesty!

Tribalism in a New Guise

Let us examine these *symptoms* at closer range, what are people *aspiring towards* in the emerging fluidity of relationships? Is there some mysterious (perhaps, ambiguous) sense in which people are trying to transcend traditional categories of friendship, love, intimacy, even sexuality? Is there a subconscious reiteration of basic tribal values which dominated our existence prior to the mechanisation of life which came to the fore with the agricultural revolution and became excessively pronounced since the sixteenth century? Are we embarking on a new tribalism? Is there an implicit reaction against the restrictive institutionalised forms of relationships in favour of a more fluid and polymorphous expression? And if there is, could it be positive as well as negative? At least, let us be open to consider this possibility!

William Kilpatrick (1975), in a work of outstanding lucidity, explores the thesis which suggests that we as a species are returning to a form of *neo-tribalism* (cf. p. 155). Marshal McLuhan (1967) in his now famous *The Medium is the Message*, announced that we were entering the electric age of television, stereos, computers, etc., thus severing contact with the more linear and mechanical era wherein lifestyle and its values were determined by the printed word and the time-clock. Formerly, we controlled and stood outside our environment, aided by the printed word, the visual perception and a vast array of mechanical gadgetry. But in the electric era we're surrounded, even absorbed, by multisensory, immediate impact:

> Unlike print which is specialist and fragmenting, electricity is non-specialist and all-enveloping. Electric sound, electric light and electric communication can surround us as print cannot. Electric communication and especially electric sound are the new tribal drums that recreate the oral-aural bond. Instead of dividing one man from another as the sword of print does, electricity casts him into a tribal web of interdependence, this time on a global scale. Moreover, since electricity is instantaneous. . . we begin to experience life in its simultaneity rather than its sequence, much as does the primitive. (Kilpatrick 1975, p. 87.)

McLuhan's neo-tribal man marks a cultural shift from the privacy, independence and individualism of our print-dominated, mechanical culture to a corporate interdependence, which McLuhan considers to be a feature of primitive tribalism, but which I suggest, is the fruit and product of our emerging, holistic worldview. To describe it as *tribalistic* is appropriate in the sense that it shows the essential pervasiveness of the *archetypal values* of our prehistoric ancestors (i.e., the power of the collective unconscious), but inappropriate if it denotes a regression to a former cultural immaturity. We quickly and naively jump to this latter conclusion when contemporary values are threatened; we need to acknowledge humbly that these values may not be that sacred after all.

Nor must we castigate and condemn with the dogmatic certainty of the West, because beneath the external facade is an orientation towards a new holistic integration:

FEATURES OF NEO-TRIBALISM*

1. Lessened personal responsibility: 'find shelter in the crowd.'

2. Indifference towards defining the self.

3. Individualism: each person doing her own thing.

4. Difficulty with abstract thinking.

5. Reaction against the etiquette and social norms of society, as in dress and lifestyle.

6. Follow your feelings: satisfy your needs as they arise.

7. New spiritual search often confused with a psychological 'high'.

8. Moral values and guilt-feelings tend to be suppressed.

9. Return to nature: hence, the upsurge of 'natural' lifestyles and customs.

10. New cooperative enterprises but also a high risk of social chaos.

* *The reader is reminded that each of these negative features includes an unarticulated (perhaps, subconscious) aspiration towards a positive, e.g., the overemphasis on 'feelings' tends to arise in a culture dominated by rational, cerebral, 'thinking' behaviour patterns.*

As McLuhan and other commentators describe him, this new man finds his identity in the group – not apart from it. Among this new breed, communion with others is valued over self-reliance or character development, and collective participation is favoured over individual initiative. Commitment to privacy and private property is not esteemed and, in general, communal and shared values predominate over private personal ones. Property may be communally held or, if it is privately owned, it is easily available to others. (Kilpatrick, p. 94.)

Kilpatrick goes on to describe neo-tribal man as 'egoless', absorbed by the group, as it were, a stance almost completely at variance with the strong individualistic tone of the Human Potential movement.[7] Undoubtedly, this latter group, on occasion, has created an exaggerated individualism, an outcome of chance rather than design (I would suggest) because the mainline emphasis is, and always has been, in finding my true self, not in isolation, but in *meaningful relationships*: hence, the Rogerian perspective of the encounter group.

Similarly, Kilpatrick's analysis of McLuhan's neo-tribalism seems one-sided. Alignment with the group consciousness does not necessarily mean being 'egoless'; in Jungian terms it may mean the transcendence of (not the denial of or escape from) the *ego* for the sake of the *Self*. We are now into the realm of mysticism and the only examples that come to mind which, hopefully, will make some sense to christian readers, are those of the *mystical body* (incorporating all but safeguarding each person's uniqueness) or St Paul's concept of *the Church as the body of Christ* with many gifts but one unifying Spirit.

This very positive approach is not intended to be a denial of or a camouflage for the very real evidence that exists to the contrary. It is an attempt to discern the underlying dynamic of cultural evolution rather than judging by mere external manifestations, however dramatic or exaggerated these may seem. Nor does one wish to exonerate what is frequently perceived as destructive, immoral behaviour. As a social scientist, my task is to *observe, intuit* and *discern*, acknowledging *all* the evidence and drawing on my personal spiritual conviction that somewhere in this contemporary mess, the Spirit of God is recreating out of chaos and renewing all things.

What does all this mean for the future of the family? If the above analysis is basically correct, it means that people will seek deeper and more intimate fellowship within a wider social circle than that embodied in the traditional family. Here we touch on what seems to be an archetypal human value: deep in the heart of every person is a longing, a yearning (what Jean Vanier calls a 'loneliness') which drives us towards fellowship and intimacy of a quality which may only be attainable in some type of 'spiritual' fellowship, akin to a religious or monastic community. To many people this sounds ridiculous and even preposterous. Let us elaborate a little further.

Sexuality and Polymorphous Perversity

In our understanding of human relationships throughout the twentieth century, sexuality, as an expression of the closest bond between married partners was considered to be a very private matter. A great deal of taboo, fear and guilt surrounded the notion of sex. Formal religion tends to be wary of liberal sexual mores and up till recent times dictated the personal and social norms for appropriate sexual behaviour. Beginning around the mid-50s, one notices a distinctive swing in attitudes and values, leading to an avalanche of sexual freedom, permissiveness and, at times, outright promiscuity.

Today, we hear and read of a new 'Victorianism', as people disillusioned with trivialised genitality or scared by AIDS, are trying to be 'straight' again. Meanwhile, Western civilisation has been through yet another cultural shift from McLuhan's print-oriented civilisation to what Norman O. Brown (1966) calls 'Penis-oriented culture'. In fact, this is quite a logical by-product of our mechanistic world view – attention swings from the whole machine (the body) to one part of it (the penis), perhaps, better expressed as a *genital* orientation.

According to Brown, this perverse and fetish slant (very much the product of emphasis on sexual *technique*) is yet another mis-guided response to a new breakthrough which he describes in the unfortunate term: *polymorphous perversity*. These words are employed to describe the sexual condition of the infant in which pleasure is located not merely in the genitals but dispersed throughout the entire body. In passing, let us note once again, the transition from the *particular* (part) to the *universal* (whole):

Polymorphous perversity is a refusal to let the erogenous zones be culturally determined. It is the diffusion of sexual feeling throughout the whole body, a return to the pregenital condition of infancy where, before the impositon of fine discriminations, all the senses combined in global interplay. . . Polymorphous perversity means an end to all the exclusive one-to-one sexuality which now limits us and the beginning of pan-sexualism – the first step towards a new mystical body. The new, egoless sexuality will help us go beyond the exclusivity and possessiveness, the emphasis on private parts and private property that plague the West. The whole stress on private parts is wrong, since we are all members of the same body. Genital sex is private sex, performance sex, partial sex: polymorphous perversity, on the other hand, is universal sharing. (Kilpatrick, pp. 126, 138.)

A sexual revolution of the 1960s and 1970s may be more accurately perceived as a prelude to a revolution than an actual one. Because so many people still operate out of an awe or fear of sex, they perceive Brown's vision as extremely pernicious and disgustingly irreverant. People assume that the articulation of these ideas can only lead to the unleashing of a rash of sexual abuse which they fail to see is already rampant both *within* and *outside* marriage. Genitality rather than sexuality has become the false God of our age.

Human sexuality is not merely about sexual intercourse – special and unique as that dimension is – but about the entire range of human feelings, moods and emotions. Sexuality is about the integration of the diverse elements of our humanity, something we can only do through the medium of relationships – with God, with people – a goal which no longer may be attainable through the traditional family unit.

And what of our sexuality in a polymorphous society? Do we just mate as we wish and breed like rabbits? This very fear is a perception governed by a level of consciousness we are invited to transcend, that mechanistic, utilitarian world view which no longer serves our best interests. Polymorphous perversity does not belong to the present order, but possibly to the evolutionary consciousness which is beginning to unfold.

It is also an incredible proposition for those who view evolutionary progress in linear progression, moving from a primitive to a more sophisticated mode of being. Evolutionary growth seems to follow neither a linear nor a cyclic progression. Peter

Russell and other writers intimate that the pattern exemplifies that of exponential growth, the type explained by geometric progression, increasing by qualitative leaps as it advances on its course.

This is one possible explanation for the growth in knowledge and other scientific advances of the present century, but it is by no means comprehensive. Evolution also seems to include a process of recapitulation, each new wave bearing with it cumulative wealth of each former one, but also bringing into clearer relief the primordial, archetypal values of our species. In this sense, we can grasp the meaning of Bede Griffith's cryptic phrase: 'The way to the Truth is not that of progress but that of return' (Griffiths, 1976, p. 68). The return, however, is not to infantile primitive, undifferentiated chaos, but to the *mythic* simplicity and fraternity of the primitives, untouched by the conditioning and enculturation of later developments.

The place and potency of *myth* for our primitive ancestors has been lucidly documented by ethnologists such as Mircea Eliade, Joachim Wach, Bronislow Malinowski, Paul Radin and Ninian Smart. *Myth* is a form of story which powerfully encapsulates our deepest dreams and hopes; it may not resonate with historical fact, nor is it necessary that it should but it seeks to express fundamental truths that can never be fully realised either in factual experience nor in rational thought.

Therefore, when we propose a return to polymorphous perversity, we are not suggesting a re-enactment of a state of affairs that once existed, because it may never have *actually* existed. What did exist was the dream, the vision and its articulation in myth which so gripped our primitive ancestors as to be 'more real than reality itself'. In a sense, therefore, the myth was (and *continues to be*) a projection of an ultimate state of affairs to which mankind feels called and destined – a final state of perfection, not one in which we lose all feeling and emotion, but in which we experience the fullness of life at all levels (including the sexual) in an integrated and holistic way.

Polymorphous perversity, therefore, may never be fully realised, but as a pervasive myth of the human condition, it needs to be continually reiterated. In former times, its articulation may have been predominantly verbal, although, presumably, experiential also in modes appropriate to the culture of that time. In our day, the myth may be primarily *experiential*; at least, the trend seems to be pointing in that direction. As our next evolutionary stage continues to unfold, our *psychic* development is likely to entail transcendence of the spoken word in favour of a new mode of expression and experience. What that new mode might be can be gleaned vaguely from Kilpatrick's concluding remarks:

> Of all desires, there is none so powerful as the desire for union, and of all fears there is none so fearsome as the fear of loneliness. Who has not experienced the sense of personal isolation, of being impris-oned in one's own ego, of being unable to break through to others? Who has not despaired of the emptiness of it all? And who has not wished to be born again into a more encompassing fellowship? When Brown echoing the words of Christ prays 'that all may be one' , he speaks for a yearning deep in every person. (Kilpatrick, p. 140.)

Celibate Values and Human Aspirations

These observations have interesting ramifications for sexual behaviour. Contrary to popular opinion the outcome may not be – probably would not be – uncontrolled sexual activity (cf. Savells & Cross, 1978, pp. 347-354). There is much evidence to suggest that sexual abuse is the fruit of repression rather than that of sexual licence and the desire for sexual pleasure often comes second place to an unconscious wish to control another person or overcome an inferiority complex. Nor must polymorphous per-versity be identified with a new prudishness or some type of universal celibacy. However, there is a vital clue to the future in what the celibate way of life stands for and this merits brief elaboration.

Celibacy, as popularly understood, is perceived as a lifestyle adopted by those who have made a special consecration of their lives to God in Priesthood or in Religious/Monastic Life. In prac-tice it entails non-marriage and abstinence from all form of sexual intimacy and pleasure. We assume celibacy to be a norm or life-style introduced by formal religion. Occasionally, it is associated with a disdain for the body and for sexuality, implying a turning-away from the world, the flesh and the devil.

After that explanation is it any wonder that most people dismiss the celibate lifestyle and values as being irrelevant to the majority of mankind who live a married 'sexual' life? It is only one of the many unhealthy dualisms that fragment and distort the deeper meaning of our existence. Firstly, celibacy was practiced long before any formal religion came into being and 'celibate' values, suggesting the appropriate manner, frequency and expression of sexual intimacy in the married state, can be detected in the lives of prehistoric peoples. In time, the 'celibate' values became institutionalised, firstly in the life of the *shaman* (Eliade, 1964), the sacred, prophetic figure of primitive times, subsequently in the monk, the virgin and, only in relatively recent times, in certain forms of priesthood (as in the Catholic Church).

Celibacy is not so much a religious phenomenon as a cultural value, with wide application and a profoundly nuanced meaning. In its cultural, archetypal context, it seeks to express something of the sacredness of sexuality and genitality, of the human need for intimacy and warmth which include but also transcend genitality (i.e. sexual intercourse), of a deep human need for closeness and tacility (touch), without absorbing the other in one's own self-gratification; of the desire – in fact, the innate capacity – to relate and communicate at a level transcending words and actions. As an archetypal experience it also expresses something of the mysterious, divine force at work in each loving and procreative act of humanity.

The story of the Virgin Birth, with its counterparts in many of the other major religious systems, is a mythic articulation of the celibate archetype:

> The myth of the virgin birth is universal and represents one of the profoundest aspirations of humanity. The instinct of love in our nature can never be satisfied with anything less than God, that is with the infinite. Human marriage is but a shadow and a symbol of the spiritual marriage which has to take place in the 'cave of the heart'. This is the return to the womb, the marriage with the mother, which depth psychology has discovered to be a basic human desire. Man and woman were once whole and undivided, enclosed in the womb of nature, in the paradise of God, and man has ever since suffered from the nostalgia for paradise, the desire for that perfect unity. . . Marriage, like all other earthly pleasures and achievements is only a temporary resting-place, a foretaste of the fulfilment of love which (man) seeks. (Bede Griffiths, 1976, pp. 65-66.)

Now all this is a far-fetched ideal, alas, a bizarre rationalisation, for a generation immersed in sexual technique and hungry for sexual stimulation so that they can perform more effectively in what Erich Fromm once called 'the game of sexual gymnastics'. However, there are signs of tiredness and weariness in the sexual game. Apparently, impotence is on the increase and women, in particular, are opting for less sex both within and outside the married state. In subtle, and obviously non-popularised way, the celibate archetype is in vogue again, not so much in institutional celibacy, which sadly has lost virtually all meaning because of religious camouflage, but in the new sexual and relational attitudes we have explored in this chapter.

Sexual behaviour, therefore, is more likely to veer towards prudishness rather than towards promiscuity. On the other hand, sexual, genital activity will no longer be confined to marriage, which in itself is also likely to become more fluid and flexible. These statements are not intended to be predictions of things to come. They are simply trends quite well established and likely to prevail as we move into a new evolutionary era.

In this light, homosexual and lesbian partnerships may also be understood anew. These are yet another misguided attempt to express the new latitude, the wish for broader and more fluid outlets for the expression of intimacy and filiation. The current trend, therefore, to establish homosexuality as a way of life may be based on false assumptions. Like other developments in the sexual and emotional areas, homosexuality serves more as a *symptom* of a new consciousness, than a phenomenon meriting status and permanent recognition in its own right.[8]

It is not the first time in human history that the 'internal barbarians' are likely to become the saviours of civilisation. Even in the christian gospel, we find those who considered themselves to be righteous and law-abiding chided with what must have been a cruel and hurtful castigation: 'Truly, I say to you the tax-collectors and harlots go into the Kingdom of God before you.' (Matt. 21:31.)

The thesis outlined in this chapter is not mere fantasy. There is an abundance of historical precedent and an increasing weight of anthropological evidence to substantiate the argument (cf. Clarke & Hendley, 1975, Chaps. 7 & 8). It is rather a cruel paradox of experience which, initially, nobody is prepared to accept and it demands a quality and quantity of change which will push many to the limits of their sanity.

THREE MODELS OF FAMILY LIFE

Source: McGinnis & Ayers, 1976, pp. 16-17.

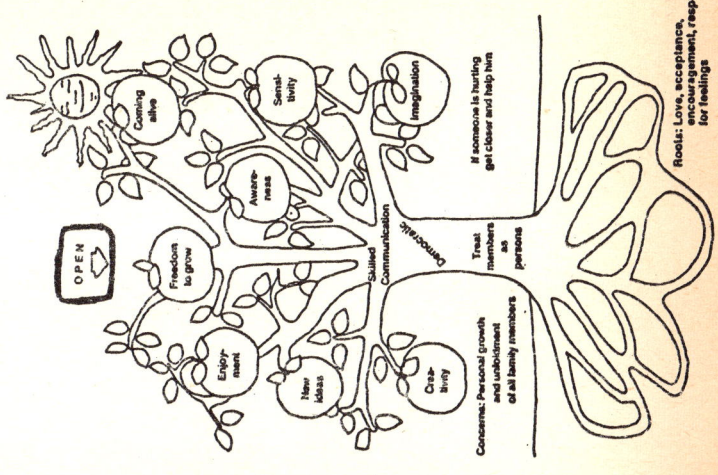

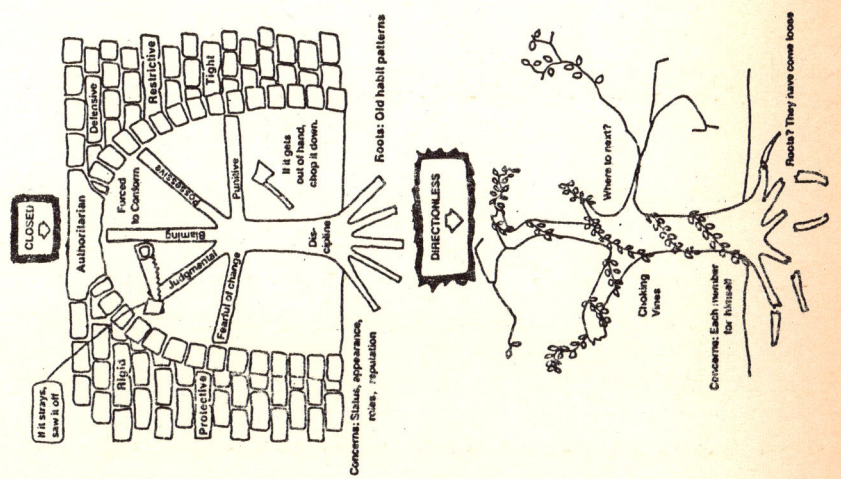

Family and Environment

As a final word, however, we assert that people can adapt to this kind of change. Humans are remarkably adaptive creatures and in a supportive environment can negotiate mutations of attitude and behaviour, at very profound levels. To cope with the change envisaged in this chapter, let us firstly examine what a 'supportive environment' may entail.

As already indicated, the focus of attack from critics of the family, is not the concept itself, but rather the 'closed' model which has come to the fore in the West in recent decades. The nuclear family has become highly introspective and impervious to outside influences. This, in turn, creates reaction, especially among young members, followed by the all too familiar trail of crime, violence, drug-abuse, etc. These negative influences we tend to attribute to poverty and unemployment; many families, afflicted by neither of these evils, also contribute to social disarray, venting anger and frustration, unintentionally fostered by oppressive and over-protective parenting.

A 'supportive environment', therefore, demands a commitment to the revitalisation of family life. The current polarisation between those set on undermining the family unit and those rigidly committed to preserving the traditional image is likely to be totally unproductive, at best, counterproductive. And the solution is not one of striking a happy medium. The traditional family concept is outdated and inadequate to meet modern challenges, personal and cultural. The only way forward is a new type of family which can only come about by:

a) An openness which acknowledges, without recrimination, the limitations of family life today;

b) A willingness to move out of the (false) comfort and security of the closed system (see diagram on p. 163);

c) A sense of tolerance and patience with the clumsiness and untidiness of the open system; creativity of its very nature demands a measure of fluidity and flexibility;

d) A move towards a value-system emphasising love and freedom rather than rules and regulations. This is not intended to be a subtle permission for immorality and recklessness which are, in fact, the products of the *closed* system;

e) A new openness to *counselling*, not as a remedial solution to serious problems (when it is often too late) but as a *service* (like the health service) directed to the ongoing growth and well-being of both the family unit and its individual members;

f) Reinterpreting the *spiritual* role of the family; statements such as: 'The family is divinely instituted'; 'the family and the church are God's gifts to humanity', tend to militate against responsible family life. We consider the family so sacred that we deem it inappropriate to intervene. This attitude is spiritually naive and culturally irresponsible.

Under the influence of cultural and global change, the family, like all contemporary institutions is in *transition*. This movement from being a normative entity to one with fluid, varied and questionable characteristics is often and wrongly attributed to the family being 'under attack'. Opposing the attackers, even getting rid of them is not likely to accomplish much. The problem is a great deal more complex and profound.

Because the family embodies and articulates deep emotions and strongly-held views, any disruption of the family system creates powerfully strong ripples, tinged with intimacy, ecstasy and delight, or alternatively, with anger, eroticism and hatred. In former times, the emotional intensity tended to be held within the family system, often leaving a travesty of superficial harmony and emotional blackmail. One ventures to suggest that the current disarray, often marked by reckless eroticism, is a backlash to the emotional suppression caused by the closed family system, or alternatively the over-spill of the negative build-up.

One thing is certain: the demolition of traditional family values is in large measure generated by the family institution itself (see R.D. Laing, 1969). Consequently, remedial action must address the corruption within the system rather than the evils in society which supposedly are undermining the family. When our cherished perceptions are under threat we always seek a scapegoat to rationalise our predicament. Society, the government, the media may contribute to the malaise of family life, but they are not the sole or original cause: the family institution itself is in disarray.

And the remedy? Throughout this book I refrain from answers and solutions. My objective is to explore the evolutionary process activating change in contemporary life. My hope is that I am posing the right *questions*, submitting appropriate critiques and suggesting practical possibilities for an indefinite but challenging future.

In the case of the family, and those close relationships within and outside the family which we all need, the way forward will be one of broadening horizons. Closed systems and neatly structured institutions whether in the international, national, social or familial context belong to the old order and cannot possibly survive. The breakdown of family life is essentially that of a closed system disintegrating because of *internal* pressure. It can no longer contain its reality. What the new structures will be like is up to each and all of us to determine. Apart from the possibilities in networking (outlined on p. 58), research on family coping strategies has been in progress for some time and is reviewed by Olson and McCubbin (1983, pp. 135-162).

Perhaps, the greatest challenge for the future of the family is that *we ourselves* must create that future. A new model, complete and redesigned is not awaiting us, either from heaven or from earth. We must design it ourselves: perhaps, with trial and experiment (which may be happening already amid the dubious and ambivalent practices inside and outside the contemporary family). We must take ownership and responsibility for it; above all, we must recreate the context in which family life will once again become vibrant and alive, emotionally and spiritually enriching.

9: Work and Unemployment

It is on behalf of all of us and in advance of all of us, that the unemployed will develop new work values, unrelated to money, and new lifestyles not based around paid work. It follows that those of us still in paid employment must provide the framework, the opportunity, the means and the resources needed to mount this experiment. – BILL HALL

There's enough for everyone's need, but not for everyone's greed.
– MAHATMA GANDHI

Bureaucracies. . .fail to survive when they are no longer funded by fear.
– JOHN HARRISON

In 1985, in the EEC,[9] some *thirteen* million people were unemployed. Each year the number rises as more people become redundant or fail to find paid work. Being without a job has become a way of life for many people. An estimated 25% of European teenagers will never hold down a permanent job; many of them will never even have one.

The study of 1,000 unemployed people in 1984 revealed that almost two-thirds of the group had failed to give any new sense of direction to their lives. A feeling of powerlessness and uselessness predominated to such a degree that they just drifted from one day to the next on an aimless course without purpose or meaning. Moreover, a significant proportion, on the initial experience of being unemployed, followed a timetable similar to the working pattern of their daily and weekly schedules.

The Experience of Being Unemployed

This study reveals something of the traumatic effects which unemployment has on our lives, personally and socially. Unemployment means *change*, one that is forced upon us, a change for which the vast majority of people are totally unprepared. The first reaction is *denial*, even to such an extent that the unemployed person will rise at the normal time of going out to work and will spend as much money at weekends as he/she did when working – although one's weekly allowance may be less than half the former wage. The unemployed person will seek to deny his predicament to friends; the spouse and family will respond similarly; they feel a sense of *shame* while the unemployed person can be riddled with guilt and a feeling of uselessness.

But the pretence can only be kept up for a limited space of time and then all hell breaks loose. *Anger* is directed at many innocent victims, especially on spouse and family. It may also express itself in destructive behaviour – crime, violence, drug-abuse – one way of getting revenge on society. At this stage, unemployment is no longer a personal issue; it has become a major social problem, with horrendous consequences for the entire community.

In Chapter Two, we outlined the five stages of death as developed by Kubler-Ross (1969) and indicated how these can be used to understand the attitudes and reactions to modern change. This model is extremely helpful in understanding the attitudes and behaviour of unemployed people (see Roger Clarke, 1982, especially, Chap. 10: 'Mourning the loss of Work'. pp. 78-87). Losing one's job is like losing a close friend or relative; it is a form of *death*, experienced as loss, uselessness, rejection and strong feelings of shame, guilt and inferiority (see Diagram, p. 169). As a form of change it is traumatic and extremely painful. Apart from the personal agony for the unemployed person, it causes massive disruption in family life and in social life generally. It is, probably, the single greatest challenge facing modern civilisation.

Perceived in such a negative light – and this is by no means an exaggerated one – the first reaction is: 'Let's get rid of this evil, let's strive to wipe it out.' This is the dominant personal response and also the one adopted by governments in all continents. Everybody wishes to create more jobs and everybody is failing dismally. We have set up work-incentive schemes, temporary-work projects, job-sharing experiments, work-experience programmes and a vast array of employment agencies, but the unemployment curve continues to rise and the jobs continue to decline.

Unemployment affects every nation in the world today. In Third World countries, the problem tends to be one of *under-employment* (not only are jobs unavailable, but the quality and quantity of available work is so inferior that much skill and talent goes amiss). In Western nations generally there is no shortage of work, but opportunities for *paid* employment have dwindled considerably in the past ten years.

EMOTIONAL IMPACT OF UNEMPLOYMENT ON PERSONAL LIFE

Source: Roger Clarke (1982), p. 81.

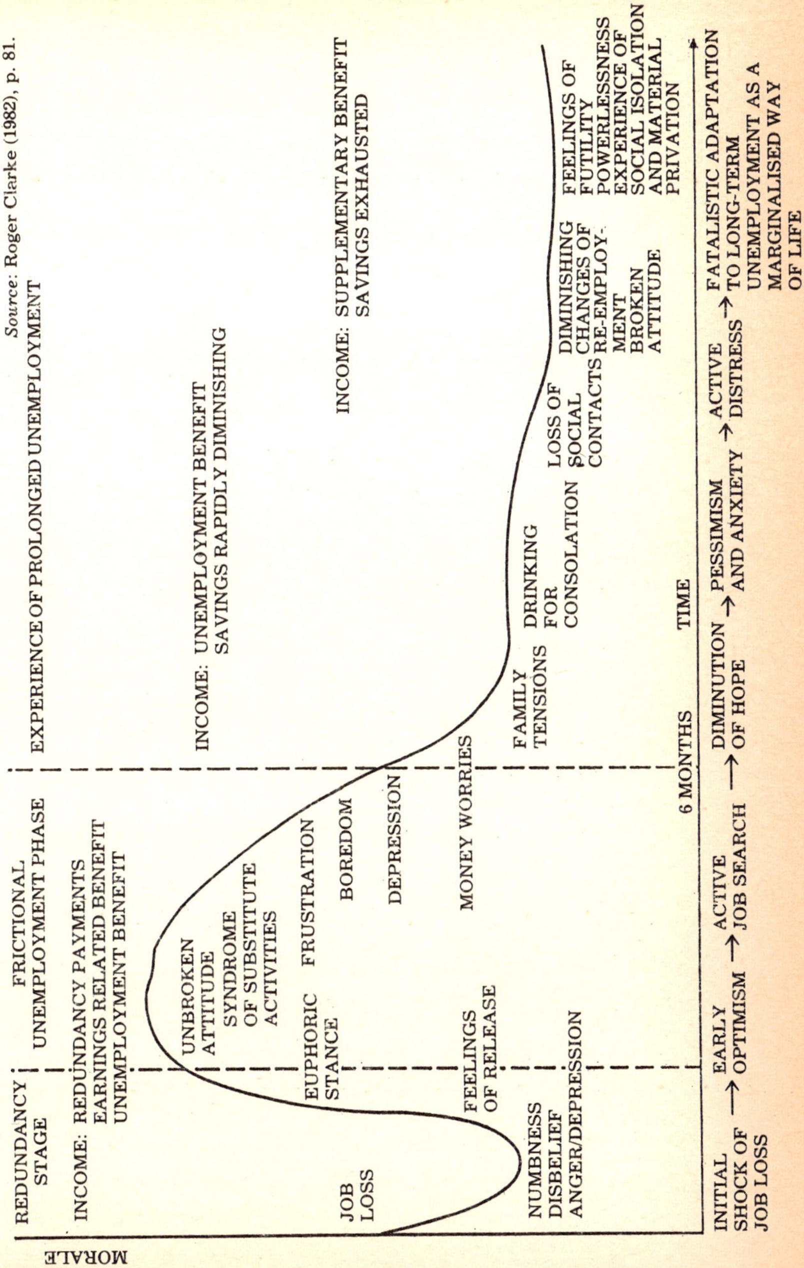

The USA is a notable exception to this pattern. Between 1973 and 1982 the Americans created 12 million paid jobs and unemployment actually decreased from 9.6% of the working population in 1983 to 7% in 1984. In large measure this achievement is attributable to wage restraint; between 1973 and 1982 wages in the USA increased by 4% compared with 22% in Europe for the same period.

This comparison reveals something of the American sense of loyalty and patriotism. Not alone were workers prepared to make sacrifices of income, but many new jobs, especially in the service sector, were created through enterprise and co-operative experiments. Job-sharing along with flexibility of time and incomes also led to the creation of new work outlets. In some measure, these developments relate to the fact that trade unions in the USA are less militant than elsewhere in the Western world, but credit must be given to the American people generally for facing this challenge with vision and creativity.

Confronted with unemployment, the USA presents a challenging and optimistic scenario. However, it is not without its negative side-effects, the outstanding one being a notable increase in the poverty index, from 26.1 million in 1979 to 34.5 million in 1983. It is also well known that an estimated one-third of the USA workforce is involved in arms' production, a form of employment with grave human, ecological and global ramifications. High-technology no longer provides new jobs on the scale of the 1960s and 1970s; in fact, if unemployment is to continue to decline, Americans must find an estimated 1.5 million new jobs in the service sector* by the early 1990s.

* According to Handy (1984), p. 7 many new jobs in the USA are located in one or other of the following 'services':
Contract Domestic Work: cooking, cleaning, garden maintenance, child-care, building and maintenance.
Eating and Drinking (e.g. restaurants, wine-bars, fast-food chains, hotels and motels).
Business Services: Accounting, tax-advice, courier services, telex and typing bureaux.
Craft Work (Handmade domestic objects, furniture, paintings, sculpture).
Education (Music, drama, literature, special tutorials, skill-training and retraining).
Tourism (e.g. fairs, exhibitions parks, guided trips and special tours).
Health Service (e.g. fitness and beauty places, sports, hairdressing, dentistry).

To date, unemployment is not a major social or personal issue for the USA, but by the end of the century a trend resembling that of other Western nations may well ensue. Indeed, if the American people ever choose to rectify the gross immorality and lethal potential of the arms' trade, then Americans may well be faced with an unemployment crisis far exceeding that of any other Western nation.

Whither Unemployment

A bitter, painful truth is beginning to seep into our consciousness: *unemployment is here to stay*. The situation is *not* going to improve; there is not going to be an economic recovery. Governments and state agencies are pulling wool over our eyes, *unconsciously* for the greater part, although one assumes that by now they, too, are beginning to perceive their own naivety.

Unemployment is both good and evil, good in the sense that it is the goal of all our endeavours since the beginning of the industrial revolution, namely, to reduce the pain, hardship and boredom of labour and allow more time and space for creative and artistic development. A society where leisure would be a dominant value has been the deep aspiration of many generations. It is about to arrive and, alas, what a shallow welcome we give it.

At long last we have created living conditions where we can endow our lives and our world with those creative skills and potentials which formerly had to be sacrificed for more gross, survival needs. It sounds almost banal, something akin to a parent who is unwilling to welcome her new-born child. The leisure society has arrived: nobody imposed it upon us; in fact, we ourselves have created it. So, let's take ownership of it and respond more creatively. In fact, we have only one choice: *accept it!* Rejecting it means ignoring a reality that is here to stay.

Negatively, unemployment may be perceived as the primary symptom of the declining Western culture. In this context, the loss of jobs is only a foretaste of the imminent downfall of economic and industrial institutions, of that value-system based on profit and productivity for the accruing of capital:

> The world faces a crisis that is endemic to the capitalist system itself. . .
> The modern economic system has been built on the basis that might is right, that profits can be maximised regardless of the effects on

others, that productivity is for profit rather than needs, that persons can do what they want with the resources of nature for their own advantage, and, ultimately, that ethical norms have no role in economic activity. (Tissa Balasuriya, 1984, p. 38.)

Western economic systems are rotten at the core, a fact well borne-out by wine-lakes and butter-mountains,[10] monuments of capitalistic greed and selfishness while millions of our fellow-humans starve to death on the African continent. In the West itself, it is the unfortunate rank-and-file, and not the monetary and industrial giants, who suffer most.

Once again, we encounter the *polarisation* between the dwindling institutional reality and the new order striving for realisation. Guardians of the old way cling ever more desperately to crumbling structures, trying to convince their followers that an utopia lies ahead. What governments in the West fail to realise is that the proletariate itself, for the greater part, is quite well educated. They can detect the shortsightedness and deception; sadly, many are unable to move further to the creative challenge of designing alternatives; that will be the major challenge of the twenty-first century.

Paradoxically, it has taken something akin to the unemployment crisis to alert us to our warped attitudes both to work and to the economy. According to Tony Walter (1985, pp. 14-15) there are four economies, relating not just to four different types of work, but rather to four different kinds of *relationships* within which work is performed. There is the *formal*, economy, the sphere of paid employment; the *household* economy in which work is performed out of commitment to family associates, usually without exchange or remuneration; the *informal* economy, consisting of voluntary work, doing a good turn, standing in local elections, holding a dinner party; friendship, neighbourliness, loyalty, generosity and pleasure in sharing are the motivating factors in this behaviour: the *black* economy, involving paid work that is not declared for the purpose of taxation.

What may come as a surprise to many readers is that the majority of people in Western industrialised nations operate within the three 'informal' economies and not within the formal one. In all European nations, under 50% of the population operate in the formal economy; in some cases it is under 40%. Nobody can, and indeed few do, denounce the remaining 50% as being a financial burden or an economic liability. The energy, effort and love, whether expressed through the nurturance of the homemaker, the commitment of the voluntary worker, the ingenuity and fun of youth, the diligence of the student or the gentleness of the elderly, go largely unnoticed and frequently unappreciated. Yet, few can deny that these 'services' comprise the highest values that animate and motivate a nation (or a people) without which the formal economy would be lax and lifeless.

Moreover, the maintenance and survival of the formal economy is based on a number of assumptions, which rest on very shaky foundations. For a start, the proportion of the population in paid work is declining and all indications are that this trend will continue as automation accelerates. Secondly, automated work does not necessarily alienate the worker as people of existentialist orientation have predicted; quite the opposite in some cases, e.g. Japan. Thirdly, extended automation need not create massive unemployment; once again the Japanese have mastered this development by a combination of house-based industries operated largely by robots, thus allowing for the consequent time and space for leisure activities. Fourthly, the immoral practices of the *black* economy are minimal compared with the tax-evasion and pilfering practised in the formal economy (petty theft in British industry amounts to an estimated one million pounds – 1.48 million US dollars – per *day*). Fifthly, unemployment can be a blessing in disguise; it has proved to be a crisis of opportunity and breakthrough for a small but significant number of people. Sixthly, the proportion of unemployed people doing 'nixers' (illegally earning money while obtaining unemployment benefit) is significantly smaller than the number of employed people involved in 'moonlighting'. Similarly, the proportion of working wives is much higher among the employed than among the unemployed.

The formal economy, as we have known it, with the emphasis on productivity, wages and profits is in a state of disarray, riddled with contradictions and smeared with corruption and deception. It is in decline and its chances of recuperation are very poor indeed.

It will be some time yet before a new economic order will emerge. Meanwhile in the work place itself, workers will experience quite a degree of confusion and disruption. This is inevitable. In the past, the dominant pattern was that of large workforces

with relatively stable employment in a bureaucratically-run
system. But that model is dwindling and as Richard Brown (in
Thompson, 1984, p. 270) suggests the emerging job-pattern will
consist of:

> Temporary work, part-time work, work under short-term contracts
> (perhaps interspersed with periods of unemployment), work (for pay)
> outside the 'formal economy', home-base work (as home-workers and
> on a 'self-employed' basis), job-sharing and households with multiple
> breadwinners, all seem likely to increase. Patterns of employment
> have never been as neat and uniform as the dominant images of work
> assumed, but they are likely to become messier, more varied and
> more complex.

The application of new technology to industrial output is still
very much in its early stages. The popular view that the factory
of the future is a person-less place with raw materials coming in
one end and going out the other as robot-manufactured goods, is
largely erroneous. The leading idea in contemporary industrial
engineering is that of computer-integrated manufacturing (CIM)
(cf. Davies & Jates, *New Scientist*, 2/1/1986, pp. 40-42). What CIM
essentially means is that the work of engineers and management,
sales and marketing staff is fully integrated by means of a compu-
ter system that stores information centrally and communicates it
to all departments. Machines and workers alike receive information from the same data base.

With CIM and other related systems, the role of people will
change markedly. Manual and clerical activities will largely disap-
pear while those equipped with management, engineering and
sales skills will participate in an industrial enterprise marked by
flexibility and interdisciplinary competence. Although numbers
in the official work place will continue to decline, output will tend
to be more sophisticated and of improved quality for a more competitive consumer market. The current scene marked by industrial unrest and trade union-based squabbles has nothing to offer
in facilitating the transition into tomorrow's world.

Meanwhile, unemployment will continue to rise, becoming the
proverbial double-edged sword, signalling the death of the old
order with its accompanying pain and anguish, but serving also
as a 'light in the dark' announcing a new reality, one in which
the bulk of 'working' people are already grounded, although

largely unaware of that fact. Jobs continue to decline but there is no shortage of work and there are numerous opportunities for creativity and imagination, most of all in the discovery of that as yet illusive way of being able to remunerate everybody with or without a job.

Living on Social Dividend

Tony Walter (1985, pp. 188-196) proposes a system of *social dividend*, otherwise know as a national dividend, guaranteed minimum income or negative income tax. Basically it means that everyone, apart from those in prison and in psychiatric care, receives from the state an amount of money sufficient to live on; it is paid for by income tax of around 60% on wages earned. The wage-earners will be rather worse off, but since dependents are also receiving the social dividend (*children* included) then the average household income stands to gain rather than to lose.

The advantage of this system is that it bridges the artificially created gap between the wage-earner and the so-called unemployed. In between are those millions of people who rear children, maintain a home, do good turns, participate in a wide variety of voluntary services, contribute to fun and enjoyment, explore spiritual and aesthetic lifestyles, take time to think and reflect. These are the people who humanise civilisation, create culture and enable their fellow humans to transcend the drabness and greyness of daily life. These are the guardians of our sanity, the breadwinners of our dignity, integrity and uniqueness as a human species. And yet we crudely dismiss them as 'dependents', financial burdens, unemployed, a drain on the national economy!

Under a system such as the *social dividend*, a greater degree of equality, opportunity and recognition of gifts and talents prevails for all our citizens:

> The social dividend is the *only* way in which the market can be freed, because it disconnects wages from the need to subsist. Everyone is freed to engage in paid work as much or as little as he or she desires, trade unionists are freed from the spectre of a wage too low to live on, and employers are free to pay the market rate for the job. Most people currently in paid work want to continue in it either because they enjoy it or because they want the money. But those who would rather retire from paid work and do other things are enabled to do so, without stigma. Part-time work would increase. (Walter, p. 189.)

Despite its economic equity and distributive justice, apart from its bureaucratic simplicity, one envisages much resistance to this suggestion. It poses a threat to the power, control and domination of that minority which already masters the fortunes of millions of working people, employed and unemployed. It tears the soul out of the capitalistic system. It is based on a socialist philosophy which quickly and ingeniously will be daubed with overtones of communism. It demolishes the bureaucracy and economic/political structures whose complexity convinces economists and politicians alike that they are responsible for maintaining and servicing this elaborate infra-structure. It would prove that the economic and political status-quo has been a type of self-fulfilling prophesy: the institutions which have taken so long to create must be preserved at all costs; the institution itself has become self-perpetuating.

Meanwhile, the people perish and our culture becomes further polarised between the haves and have-nots. Indeed, it appears that this social/economic divide may become a great deal more pronounced before remedial action is considered. Such is the resistance to change, especially for those with vested interests, which includes the governments of most Western nations. The change will not come from those who govern us, nor from the economic wizards of our age. Change tends to arise from the rank-and-file, especially from the disenchanted middle-classes.

The 'proletariat' of society has not yet attained a sufficiently altered consciousness on alternative economic possibilities in order to influence change 'at the top'. The economic conscientisation of the masses (which, perhaps, should be the primary purpose of trade unions) is a prerequisite for a new economic order. And this implies a whole new way of relating money to work; more important, of divesting work of its economic shackles and seeing it instead as that innate, personal and societal propensity, essential to mature personhood and to the humanisation of our planet.

Coping with Unemployment

In the light of these observations, we can assume that unemployment will continue to be a major cultural and human issue well into the twenty-first century. In this context, also, unemployment is seen not so much as a feature of our age which we should strive to get rid of at all costs, but as a *symptom* of cultural, global change.

Accordingly, an appropriate, initial response will strive to accommodate the following elements:

1. Unemployment is primarily about *people* and not *jobs*. Jobs and wages are human inventions, so deeply ingrained in the fabric of social life that we *unconsciously* consider them to be of divine origin. If we invented them we can always choose to modify or even destroy them. This may sound unreal and mere speculation, but *it is our reality*. We must learn to acknowledge it before we can confront it realistically.

If *people* come first, then the unemployed people themselves have a special claim on our love and support. Blaming the unemployed for their predicament is a brutal and gross form of rationalisation, one frequently adopted to alleviate our own guilt. Nor must we immediately opt for alternative employment as the only appropriate resolution; for most people over *forty* this is a non-starter, anyhow.

Our first challenge is to *understand* the plight of the unemployed and *befriend* them through that process. This may seem a very passive and insipid attitude which we tend to dismiss in an age of *action*, where people are rated primarily in terms of function and productivity. We must relearn that people are precious in their *unique capacity* as human beings. We are much more than what we can do or achieve. We are more than the money we earn.

Befriending unemployed people demands an awareness of the process of grieving as outlined by E. Kubler Ross (see Chap. Two). We learn to support people in experiencing this sense of loss with its complex array of feeling and emotion (see Diagram, p. 169). Only in this way can the transition from one life-experience to another be negotiated so that it enhances people's growth and dignity as human beings. Befriending of this nature demands new and appropriate structures ensuring a measure of support, solidarity and confidentiality. Churches and local authority agencies should seriously and urgently consider appropriate initiatives in this area.

2. Every human being is endowed with a creative potency of which *work* is a primary experience. Work which can accommodate and foster simultaneously manual skills, intellectual awakening, emotional expression, social interaction and creativity development is the only type that satisfies the human spirit (cf. Roger Clarke, 1982, pp 21-28; see Diagram, p. 178). In this con-

SOCIAL/PSYCHOLOGICAL CONSEQUENCES
OF BEING EMPLOYED/UNEMPLOYED

Employed	*Unemployed*
Power	Powerlessness
Access to goods and services	Relative poverty
Dignity and social honour	Stigma and social unease
Structure to life	Structureless lives
Purpose in life	Purposeless lives
Satisfaction of being	Frustration leading to hopelessness
A contributor to society	Enforced dependency on the State
Sharing life with others	Socially isolated lives
Having a voice	Voiceless position in society

Source: Roger Clarke, 1982, p. 28.

text, most traditional work-forms have been (and still are) stifling and stultifying for the human personality.

The fact that work has been waged and evaluated in terms of monetary productivity has largely numbed the human capacity for creative expression. We pour so much energy and enthusiasm into mechanical, profit-based outlets, that often we have nothing left-over to energise our love for spouse and family, never mind for the exploratory development of human potential, our own and that of others.

Work, therefore, is a great deal more than the eight-to-five stint, remunerated financially at the end of the week. Beyond the functional and utilitarian pursuit, which we call 'a job', are vastly unexplored areas of human and social creativity. It is in this latter capacity, I suggest, that we humanise our world and in evolutionary terms our earth will remain grossly under-developed until we begin to cultivate these hidden talents. The decline of the job market becomes the precondition for a new quality of productivity, touching the kernel of human, social and earthly life.

3. In suggesting that we accept the permanence of unemployment, we are not proferring passivity, apathy, disillusionment or irresponsibility. Quite the contrary! It is becoming already obvious that we cannot reverse the unemployment trend and, as indicated above, it may be highly inappropriate to do so. We went on to assert that *jobs* (employment) and *work* are not synonymous, the latter being a dimension of human experience which, at best, can be expressed *partially* in a *job*. In the absence of jobs, therefore, how do we create work-outlets.

Our initial task may be one of *undoing* rather than *doing*. So many of our contemporaries look to society, government, industry, to provide work opportunities. This attitude seems to be the inheritance of a parenting and educational system whereby we are conditioned into looking to those *at the top* for all our values and guide lines. Individually, we seem to lack a healthy and creative independence; equally, we are socially deficient in our creative ability to explore the resources of our environment. We develop a degree of personal independence that militates against, rather than enhances, co-operative exploration. At both a personal and social level, we bury (i.e. leave undeveloped) a huge proportion of our potential.

For a start, therefore, we need some radical changes in parent-

ing skills and in educational systems, still far too rigidly committed
to producing servile, lucrative agents for a rapidly declining pro-
duction-based economy. Instead, we need to cultivate skills of
enterprise, self-confidence, co-operation, originality and creativity, along with accompanying structures to express and articulate
these values. Young people then begin to grow up differently,
fostering attitudes and values based on what they have *to give* to
society, knowing full well that the propagation of these values
rebounds to their own advantage.

It is a massive undertaking, demanding radical change in the
already established structures and institutions and, moreover,
change in value and perception on the part of those who maintain
and propagate the status quo. The odds seem weighted against
a positive outcome, but people are often more adaptable than we
give them credit for and in what will become progressively
apparent to be a 'do or die' situation, one may be cautiously optimistic about a positive outcome.

4. The greatest challenge of all must be that of separating work
from money. At the moment it is almost inconceivable that one
could be considered without the other. For many, work is valuable only in terms of its monetary value. *Money* rather than *work*
has become the supreme norm. And this leaves us with a rather
confused and split personality, denying a basic part of ourselves
because it does not earn us cash. It also puts us in a conflictual
relationship with our fellow beings who become primarily important as monetary beneficiaries, depending on our perverted skill
to exploit and demean them. Prostitution is the supreme example
of this evolution, a practice we associate with the 'lowest of the
low', but one heavily subscribed to by many of the monetary male
giants of Western capitalism.

The dichotomy between work and money can only be resolved
by an economic revolution which will lag behind the unemployment rate, prolonging the latter and inhibiting a creative and progressive outcome. Since money has become the supreme God of
our age, economic bastions will withstand many a hammering
and may not succumb, well into the next century when many of
the world's raw resources, especially oil, reach critically low
levels. With the crisis in resources, the 'foundation stones' of the
economic system have shifted, the multi-nationals are likely to
experience the financial insecurities many of us, the proletariat,

experience today.

Since the only alternatives to these resources are localised 'soft' technology based on recycling of waste and solar energy (demanding new global, co-operative strategies), the traditional strongholds of the economic system can scarcely withstand the upsurge of local creative efforts. A new wave of localised autonomy will reclaim the human creative energy, which, in the first place, should not have been so exclusively invested in a handful of superpowers. The current economic crisis of global proportion and the rise of alternative 'soft' technologies, already verifies the trends we outline.

Hope on the Dole

For many of our contemporaries, unemployment allowance, or 'being on the dole' is about the most humiliating role they could be asked to assume. It will take a considerable time to reverse this perception. For the few, unemployment has supplied the long-sought opportunity to explore and develop other creative gifts and for those people the dole is a blessing rather than a curse.

It's all a question of attitudes and perceptions. If we perceive ourselves as being valuable in terms of a system we service (a functional role we play) or if our life-meaning is strongly centred on financial status, then being out of a job becomes a very negative, potentially destructive experience. On the other hand, if we can bring ourselves to accept an alternative set of values, with job and money having a diminishing importance, unemployment can be seen as an opportunity rather than a catastrophe.

The courage to opt for the latter course of action very much depends on one's ability to assume a *holistic* outlook. While people operate out of a mechanical, functional vision, lifestyle will tend to be governed by fragmented and partial values; life itself is experienced at a level which leaves untouched and grossly under-developed the variety of our gifts and talents.

Being on the dole can become so exclusive a concern that it overrides all other dimensions of life. When we adopt a life project, based on a holistic and creative vision, our unemployed status becomes what humanity has always intended it to be, the opportunity for new growth, based on the fuller exploration of our God-given, creative potential.

We do not wish to under-estimate the *change* involved in this transition. For the majority of people it is quite traumatic and touches the lives of many others, with often detrimental effects for the social fabric of family and close friends. The changes facing the unemployed person and something of the emotional trauma involved, can be gleaned from these scripts:

1. 'The context in which I have lived my life, earned my livelihood, made some of my best friends and achieved some of my greatest joy and satisfaction, is gone. I am left with this terrible vacuum which in the hour of disaster seems incapable of being filled and in my pain and frustration I am not even sure that I want to fill it.'

   The befriending process (outlined above) is important here: the person is mourning a severe loss; it is irresponsible and uncaring to drown it out with drugs or alcohol. The person really cannot carry this load on her own; it can only become a lived and integrated experience through the fellowship and support of good, understanding friends.

2. 'It is so awkward, hanging around the house, wondering what to do. The wife is depressed and the children feel ashamed. Everybody seems out of sorts; we bitch and bark at each other over the least disagreement.'

   The family on its own cannot cope with this travesty; it was never intended to, especially in those families where husband and wife have tended to lead more segregated lives (cf. Elizabeth Bott, 1971). A supportive network, incorporating counselling, befriending, advice and recreational services is urgently needed to supplement what is no longer a marginal issue in our society. The onus is on locally based organisations, such as churches and local government agencies to take appropriate initiatives for the betterment of the unemployed, their families and friends.

3. 'One feels an awful fool going around to employment agencies. They all take your name and address, but you never hear from them. Increasingly, you begin to realise that you are just another *number*, an anonymous entity.'

   Appropriate advice about job-seeking, especially for those applying for the first time, is not as readily and widely available as would be desirable. Most urgently needed are counselling services and advice centres which enable the unemployed person to face and accept the fact that she may not get another job, but can live a rich and fulfilled life through the exploration of alternative gifts and talents. Again, the responsibility for this provision rests with local groups rather than with central government agencies.

4. 'Going down every Tuesday to sign on is the most debasing and degrading experience I've ever had. Everybody seems so apathetic and lifeless and most of them head for the pub afterwards, the only safe refuge left for all of us.'

This kind of statement illustrates the fear and humiliation of unemployed people, attitudes and feelings which often cripple any hope of a meaningful reorientation in life. Even external deportment, especially that of men, exhibits a feeling of desertion and betrayal: they are frequently unshaven, slovenly dressed, drooped in posture, and sluggish in speech. Affirmation at a very basic human level is acutely needed.

5. 'There is no more money left: we just go on hire-purchase and make whatever sacrifices we can. I knew all along it would come to this.'

Frequently, unemployment spells poverty and deprivation. In many countries, unemployment benefit does not match the cost of living, nor does it keep pace with inflation. Moreover, the belief that unemployment earnings exceed those of a working wage, is widely exaggerated. In one European study it was discovered that only 3% of those on the dole earned more than they did in previous employment. For at least 90% of workers, unemployment means a drastic cut in financial resources.

On the other hand, the situation is often aggravated by the family's (and by the unemployed person's) slow and unwilling adjustment to a more modest lifestyle. Occasionally, cars, videos, even weekly entertainment is budgeted for, while children are left hungry and deprived. In a rather ironic way, unemployment can be a salutary reminder of wrong priorities. Again, the adjustment involved, both for the person and the family, demands skills and expertise, which in most cases, is simply not available, though most urgently needed.

6. 'Apart from odd jobs, our Simon hasn't worked since he left
   school, six years ago. We're beginning to wonder will he ever
   get a job.'

We find it difficult to comprehend that many (perhaps 50%) of
today's youth will never have permanent employment; an estimated 25% may not even have a part-time job. How do we prepare
people for such a future, so that creative talent is not wasted and
sublimated in criminal and destructive outlets? How do we offer
our youth a future, enable and empower them towards a life of
joy and fulfilment, *without a job*? It is a daunting challenge – where
does one even begin?

I suggest that we start with a reform of the educational system
itself – still largely geared to academic achievement of a type best
suited to technology and industry. Not alone is this system
unsuited to a leisure-based society, but counterproductive in so
far as it creates false hopes and unreal expectations resulting in
feelings of frustration and failure which become the breeding
ground for crime and violence. Advocating reform in the educational system is a classic example of bashing one's head against
a stone wall; change is slow and piecemeal and usually a number
of decades behind the times. But reform in this area is so basic
and fundamental that it cannot be ignored. Despite the massive
resistance, we must keep calling for such reform.

The community at large, including parents, are rather limited
in what they can do by way of preparation of youth for unemployment. A significant number of the adult community have been
and still are employed; those made jobless in recent years have
not integrated their experience to a degree that enables them to
assist in the creation of new attitudes towards unemployment.
Consequently, we push the problem over to schools (career-
guidance teachers, in particular) or to youth associations and
expect them to provide the answers.

Challenge of Our Time

Preparation for unemployment is the responsibility of the entire
community. Initially, it demands a change of attitude and perception – of the type suggested in this Chapter – on the part of the
adult community. That may well be the major hurdle, one which
a significant number will negotiate unsuccessfully. Only with such
a change of outlook, can we develop the good will to gather

together the resources of the community (and they do exist) and plan programmes for the future growth and development of our youth.

Vigour and enthusiasm, freshness and originality, enterprise and creativity, are the qualities we wish to awaken. Beautiful words, but difficult to translate into appropriate action unless the community imparting the wisdom is itself a living model of that which it seeks to transmit.

Once again, it becomes apparent that the curse of unemployment is paradoxically a movement of our time with a vast potential for social and personal transformation. Can we rise to meet this challenge? If not, we spell our own demise and the ruination of future generations. It is a vast and onerous task and extremely urgent because time is running out.

Unemployment is no longer an issue merely for those out of work or unable to find a job. It is a major social, cultural and global phenomenon necessitating a concerted effort, based on vision, initiative and creativity, on the part of all humanity.

The change involved is quite profound and very disturbing for employed and unemployed alike. What becomes equally clear is that this transition can be made very much easier if society at large, especially in the local community context, became aware of its social responsibility to the unemployed. In fact, there is no long-term solution to the predicament apart from concerted community action. In other words, if unemployed people are to *change* in a life-enhancing way, then all of us must *change* in terms of our social co-responsibility.

Unemployment is not just about unemployed people. It is a challenge to all humanity. If it is left unaddressed and unattended to, massive apathy and indifference will erupt and these form the breeding ground for crime and social disruption. Already, society has embarked on this course and society alone can change the course. In this way, unemployment has become not merely the greatest evil of our age, but the supreme challenge of our time. How we handle it determines our aptitude to handle all social change confronting mankind today.

Part Three

Personal Change

10: From Individualism to Individuation

Change begins with individuals becoming clear and ceasing to act out of misunderstanding and ignorance. . . Nothing less than planetary survival hinges on the outcome. – KENNETH R. PELLETIER

The peak of ourselves, the acme of our originality, is not our individuality but our person; and according to the evolutionary structure of the world, we can only find our person by uniting together. – TEILHARD DE CHARDIN

The greatest formal talent is worthless if it does not serve a creativity which is capable of shaping a cosmos. – ALBERT EINSTEIN

With the rise of *existentialism* in the nineteenth century, the individual came to the fore in the philosophy and thought-patterns of the West (cf. Lukes, 1973, pp. 3-42). This development was the product of the scientific consciousness of the two previous centuries but, more significantly, it marked a strong protest against the impersonalisation of the system itself and its effects on human dignity and uniqueness. The existentialists sought to exalt the individual in his uniqueness so that he could reclaim his autonomy and dignity amid the *angst* and meaninglessness of life. In so far as this new trend resonated deeply with many people's experience it gained strength and popularity, a much-needed emphasis but one that, in time, proved to be grotesquely introspective and unashamedly selfish.

The existentialist's goal of individual autonomy contained a number of inbuilt weaknesses, not least being its perception of the individual as an isolated, independent being. This image has frequently been misrepresented in the independent, self-effacing individual who functions with little or no reference to his fellow men and women. It has been further reinforced by the male-chauvinistic dominance of Western society, exemplified in the status and authority of the boss-man, so essential to capitalistic equilibrium. As a model it contains many of those popular Western values such as toughness, power, decisiveness, objectivity and clarity of purpose. But it also contains the seeds of what may be the most devious and pernicious force of any culture: *individualism*.

Individualism

We all use the word and we know something of its meaning. It denotes an attitude and value-system focused primarily on the individual and his/her individual needs. According to Lukes (1973, pp. 45-78) the conceptual frame of reference is that of *dignity, autonomy, privacy, self-development and abstractness* (i.e. not capable of being 'socially arranged' like society or the state). *Individualism* seeks to pursue personal goals in spite of or irrespective of the wishes and desires of other people. The social dimension is poorly developed, if developed at all. Greed, selfishness and personal progress dominate both thought and action. Stubbornness and a strong sense of self-righteousness tend to accompany this lifestyle.

Individualism is rampant in contemporary society, especially in the West. Some trace its origin to family upbringing with the emphasis on personal pursuit and self-perfection. Religious attitudes sometimes reinforce this outlook. What we often fail to understand is that the person operating out of such a model poorly understands – in fact, may be totally unaware of – her own value-system. Attitudes and behaviour may be largely governed by *unconscious* drives towards power, glory and self-assertion.

In many cases, individualism is a form of reaction against past or present structures which are perceived (consciously or unconsciously – usually the latter) as threatening. To cope with this threat, the personality has developed 'defence mechanisms' which automatically come into play, especially under pressure or challenge. Individualism is a survival mechanism which owes its origin more to systemic oppression than to anything within an individual human being.

We cannot comprehend this mode of behaviour without some

understanding and appreciation of the underlying causes. Personal autonomy (even survival) may have been so undermined or lacking in one's childhood that one spends an entire lifetime selfishly guarding one's 'niche'. Persistent illness or the acquisition of disease may be the 'child's' final hope to attract the attention and recognition long sought after (cf. Harrison, 1984). Affection and warmth may have been in such short measure that a person simply has not acquired the inner freedom to give and share with others. Contemporaneous factors in family, work or relationships may pose threats that put one on the defensive. Even when we know the source, or think we do, the other person genuinely may not understand what we are trying to say.

People with this disposition find *change* extremely threatening and consequently will resist it strongly. Can we enable them to cope more effectively? To this question there are a variety of responses: those who suggest that we should accept 'individuals' for what they are; expecting them to change may be asking the impossible and will only alienate them further; those who submit that 'every man has a right to go wrong'; freedom is our supreme right as human beings, nobody is entitled to interfere with our freedom, even when we misuse it. Alternatively, there are those who realise that when we fail to challenge people to change, then we automatically condemn them to stagnation – as responsible, social beings we have no choice but to challenge individualism with its destructive consequences.

There seems to be a very thin line between the *right* to respect an individual's uniqueness and the *duty* to interfere in order to activate (or facilitate) new growth. In human relationships and personality development we either *progress, regress* or *stagnate*. Equilibrium and balance are scientific categories which are no longer applicable to human growth and development, nor indeed to science but as little. Individualism is essentially an arrested form of growth. The person is 'stuck', and if we seek to foster a caring humanity we seem to have no choice other than helping him/her to become 'unstuck', painful though that process may be.

Individuality

Individualism has been recognised as a blockage to growth and progress in many different areas, personal, social and cultural. The suggested substitute has been that of *individuality*, a term

which initially seems to transcend the self-centredness and nar-
row limitations of individualism. Essentially, *individuality* implies
a conceptually clear and convincingly strong awareness of my
uniqueness as a person on par with the uniqueness and dignity
of every other human being. From a deep appreciation of my
own value and worth comes the ability to perceive and respect
the individuality of each other person. Conversely, my own
dignity and status is enhanced through my interaction with other
people.

The basic emphasis is on the value of the person above and
beyond the group, the social system and creation at large.
Humans as individuals are deemed to be supreme, just as the
individual God is supreme over creation. Statements like: 'The
person is all that matters', 'Human beings come first', 'People are
more important than things', all belong to this category.

In an effort to assert the absolute sacredness of the person,
individuality veers towards a form of superiority which is both
subtle and dangerous. The tendency to juxtapose the individual
to everything else in creation can easily lead to exploitive and
manipulative abuses of other life-forms, inanimate objects and,
indeed, other people too. It leads to forms of fragmentation which
militate against holism.

What initially seems to be a very coherent and humane concept
can easily become devious and destructive. Western democracies
pride themselves in safeguarding individuality; so do the multi-
nationals! The West has progressed and still proceeds on the basis
that man is master of creation, a concept which has led to the
gross abuse of other life-forms and of nature. It has led to an
exaggerated self-concept, very different from individualism, but
ultimately no less lethal and destructive.

Individuality is also a concept warmly cherished by the christian
churches. The supremacy of God is a prerequisite for the supremacy of man, which in turn validates categories of leadership at
various organisational levels of society, e.g., Pope, Cardinals,
Bishops, Clergy; or politically, President, Prime Minister and a
host of elected representatives at different levels. What we have
created in the name of democracy – in order to safeguard human
individuality – has, in recent times, led to many subtle forms of
subversion and corruption. At the end of the day, nature has been
polluted, other life-forms have been brutalised and even humans

themselves have been degraded.

Escalating unemployment, especially in Western nations, has dealt a severe blow to *individuality*, thus highlighting the ambivalent underpinnings of this concept. According to Krishna Kumar (cf. Thompson, 1984, p. 3) traditional Western employment (what formerly was known as the Protestant work ethic) was characterised by work, job, identity and *individuality*. In this context, the self-concept tended to be one of achievement, control, function and monetary reward. It conferred status, power and a sense of usefulness. Strictly speaking, the self-referrant terms were from *without* rather than *within*: the automan, the functionary, Marcuse's one-dimensional man, held pride of place. The job-oriented individual may not be well developed emotionally or even socially and spiritually. Behind the outward performance, whether it be one's duty to state (work) or church, there may exist a superficial and underdeveloped spiritual life.

Individuality is not so much an evil as an inadequate, conceptual category for a world yearning for a more global, interdependent and holistic set of values. Confronted with change, our individualist (individualism) resists because of fear, the individual (individuality), because it poses a threat to his power. The individual welcomes change so long as he is able to manipulate, control and structure it to his own wishes; change he cannot control is dismissed as either meaningless, trivial or superfluous.

Individuation

Our third category is borrowed from Jungian psychology, wherein it denotes a *process* of personal growth through which the person integrates the conscious and unconscious elements of human experience. For Jung, this often happens in the successful negotiation of a trauma, a neurosis or an illness of some type, and is characteristic more of people in the latter half of life than in their youth.

The emphasis is very much on *integration*, and for the purposes of this book, *individuation* may be described as that *ongoing* process whereby I experience my life as part of a larger reality – social, ecological, spiritual, cosmic – to which I am responsible and which nurtures and nourishes my being as a person. It is a state in which I hold together in a creative synthesis the polarities of life. I belong to the process but I am not absorbed by it. I retain

INDIVIDUATION PROCESS AND
NEED SATISFACTION

Stage/Experience	*Dominant Needs*
Individualism	Survival and safety Belongingness and love Gratification Control Self-determination
Individuality	Esteem by self and others Dominance Achievement Self-actualisation
Individuation	Inter-relatedness / interdependence Cosmic-centredness Transcendence Intimacy

and maintain my dignity and uniqueness in so far as everyody around me – and creation at large – is able to enjoy the same right (cf. Goldbrunner, 1955, pp. 119-145).

This is a radically new way of understanding humanity and comprehending the mystery of our existence. It is neither *pantheism* (being absorbed into God) nor *creationism* (being absorbed by creation). We lose nothing of our uniqueness, dignity and personal worth. In fact, we rediscover them anew and continue doing so every day of our lives. The urge to control and manipulate is gradually abandoned, while the care and cultivation of life takes on a new sense of urgency. We begin to feel a sense of oneness with our universe: 'Individuation. . . breaks down the barriers and walls which the ego has erected between itself and the surrounding world' (Goldbrunner, 1955, p. 122). We begin to realise that everybody and everything need each other, not in a competitive and manipulative way, but in an orchestrated interaction which seeks to extrapolate and utilise the best which each person and each reality has to give for the benefit of the whole.

Individuated people welcome change, since they themselves feel most at home in an ever-changing universe. And they perceive change as a gracious challenge of which they are primarily beneficiaries. Both individualism and individuality feel victimised by any form of change they cannot control. Individuation is a corollary of the thesis that the whole is greater than the sum of the parts and yet the whole is contained in each part giving the individual parts something of the power and dignity of the whole itself (cf. the *hologram,* pp. 80-81 above). The individual is meaningless apart from his relation to the whole; it's not a question of opposition or juxtaposition; neither is it cause and effect and it is definitely not polarisation. We are dealing with a new conceptual, *mystical* reality for which modern writers have coined terms like *interdependent, interconnected, holistic*.

Change in the Personal Life

These three categories provide a useful conceptual framework to explore the nature and impact of personal change in today's world. We cannot escape the influence of change; it is all pervasive. Neither can we control it, because its origins are global as well as human, and predominantly the former rather than the latter. We live in a time of (approaching?) evolutionary transition;

we are being swept along in a wave of change in the face of which:

a) Some ignore it and go along doing their own thing. Occasionally they realise that they have been ensnared in some new strange experience; defence mechanisms quickly come into play and they either rationalise their way out or otherwise just grin and bear it. These are the *victims* of change, largely unaware of what is happening, trapped in a net of *individualism*.

b) Others acknowledge it within their own *managerial* frame of reference and quickly seek to devise a way of circumventing it, perhaps by creating a new product to answer a new consumer need. Change is perceived to be happening in the *parts* rather than in the *whole* of the machine, dampen the effect or alter the procedure and in that way we'll keep things at bay. It's all neatly worked out in the *head*, the *think*-tank on which *individuality* thrives.

c) What is still a minority, accept the reality of change, acknowledging it as a birthright we have inherited from our past, one we pass on to future generations with the imprint and contribution which we add to the cumulative wisdom of our universe, technically called the *Collective unconscious*. In this wave of change, we find our lives by losing them. We are beneficiaries of change, not its victims. This *feeling* for change as something gracious and positive comes, not from the head, but from the *heart*, the intuitive centre of *individuation*.

Individuation is neither a state nor a stage; it is an ongoing process of growth and integration. Although normally experienced in adult life – by those over *thirty-five*, according to Jung – its seeds are sown in those miraculous hours and days in the mother's womb. And if we allow those seeds to flower and subsequently nurture them in a tender and caring environment, they continue to produce ever richer and luxurious foliage over the span of an entire lifetime and, indeed, beyond. We'll explore this topic in our next chapter.

The progressive development from individualism to individuality to individuation is not based on deliberate decisive moves from one state to the next. We find something of ourselves at all three levels most of the time. As our awareness increases, however, we become empowered to move in a direction best suited to our own growth and development. Willy-nilly this also means adopting the approach best suited to the progress of all life-forms.

And this process is not merely *personal and individual*. As already indicated, it is also *cultural*. Individualism is rampant at many levels of life; unfortunately, the alternative we opt for tends to be individuality with its subtle and oppressive characteristics, as outlined above.

Our new global consciousness brings with it a fresh, cultural image of people and their uniqueness. Because this mutation of consciousness leads us away from the control and domination we tend to associate with mature adulthood, it does not elicit massive support. Many people are so choked and stilted in their cultural conditioning that they cannot even recognise the process. Others acknowledge it but having to sell everything they possess in order to buy the pearl (cf. Matt. 13:46) is a mighty risk that many rescind from. A minority take the risk, often amid pain, suffering and confusion; in all probablility these are our contemporary prophets leading us into the promised land of tomorrow's world:

> Change begins with individuals becoming clear and ceasing to act out of misunderstanding and ignorance. This task of moving out of the bondage of individual anger, malice, greed and self-service is the most formidable challenge of a lifetime. Nothing less than planetary survival hinges on the outcome. (Kenneth R. Pelletier, 1978, p. 31.)

11: Change and Growth on the Journey of Life

Human knowledge is personal and responsible, an unending adventure at the edge of uncertainty. – JACOB BRONOWSKI

To change is to grow; to be perfect is to have changed many times.
 – CARDINAL NEWMAN

Friend, the road is long and difficult because you are trying to reach the end ahead of time. The true purpose of the road is not to reach the end but to make the journey. – THE BUDDHA

Why are we so frightened of change? When we look at a human life unfolding we cannot escape the simple but all important realisation that change is the very essence of our being. From birth to death – physically, socially and mentally – we change and continually adapt to new challenges. Change is imprinted in the very fabric of our lives; it is inherent to our nature. Its elimination or suppression, on which we expend so much energy, especially at a subconscious level, is the greatest crime of our civilisation. We deprive ourselves and our universe of so much beauty and vitality, variety and creativity. Our resistance to change is one great denial, an insult thrown in the face of our creative God.

The Human Life-Cycle

Over the centuries scholars have debated the problem of the origin of human life: when does the foetus become a human being? When does the soul enter the body? Nobody has yet thought of abandoning the mechanics and asking a more dynamic question: 'When will we begin celebrating life not as an *object* but as a *relationship*?' Every sexual encounter, whether reproductive or not, is intended to be life-giving, nurturing, an assertion that life is ultimately delightful and ecstatic. Even before the sperm fertilises the ovum, the wish on the part of the couple to create new life is itself a dimension of that life – indeed a most important aspect of caring and nurturing. Love, not the soul, is what animates life.

In recent years, we have acquired valuable insights into pre-natal development. Already, some forty-eight hours after conception, the human zygote contains in embryonic form, the full genetic equipment for an unique human being. It is also believed that the capacity for memory may already be active at this early stage, which means that we humans may be capable of recording and retaining (to our advantage or disadvantage) everything that happens to us from the first hours of life.

The miracle of the human zygote is not merely in its personal uniqueness but also in that beautiful and delicate interaction of life-balancing fluids and chemicals within the mother's body that enable the potential person to float down the fallopian tube, become embedded in the wall of the womb and begin to draw nourishment for its growth, initially from the endometrium and subsequently through the umbilical cord. The fact that a significant proportion (between 30%-60%) of fertilised ova fail to negotiate the 'journey' and consequently die, is a poignant reminder of the delicate interdependence and mysterious interaction on which early life is dependent for survival. It is banal in the extreme to argue the moral appropriateness of the Morning-After pill, 'since up to 70% of zygotes die anyhow'; this is a classic example of mechanistic thought and crude manipulative interference.

Life begins in a relationship, the procreative encounter of woman and man. It negotiates its first journey (taking six to eight days), aided by minute 'life-carriers' within the mother's body. Over the next nine months the new creature grows to the physical and psycholgical stature of an infant capable of living and surviving outside the womb. Meanwhile, much has been taking place and already the future pattern of this new being's health and happiness may be ingrained in her personality. Everything mother says, does, feels and thinks during pregnancy, affects baby's well-being and is now believed to have long-term effects for physical and mental health.

Blockages in emotional growth, occurring in adult life, may have their roots in pre-natal experience (cf. Frank Lake, 1981, pp. 15ff., 39ff., 50, 153). We have abundant evidence to show how toxic substances can be passed from mother to child; babies have been born drug-addicts and had to be taken through the withdrawal process. We are loath to accept that a similar relationship exists regarding mental well-being. It is only a matter of time until this relationship is more definitely established.

The earliest studies in child development were pioneered by the phychologist, Sigmund Freud. Today, few would adhere to his deterministic, sexually-based model, with particular exphasis on the oral, anal and oedipus stages. What still carries a degree of credibility is the influence of childhood development on adult behaviour: the values and behaviour patterns we adopt as children determine the kind of adults we become.

Many would challenge that view today, but would submit that our childhood *emotional* experience influences our adult emotional development, e.g., a child who lacks love and affection will crave for this warmth from others and may unconsciously express this desire in attention-seeking behaviour, in sexual exploitation, in aggression or, alternatively, in severe depression with a relatedly poor self-image and inferiority complex. The potential for change in adulthood may be seriously hampered because of negative childhood experiences.

No longer, however, do we subscribe to the theory that the human personality is changeable and adaptable up to late adolescence, but pretty well 'fixed' and unchangeable from there on. This view flourished up to the early 1960s; psychology and human-development text-books gave the distinct impression that development ended at *twenty*. Occasionally a short final paragraph was devoted to death and bereavement, but practically nothing was said of the rich and turbulent intervening years which, for the majority of mankind, are the most creative and productive.

Stages in Human Development

In the 1950s Erik Erikison (1950) developed a new model of developmental psychology, covering the entire life-span. His initial outline has been adapted, modified and refined; the diagram (p. 198) provides an overview of the main stages as elucidated by various theorists. The danger with this model is that people tend to absolutise one or other stage and seek its application in a mechanical and stereotyped way.

The work of Erikison and his followers adheres to what is a crucial distinction of the holistic vision, the priority of *process* to *product*. The stages outlined in the Diagram do not refer to 'tasks to be completed', by a certain age. Instead it is an attempt at

STAGES IN PERSONAL/RELIGIOUS/MORAL DEVELOPMENT

Stage	Personal	Religious	Moral
Infancy (0-1½)	Trust v. Mistrust	Undifferentiated Faith	
			Precovential
Early Childhood (2-6)	Autonomy v. Shame Initiative v. Guilt	Intuitive-Projective Faith	Instrumental Exchange
Childhood (7-12)	Industry v. Inferiority	Mythic v. Literal Faith	
Adolescence (13-21)	Identity v. Role Confusion	Synthetic–Conventional Faith	*Conventional* Mutual, Interpersonal relations
Young Adult (21-35)	Intimacy v. Isolation	Individuative–Reflective Faith	Social System and Conscience
Adulthood (35-60)	Generativity v. Stagnation	Conjunctive Faith	Social Contract Individual Rights
Maturity (60–)	Integrity v. Despair	Universalising Faith	Universal, ethical principles
	Source: Erik Erikson & D. J. Levinson	*Source:* James Fowler, Sam Keen & Others	*Source:* Lawrence Kohlberg

Source: Ó Murchú, 1986, p. 61.

naming the experience which *tends to predominate* during those years. Success or failure cannot be judged by allotting a person to one or other category. The models enable a person to identify and name one's experience and feel at home with its ongoing development. Stages-theory can also indicate, quite poignantly, where one's blockages are and what one needs to do to transcend or release them.

In this approach *change* is considered to be a normative and normal dimension of life. Some stages may be more critical than others, e.g. early childhood, adolescence, mid-life transition and retirement, but *all* are inherent to our growth and development. All of us live through all the stages; how we experience and negotiate their impact on our lives varies significantly from one person to the next.

A great deal has been written about *stages* in human development (in the vein of Gail Sheehy, 1976) and it continues to be a topical subject. Workshops, seminars, and lectures are also readily available. Gratefully, the educational systems of many countries are acknowledging these new insights and seeking ways of conveying this new wisdom to young people and adults alike. Hence, the upsurge in courses on parenting skills, relationships, preparation for retirement, coping with bereavement, just to mention a few. Since so much is already written and otherwise available, I will not deal with the stages in detail. Rather in keeping with the central theme of this book, I will outline ways and means of coping with the change envisaged and demanded for the successful negotiation of the various stages.

Coping Skills

In the face of anticipated or imminent change, one frequently hears the following statements: 'Surely, you don't expect someone of my age to change!': 'All this change is beyond me'; 'All this talk about change is driving me mad'. These statements are a sad indictment of a society that has conditioned and brainwashed its members into a staid and morbid stability. We have been alienated from a true perception of ourselves as changing, growing people; we even fail to acknowledge and credit ourselves for the many changes we have successfully negotiated. Most of all, we need to cultivate a basic coping skill: that of *trust* in the changing process and in ourselves as changing people. To make this possi-

ble we need to appropriate new attitudes based on:
a) Awareness
b) Decisiveness
c) Concerted action.

Awareness: i) We need basic *information* about change, at all levels of life: global, social/cultural, personal. Where and how is change taking place and how does this affect our lives? Individually, we can take a number of initiatives to procure this information.

ii) The *quality* of information in our educational systems warrants urgent attention. Much time, energy and finance is devoted to the transmission of new information, frequently of an academic quality, useful only to a small proportion of the citizenry. Instead we need to relocate our resources in enabling young people to cope with the massive quantity of information *already* at their disposal. Developing media skills, critical viewing, integrating information, perceiving change, value-formation, communications are just a few of the skills which both young and old need at the present time.

iii) We need a radically new understanding of the *origin* of change. The perception that we, humans, are the activators and agents of change (the reverse side of which is: change will not take place unless we implement it) is naively simplistic and grossly inadequate for our evolutionary era.

iv) This also means that we tend to misread the *focus* of change. Change is another name for the unfolding process of life. It encapsulates all reality and was already at work for billions of years before we humans came on the scene. We don't have a *mandate* to manipulate or control change; such power would be a prescription for self-destruction, a tendency already apparent in the efforts of the world superpowers to control and dominate life.

v) We need to cultivate an *eclectic* quality of awareness, not one based exclusively or chiefly on 'head' knowledge, but one that draws on the diverse and deeper wisdom of imagination, intuition, spirit, feeling and emotion.

vi) We need to cultivate *sensitivity* to the impact of change on ourselves and on each other; on the pain and anguish, characteristic of all loss, but also on the hope and vision which initially may seem vague and unattractive.

Decisiveness: i) Confronted with change of a global nature the alternatives we face are: *change* or *stagnate*. We are offered the option of being either the *beneficiaries* or *victims* of change. Our awareness will tell us that much; but we ourselves have to make the *choice* and in the words of the well-worn cliche: 'no one can make that choice for us'. There is a sense in which it has to be uniquely and consciously made by each person.

ii) The option for change also implies the formation of new links with other individuals, movements, organisations with whom we can discern what may or may not be appropriate lines of action. The option to go it alone is scarcely adequate at a time of so much and such complex change. A supportive network not merely eases the transition but seems well nigh imperative for an authentic response.

iii) *Timing* change will be determined by our perception of its pattern and pace. 'Waiting for the right time' may reveal a lack of decisiveness based on fear rather than a form of discretion arising from intuitive wisdom. This is one of the many issues we need to check out reguarly with members of our supportive network.

iv) Our option for change is facilitated by a cognitive and affective recognition of the sacrifices involved, both in terms of cherished values that must be abandoned and cherished friends we may have to leave behind because they chose to go another road. That is not to suggest that we either ignore or forget those who disagree with us, nor do we *deliberately* choose to abandon others to the stagnation of immutability (see no. v, below). But we must not allow others to restrain us in our response to a new future. When Jesus told his disciples to leave parents, home and family for the sake of the Kingdom, he was not advocating desertion or disloyalty, but a new state of relatedness, transcending old bonds and former relationships.

v) Our choice to bring others with us on the road of change is fundamental to the global vision we articulate. We do not have a right to abandon or desert anybody to a life of morbidity or stagnation. Neither can we push people to accompany us on the journey. Appropriate motivation must be gentle and tactful. At the end of the day, we respect each person's unique option.

vi) One cannot help thinking that large numbers will resist, opting instead for the status quo rather than for the global alternative. Against this background, the option for change, the choice to become an innovator, will meet with cynicism, misunderstanding, derision, even persecution. Like the prophets of old we must be prepared for a rough passage. There is always a price for progress.

Action i) Change can be either quantitative or qualitative, or even both simultaneously. Quantitative change is that which seeks to modify the external structures such as membership, rules, procedures of an organisation. To achieve this end one may choose to work through a trade union, through the official leadership or by direct personal intervention. We exchange the parts, discard some, introduce others to achieve a desired end. Renewal has been achieved through planned action.

ii) Qualitative change cannot be planned, monitored nor effected with the same degree of accuracy nor of human efficiency. The process is a great deal more subtle but also more sublime. In this case, the change-agent, whether individual or group acts as a *catalyst*, one who seeks to 'loosen-up' the system – at a personal, social, national, global level – so that the innate energy may flow more freely and bring about a transformation from within. Since this concept is so new, and so much at variance with the accepted mode and understanding of change, it is not easily grasped, cognitively nor practically.

iii) Qualitative change presumes a deep level of trust, in God, in life, in people and in oneself. This becomes the prerequisite for new relationships generating the cumulative wisdom and intuition for appropriate insertion as a change-agent.

iv) Qualitative change necessitates a deepening quality of awareness, not that one must know all there is to know about everything, but one stands to benefit from a holistic wisdom that progressively enables one to understand 'how things hold together', how polarities complement, and how all life-forms are interconnected and interdependent.

v) In the light of the above observations, *non-action* rather than *action* may occasionally be the more appropriate response, as envisaged in the Argus poster which reads: 'A man is rich in proportion to the number of things he can afford to let alone.'

vi) Value formation rather than structural alteration is the goal of qualitative change. CND does not set out to destroy nuclear warheads, but seeks to raise human consciousness to such a degree that the cumulative wisdom of our species will compel the superpowers to terminate their use and deployment and, in that way, bring about their destruction. The pursuit of justice, peace and a new world-order are important dimensions of qualitative change.

vii) The justice that leads to peace frequently invites us to places we would rather not go: the picket line, the protest march, the peace rally, often dominated by scruffy hippies and punk rockers, vintalating righteous anger. We like to be on the side of change but not in those kind of situations, so much at variance with our middle-class values.

viii) Keep an eye on *stress*: so many potential catalysts never leave their mark because either they *rust out*, waiting for the right time, the right place, the right people, or they *burn out* from excessive activism, exhaustion and over-involvement. To strike the happy balance is not so much a skill of measuring the *amount* we can take-on as rather blending quality with quantity. Activity, if it is to be fruitful, must be combined with appropriate rest, space for reflection, time to pray and meditate, discourse with friends and discreet care for health and well-being.

ix) Seek to transcend stereotyped, formalised modes of behaviour. Our society is sorely lacking in initiative, spontaneity, vibrancy, flexibility and creativity. Cultivating these qualities, conceptually and practically, is like setting the seeds of change.

x) Allow God (by whatever name you use) to work in and through you: in more secular language, remember you are an agent for change in a changing world. Your task and privilege is to interpret change and enable others to understand the process. In this way, you help to diminish the fear and mistrust many people associate with change and you open up possibilities for new growth and new life. In the last analysis, this is what all human life is destined to achieve.

These are basic ground rules which apply differently in our adaptation to change demanded by each new experience of life. But whatever the situation, and no matter how original the experience may seem to be, three basic principles apply:

— Keep alert, aware and sensitive to what is happening, opening yourself to whatever supportive networks will empower you to that end.

— Be decisive in your option for change, acknowledging the accompanying stress and strain, the abandonment of old ways (perhaps, still *valid* in themselves) and the assumption of new orientations.

— Seek appropriate means to translate your new vision into action; otherwise mankind and civilisation is forever deprived of the uniqueness of your contribution.

Activating the Power Within

The author of life equipped us all with the power and capacity to change, to grow through change, to meet its challenge, to be enriched by its invigorating spirit. It is not *change* that overwhelms and confuses us; it is the blockages that inhibit and distort the flow of change. Removing these blockages, our resistances and defence mechanisms, may be the greatest change we are invited to espouse. And there are a variety of support systems that will enable us to do that, counselling and psychotherapy being among the better known.

In the human community generally, people are still scared of the psychiatric and psychological professions, the 'brain-shrinkers' as they are perjoratively called. On the other hand these services have been idolised, especially by Americans for whom it seems to be a mark of status and maturity to attend a psychiatrist, something akin to the confused teenager who considers herself liberated because she has lost her virginity. Apart from these extremes, there has emerged in recent years a variety of psychotherapeutic approaches based mainly on the humanistic and transpersonal schools of psychology.

Like the new trend in alternative medicine, the focus is on the *whole* person, not on the 'sick' part. The psychological block is not envisaged as belonging to one or other facet of the personality but is symptomatic of a general defensiveness, fear which may be inhibiting (even crippling) the person in a variety of ways, largely unconscious and, therefore, beyond the person's control. According to the alternative approach, these blockages may have nothing to do with the instinctual *id* of the Freudian subconscious, rectifiable only through psychoanalysis, nor with any of those other inner recesses, dark and dangerous territory, in which neurosis, psychosis and madness hibernate.

Working on the *holographic* principle that the whole is contained in each of the parts, the new phychotherapeutic methods adopt newly developed techniques for release of emotional blocks. Thus, *Bioenergetics* focuses on tension absorbed by and locked in the musculature of our bodies; once this is released, the energy flow throughout the entire system becomes activated and will adopt new patterns. *Gestalt therapy* seeks to alert us to the impact of wrong perceptions on our lifestyle and behaviour, especially those reconstructions that prioritise the *parts* at the expense of the *whole*. *Massage* and other forms of *Bodywork* seek to stretch, lengthen and relax muscles, tendons and connective tissues, thereby freeing body functions to operate in a more spontaneous way and enabling the body to utilise more effectively its innate, healing powers. *Primal Therapy* facilitates the release of repressed feelings and emotions through the medium of voice-sound and the accompanying expression of anger and frustration.

Other forms aim more at the totality of human *experience*. Thus, *Psychodrama* enables the person to relate and integrate 'disjointed' aspects of the personality. *In-depth meditation* activates a sychronistic effect in brain activity (the precise nature of which we do not yet fully understand) which in turn facilitates personal growth and integration. *Encounter groups, Co-counselling*, etc., aim at creating a supportive environment in which people can enable one another to deepen personal awareness and integrate new perceptions and understandings of self into daily living.

The list is by no means complete, but it adequately reflects the new orientation towards psychological wholeness. As opposed to traditional psychiatry, there is a distinctly different approach. The person is not considered to be *sick*, but thwarted in growth as a result of her own or people's influence. In one way or another all humans are lacking in that quality of integration that fosters growth (a new explanation for original sin?). We all need to explore new ways of growing and becoming, and thus actualise and release, for the benefit of all, our hidden potential and resources (hence, the name, Human Potential Movement). The strategy is essentially one of releasing and reactivating our (God-given) inner resources so that they can do the rest for us. There is no intention of interference or alteration on par with that employed by the medical profession in administering pep-pills, drugs, tranquillisers or ECT.

The *sacredness of the person* and of human life is important for these new movements. Their approach is thorough and holistic and in aspiring towards human integration, they strive to accommodate all aspects of the human phyche from the physical to the spiritual. They acknowledge the person's ability and *innate* desire to change – at all stages of life; their various strategies are geared explicitly to the realisation and actualisation of this change. In this they differ radically from traditional psychiatry whose view of humanity is shallow and pessimistic and whose method of intervention tends to be rationalistic and mechanical.

The philosophy and orientation of alternative psychotherapy is supremely suited to those committed to the challenge of change. The adjustment and relocation necessitated by transition can make heavy demands on our health and sanity. At different stages of the journey we may need the support of those in the *network* specifically concerned with our mental and psychological well-being. It doesn't mean we are *sick*; it simply means we are *human*. The transformation of our humanity can be so much more powerful and beautiful when we draw on those healing agents whom God has given to be our companions on the journey of life.

12: Behold I Make All Things New! (Epilogue)

When we say God is 'eternal', we mean God is eternally young.
— MEISTER ECKHART

We are becoming so identified with revealed truth that synthesised truth is no longer necessary. Expectant waiting is more important to us than organised religion. — ARTHUR GUIRDHAM

A writer is in the end not his books but his myth – and that myth is in the keeping of others. — V.S. NAIPAUL

When I set out to write this book, I consciously adopted the stance of a social scientist. I set myself the triple task of observation, interpretation and verification. Because of personal circumstances, my methodology had to be one of collating the theory and practice of contemporary change, available to me from a variety of documentation and in the end submit conclusions based on that research. My contact with the actual *experience* of change was somewhat limited; however, my dealings with unemployed people, clients in counselling, colleagues in different professions and liaison with a variety of 'new-age' movements, proved immensely helpful and enlightening.

As the task proceeded, the role of the 'neutral observer' progressively diminished. Insight based on objective reasoning always fell short of intuitive wisdom; the social scientist lagged behind the spiritual seeker. One could observe the factors which motivated change, the manner in which change was implemented along with the resistances outlined in Chapter Two. But one could not ignore the fact that change *happens* irrespective of human interference and *in spite* of human resistance. To explain this phenomenon, which became the major thrust of the book, I chose to be more of a dreamer than a reasoner.

And yet, the book is not a wild fantasy! The theory is based on experience, albeit that of a human minority. When this minority first emerged (as in the Hippie movement of the 1960s) it, too, sought to be objective and neutral, but not for long. The fascin-

ating about-turn is aptly demonstrated in the life of one of the
first 'new-age' theologians, Harvey Cox.

In 1965, Cox published *The Secular City*, something of a
bombshell in its day. Urban man had come of age; the city with
its businesslike atmosphere and rapid pace of life epitomised the
mature technocrat. Urban man sought to control and manipulate
his destiny; what formerly was attributable to the mysterious
power of God was now reclaimed for the technological skill of
man. The pomp and regalia of popular religiousity was losing out
to the rationality and secularism of modernity.

And then came the hippies, the flower-people, the Jesus freaks
and a host of others, disillusioned with technology, turning their
backs on the city and all it stood for. Cox went back to the theological drawing-board and wrote *The Feast of Fools*. Urbanisation
was a blessing but left untouched the deeper human aspirations,
especially the human need to 'celebrate' the spiritual in appropriate rite and ritual. The vision of the secular city was, at best,
a limited one.

Three years later, Cox wrote *The Seduction of the Spirit*, a
work which portrays an ever deepening sensitivity to the inner,
spiritual search and to the reconstruction of 'sacred spaces' to
explore and articulate that search:

> The mystics and contemplatives have served as the guardians and
> explorers of that uniquely human realm called 'interiority'. I think we
> need them today, perhaps more than we ever have, precisely because
> authentic personal life is now so fatally threatened by an intensive
> technical world. (Cox, 1974, pp. 93-94.)

Finally, in 1976, Cox travelled to the Far East in search of that
deeper wisdom which the West could not provide. On his return
he wrote: *Turning East: The Promise and Pearl of the New Orientalism*, in which he explores the potential values of Eastern
culture for Western civilisation. This book seems to lack the verve
and vitality of Cox's earlier writings. Indeed, this very reticence
may reflect a new quality of wisdom shared by many today:
taciturnity in pontificating or pronouncing too definitively on the
bewildering trends of our time.

Adherents of many disciplines have been through a similar
experience and like Cox finally set out for the star rising in the
East. What I find interesting in this quest is the rapid transition

from the rather serious sociological analysis depicted in *The Secular City* to the progressively expanding spiritual depth required for the holistic vision of our age.

My own exploration of *change*, as outlined in this book, was also one of unavoidable encounters with the spiritual. Rationality functions within terribly limited parameters, as specialists in many fields are beginning to realise. To interpret change in an integrated and comprehensive way, one has to employ feeling, imagination, intuition, spiritual insight, psychic awareness along with the powers of rational thought. And one has to think *globally*: because change is essentially a global phenomenon, a feature of universal life.

It was not by deliberate foresight that this book assumed a spiritual, prophetic tone, nor does it seem appropriate to conclude without a spiritual epilogue. I base these final thoughts on the inherited wisdom of my own christian faith. It is my wish and hope that they are not so exclusively christian as to be offensive or meaningless to followers of other creeds. Even in spiritual matters, I am deeply committed to a global perspective.

Of course, global, ecumenical dialogue does not entail either abandoning or diminishing one's own cherished beliefs. In fact, genuine dialogue with another only seems possible when I feel comfortable and secure on my own ground. Moreover, if I am in touch with the depths of my own tradition, the chances are that I am connecting with the archetypal, primordial values that unite all mankind in its spiritual quest. In that spirit of reciprocal dialogue I offer these concluding reflections.

Jesus and the 'New'

The christian Bible ends with the *Book of Revelation*, a dramatic and colourful presentation of God ruling the heavens and the earth. In the *twenty-first* chapter we read the provocative statement which forms the title of the present chapter. The words, as recorded in Rev. 21:5 (re-echoing Is. 42:9), are those of an eschatological theologian describing the most intimate relationship between God and his people in the new creation. It is the first time in the book that God speaks, using words which have many parallels throughout the New Testament.

Thomas Fawcett (1973, pp. 53-70) claims that the focus on the 'new' is central to the meaning and message of the New Testament. With the coming of Jesus on earth, a new quality of life has been established (i.e. the *Kingdom of God*). The followers of Jesus recognise in his ministry a new teaching (Mk 1:27). Jesus himself compared his ministry to 'new wine' which requires 'fresh skins' (Mk 2:22). Those who are 'created in Christ Jesus' (Eph 2:10) constitute a 'new creation' (2 Cor. 5:17). For this new manner of being, the New Testament uses two Greek words: *kainos* meaning *new* in reference to character and *neos* meaning *new* in reference to time ('young' or 'recent'). Both *kainos* and *neos* each occurs *forty-two* times in the New Testament.

More important than the frequency of the idea is the qualitative thrust of the message. Jesus inaugurates a 'new Covenant', a new way of living, a new quality of relationship between man, God and creation. There is a sense in which the old order continues ('I have come not to destroy the law, but to fulfil it') but its very fulfilment means that the 'old' has now been superseded, declared *inadequate*, if not useless. St Paul brings this out forcibly in his letters to *Romans* and *Galatians*: humans can no longer consider themselves justified (i.e. in a meaningful relationship with God) by the observance of the law, the apex of the old order with its emphasis on external, measurable, rational criteria. Fidelity to the *Spirit* is what matters in the new order.

For St Paul, the coming of Christ marks the end of the old dispensation (Rom. 6:14, Gal. 3:13, 25; 4:5 & 5:1). Henceforth a new quality of relationship between God and humanity is envisaged. Through the medium of humanity, transformed and renewed in Christ, humans have a new way of relating to God, of experiencing his love and entering into his fellowship. And this is no mere individualistic, narcisstic intimacy. It also includes a material, global aspect. *All life* is under the spell of revitalisation and God's creativity is being expressed in fresh and diverse ways.

One does not wish to under-estimate the theological nuances and complexities of this view. As a vision it is rich, complex and radical; the christian tradition has under-estimated rather than overrated its significance. Since early christian times, especially since the great theological debates of the church councils of Nicea (325 AD) and Chalcedon (451 AD), we have tended to couch the christian message in language and ideas which, if anything, suppress the vitality and freshness of the 'new'. An over-conceptualised theology becomes 'heady' and 'wordy', whereas the New

Testament message is essentially one of creative and compassionate *action*. As a praxis it is unique (among the religions of the world) for its emphasis on 'making life new' (see Fawcett, 1973, pp. 273-252), and in its perception of people as central to that process of innovation.

One could venture to suggest that the invitation to renew life is the essence of the christian message and of its vision as a living religion. What does this mean? Instead of shrouding our faith in legal and prescriptive terms, instituting dogmas to safeguard orthodoxy, questioning every new endeavour lest it deviate from 'the truth', we christians should be the vanguard of experimentation and exploration, of freshness and vitality, of hope and new life.

So many people today perceive the christian church as outdated, irrelevant, cramped and stifled in archaic institutions, out of touch with reality, custodians of the ancient, opposed to change and new developments. The christian churches are in danger of undermining the central message of the New Testament, in danger too of shielding their members from the vital challenge of God's word. The renewed call of every generation is to be a *leaven*, fresh dough, a people who will bring alive with new intensity God's message and its invitation to action in the context of each new era.

The Kingdom of God

The concept of change outlined in this book is consistent with the christian biblical vision and, one assumes, very much in tune with the spiritual vision of all the great world religions. The christian message stands as a permanent reminder that we stabilise human and earthly reality only at the price of ossification. Furthermore, it verifies the assertion frequently made in this book, that profound change entails a radical break with previous reality; this does not mean an *abandonment* of what formerly existed.

When Jesus announces a new kingdom, he envisages the termination of the old regimes of power, status, domination, control, class-distinction, warfare and material acquisition. The kingdom announced by Jesus is primarily one of justice, love and peace, a reign of God not determined by geographical boundaries or political/ecclesial control, but established globally for all who wish to participate in the task of co-creating 'a new heaven and a new earth'.

In this kingdom it is not the chauvinistic male figure, no less the regal boss, who controls; the 'child' becomes the new symbol of supremacy; hence, the powerful impact of the New Testament infancy narratives with the God-child as the focus of welcome, love and admiration. And the strategy for action is neither regality nor armaments but quite simply *weakness*: the vulnerable God who overcomes our pain and misery by submitting to it, a paradox illustrated most succinctly by St Paul when he writes: 'For when I am weak, then I am strong.' (2 Cor. 12:10.)

Nor is God's new reign predominantly prayerful, gentle and easy. Injustice, segregation, exploitation are strongly contested and condemned. No matter how one interprets the life of Christ one cannot escape his espousal of political protest and agitation, exemplified most potently in the cleansing of the temple (Mk 11:15-17). With good reason this new reign has been described as 'the upside-down Kingdom': with its inauguration, earthly and political power is thrown into disarray.

Where can we encounter this reality in today's Church? Where can we meet the radical Christ in the contemporary christian world? Certainly not in the power-laden institutions of christian Europe, still proclaiming a largely lifeless message to rapidly declining numbers; perhaps in the struggling and often bewildered churches of Africa and Latin America, desperately trying to convince their colleagues in the northern hemisphere of the integrity of their approach. These infant churches may be in organisational disarray, proclaiming a gospel message that cannot conform to doctrinal rectitude if it is to reflect its human reality truthfully and honestly: 'I know that being close to God entails being too close to people for comfort' (Jean Wildgoose in the *Radical Jesus Manifesto*, p. 26). And hence the polarisation which has become so acute in the Catholic Church, particularly throughout the 1980s.

A Church in Bewilderment

In the christian churches today a double drama is being played out. Firstly, there are the guardians of institutional christianity who claim to represent the bulk of believers, who seek to stabilise church life and bring a measure of uniformity (conformity?) into christian theory and practice right across the world. What church officialdom frequently forgets is that it commands the *nominal* allegiance of some 60-70% of the christian people but only the *real* allegiance (in terms of moral observance, attendance, participation in Church life, etc.) of a mere 10-20%.

There is an *alternative* group, comprising 10-20% of christians. Nominally, they may belong to one or other christian church; less than 5% would be 'practising'. What they have in common is a deep desire to share christian values and beliefs which they hold deeply and these include a church that is fresh, vibrant and revitalised. There is also a strong social consciousness which may drive them towards Marxism, CND, alternative technologies; in any or all of these frameworks they hope to get the support-structure to articulate their wish for a more just and equitable society. Many belong to the basic christian communities of the Catholic Church or to the house churches of the other christian denominations.

This alternative church is gaining ground and all indications are that it will continue to do so. They seek a church of the people marked by intimacy, participation and community, along with being a forum to articulate and explore spiritual feelings and aspirations. Disillusioned with a church that has become impersonal and formalised, bureaucratic and moralistic, they aspire towards something small, simple and intimate. And their vision is neither insular nor deliberately divisive. They do not wish to abandon the Church; if anything, they feel the church has abandoned them.

The offical churches always strive to dampen the effect and influence of 'renewal movements'; the more they try the wider the rift becomes. The polarisation arises from false perceptions in which the new movements are considered to be the product of secularising influences or deliberate deviations from the norm. This perception is onesided and superficial.

As indicated many times in this book, change may not (in fact, frequently, *does not*) operate on the basis of cause and effect. Change is an ingredient of life; growth thrives on it, and since all living organisations, including churches and religions, are destined to grow rather than atrophy or decay, then we can assume that *growth will take place*, not according to our approved norms, but in spite of all our efforts to control and engineer it.

I wish to submit that the focus on the 'new' is the leading and dominant myth of the New Testament (and presumably would have parallels in all the great world religions). It is another articulation – perhaps the supreme one – of that power for change, arising from the collective unconscious, that impinges on all our lives (and on all our reality), moving us continually towards that growth and transformation essential for our development and progress as envisaged in the divine plan of creation. Nothing on this earth, no matter how sacredly or solemnly instituted, can finally arrest that growth and change. We can only submit to it. And in this very submission we gain our greatest freedom.

Tragically, the churches of all major religions have tended towards hindering rather than fostering change. Even the Eastern religions whose mystical writings project a profound appreciation of change as the essence of reality (see Capra, 1976) are open to a misinterpretation that tends to become normative. In the very process of perceiving and interpreting change, Easterners deem permanence and stability to be *illusory*. They go on to suggest that everything in this world is illusory, temporary, passing away. The after-life alone is permanent; even for the Easterner the permanence has to await the eventual outcome of the transmigrational or rebirthing process.

In both the East and West, the churches have precinded from the idea of *coping* with change. Instead, they dismiss it as being illusory, secondary, ultimately irrelevant to the permanence that awaits us after death.

Simplicity or Integration

Universally, we continue to suffer from what Raimundo Panikkar (1982) calls simplicity at the price of simplification, Instead, he advocates simplicity through the process of integration. The former belongs to the scientific paradigm in which religious truth was considered superior to all other forms of wisdom and beyond error in its perception and judgement. The Coperican revolution along with the birth and development of social and anthropological science has all but demolished that monstrous claim. Theology may still be the queen of the sciences but unlike the royalty of former times, she can no longer assume a role of unquestioned loyalty. If she does, she faces the demise of the few remaining political royalties: outdated but glamourous antiques, rubberstamping decisions made by their respective governments and, in practice, devoid of any real power.

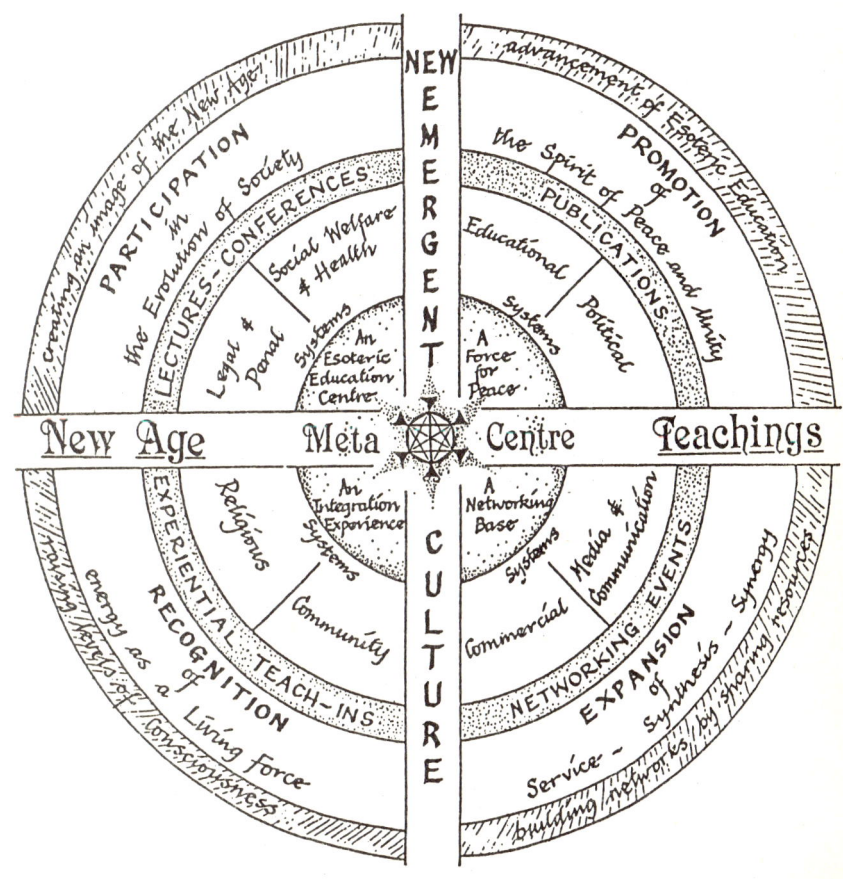

SYNTHESIS FOR THE IMPENDING AGE

Explanation: I am deeply indebted to M'haletta, Derek and Carmella of the
MetaCentre, Clent (near Birmingham, England) for permission to use and reprint
this diagram. Initially designed to synthesise and explain the philosophy of the
MetaCentre, with its new-age programme of holism and integration, I offer it to
the reader as an encapsulation of the dream and vision of this book, a reality
slowly unfolding and eagerly awaiting realisation in our hearts and in our world.

A spirituality of integration seeks to acknowledge and encompass the diversity and pluriformity of life along with the ever new understandings brought about by change and development (graphically outlined in the Diagram on p. 215). It does not consider the fluctuating state of affairs to be essentially illusory, but instead *real* in its basic nature. It goes on to point out that we tend to camouflage reality in constructs and experiences which we dissect, fragment and juxtapose, all to the advantage of our exploitative and consumerist world.

The world itself is not unreal, but we, humans, tend to be unreal in the way we treat our world. The first and most urgent challenge of contemporary spirituality (and of christianity ever since the incarnation of God on earth) is to empower and enable people to take the world seriously, to acknowledge God's hand at work in its every movement, to cherish its variety, fragmented and contradictory though it may be at times and above all, to enter attentively and lovingly into its daily change and mutation.

So often, religion and spirituality has created an ideology of *escape*. Ever since the time of St Augustine, we have, in varying degrees, disowned our bodies and especially our sexuality, probably the most creative gift with which God has endowed our species. In the face of crisis and catastrophe, we tend to employ an 'end-of-the-world' polemic, by which we comfortably condemn evil, without lifting a finger to remove it. In the name of sanctity and salvation we flee the world to the security and comfort of monasteries, which, in fact, should be the germinating ground for radical spirituality, implying the maximum of risk and insecurity, as the Taizé community is today. Our churches and religious traditions have a great deal to unlearn before adopting a spirituality of integration.

The churches and their respective religions are not superior to change. Its impact hits all alike; its fruitfulness depends on our responses. We cannot block the flow of change. We may hold it at bay for a while but ultimately it waits for neither humanity nor its mighty institutions. We become either its victims or beneficiaries.

When change becomes threatening we retract and resist. A whole range of defence mechanisms come into play and polarisation in its negative sense ensues. This is the great sinfulness of our age. This is the reaction that always says 'No' to the creative urge ever seeking a 'Yes'. In a time of transition of the type we experience today, a church which is unwilling to respond to the challenge is doomed to extinction!

And from the ashes of dying institutions spring the beneficiaries, perhaps often scared and hurt, frequently rebutted and rejected by those who choose to resist. But they have survived, equipped with a new dream, telling a new story. These tend to be very fragile people, often found on the margins of official organisations, at CND rallies, in new-age movements, in basic christian communities, exploring Eastern meditation, seeking new friendships and affiliations. Perhaps, because of the dislocated nature of their own lives, they can appreciate change more profoundly. Every society needs these people, their vision and their dreams; at this time of impending evolutionary change, we need them more than ever.

Light on the Horizon

We live on the threshold of a new era. Changes are taking place all around us. In the course of this book we have explored some of the main trends. Were this book to be written five years hence, it would, in all probability, have to proclaim a very different message. Such is the speed of change in today's world.

We live in exciting times. Whole new vistas open up before us. The old ways are dying, encircling many lives with pain and darkness. Meanwhile a new sun envelops the horizon, encircling the darkness. We humans have the choice of staying in the shadow or allowing the sun to penetrate. In one case, we become victims engulfed by the dark; in the other, the beneficiaries of warmth and light.

In the depth of our hearts we all like to be beneficiaries, no matter how painful that may be. Furthermore, it is our god-given destiny to be winners, not losers. Time is running out; we must choose! And may the God of light enable us to make the right choice!

Appendix

In the course of this book, we have explored a vast terrain of mystery and experience. Many intricacies, aspirations, unfulfilled hopes, even contradictions, still remain – hopefully, demisted a little! It may be helpful to summarise the message of this book and to isolate the main points: I offer this resumé in the form of ten propositions:

1. Change takes place continually at all levels of life, ranging from the personal to the universal. Without this change there could be no growth or development.

2. Change is activated, not only by humans, but by the energy of life itself. We cannot escape change; mentally and psychologically, we can try to convince ourselves that it's not happening; that is mere deception.

3. We humans can control and modify change only in a very limited, and usually in a self-destructive, way. Inadvertently, we expend much time and energy in avoiding and resisting change rather than directing and controlling it.

4. In the creative 'plan' of our universe, our human task seems to be that of accepting and enhancing change, 'going along with its flow'. In that way we become its beneficiaries, instead of its helpless victims.

5. Change is particularly powerful at the present time, because we are living in an 'in-between' era, a transition stage in which an old paradigm is in decline and a new supersystem is being born.

6. Because of this evolutionary transition, the most powerful waves of change are those taking place on a *global, universal scale*, at the level of what Carl Jung called the 'Collective Unconscious'. It is primarily because of this global transformation that change and mutation is taking place in our social institutions and in our personal lives.

7. Because of the impact of global change, even our most sacred institutions – the church, governments, the family, employment, the scientific world-view, economic theory – are all disintegrating. This process of decline and decay marks the death of the old

order and nothing is likely to escape its impact.

8. A major challenge of contemporary change is the ability to 'let go', especially of our compulsive tendency to interfere, control and manipulate. And the supreme invitation is to 'let be': gracefully and gently allow the new to unfold and commit ourselves to its growth and development.

9. The in-between time will be one of chaos and confusion, with much pain and suffering. Why this has to be is something of a mystery. That it will happen is verified, in different but related ways, by all the major world religions in their assertion (variously expressed) that there can be no 'resurrection' without a 'calvary' preceding it.

10. As the old declines and the new supersystem assumes a leading role, spirituality will flourish anew and it will be one of the main assets for those who will successfully negotiate the evolutionary transition.

In writing this book, I have been inspired by many people, living and dead. Foremost among them is a scientific and prophetic genius of the twentieth century: Albert Einstein. During his lifetime Einstein grappled with a dream that never came to realisation: a scientific theory that would explain how all the forces in the universe function in harmony for the benefit of the whole. The theory is still a dream, although undoubtedly closer to realisation. Towards the end of his lifetime Einstein was asked why he assumed his 'Grand Unification' theory to be true. His response was simple and direct: 'It is too beautiful to be false.'

In defending the ten propositions outlined above, I feel tempted to reiterate Einstein's mystical response. I hesitate to do so, although deep within I share the sentiment. However, I will conclude with another remark from the great scientist, one that elucidates my faith and conviction in the dream and vision of this book:

> I trust that posterity will read these statements with a feeling of proud and justified superiority. (Einstein, 1950, p. 11.)

Footnotes

1. For the reader unfamiliar with Jungian ideas, the concept of the *Collective Unconscious* can be difficult to comprehend. Firstly, it refers to a quality of consciousness or awareness rather than an absence of it: information we are not consciously aware of, although it exists all around us, as I attempt to explain in the text (pp. 98ff). Secondly, I find the concept useful in striving to make sense of those dimensions of human and earthly experience which the physical sciences on the one hand, and the religions on the other, tend to dismiss as 'superficial', 'airy-fairy', 'illusive', 'unprovable'. To the best of my knowledge, nobody has yet found a way of 'proving' the existence of the Collective Unconscious, nor does this underscore the validity and usefulness of the concept. As Zukav (1980, p. 287) reminds us: 'A "proof" does not verify that an assertion is true. . . (but) that the assertion in question is logically consistent. . . In short, when a scientist says that a theory is true, he means that it correctly correlates experience and, therefore, it is *useful.*'

2. References throughout the text to *Western* civilisation, culture, value-system, etc, refer to those values and assumptions which underpin 'our way of doing things' in Western nations, whether in politics, economics, religion, medicine or education. The Western world-view of the past two to three hundred years has been predominantly that of Newtonian science and Cartesian philosophy: we try to understand everything as if it were a machine consisting of parts (hierarchically arranged) which can be altered, repaired, or replaced. This procedure is based on philosophical assumptions which claim that (a) the whole equals the sum of the parts: (b) our rational (logical, scientific) way of analysing, restructuring is the supreme wisdom available to our world. For reasons indicated throughout this book, these values and the assumptions underlying them, are inappropriate, if not counterproductive, for the times in which we live.

3. The dwindling impact of Western Christianity is revealed by:

a) The diminished role of Church values and religious values in Western nations generally;

b) The apparent inability of religous systems to offset the gross immorality of the arms race, the nuclear threat, the social injustices which divide rich from poor, racism, etc.;

c) Declining numbers in formal religious practice, more pronounced in Western Europe than in the USA;

d) Christianity's traditional influence on personal morality (especially on sexual behaviour) has dwindled considerably;

e) The institutional churches no longer command extensive influence or respect. Secularisation (cf. Martin, 1978) has forced the christian churches into something of a crisis which some churches have not even begun to acknowledge.

A *new quality of religion* does not necessarily mean the abandonment of one's religion nor the creation of an alternative to one or other of the major religious systems. It refers to a new quality of spiritual awarness, noticeable in many parts of the world, whereby people seek to explore and articulate their spiritual beliefs in one of two predominant ways: (a) by making little or no reference to a religious system; standard religious practice is often perceived as being irrelevant and archaic; (b) by drawing on insights and experiences from a variety of creeds and belief systems (cf. Cox, 1984; Ó Murchú, 1986). In using this term I am referring to an universal trend which is not confined to any one of the 'emerging theologies' (eg. Liberation theology, Feminist theology, Creation-centred spirituality, Eastern mysticism, to mention but a few) although any of these may serve to sharpen the focus of this pursuit.

4. Throughout the book, I use the term *supersystem* to describe that set of values and behaviours that is likely to replace the present 'system', which occasionally I describe as 'the old order'.

5. In the remarks which follow I draw attention to a trend in the contemporary arts (especially in art, music and literature) which seeks to articulate the death and decay taking place in our world ('mirroring reality as it is'). It is difficult to know how much importance one should attribute to this development. Critics of the arts depict modern exponents as being 'at a crossroads' or as 'having lost direction'. However, artists themselves strongly disagree and maintain that their apparent 'confusion and chaos' is only a reflection of the disorientation of our age.

Space does not allow a detailed exposition of this topic, nor do I claim the expertise for such an undertaking. However, to ignore the subject entirely would be a gross omission. One hopes that by including a brief coverage, others more versatile than I will explore these observations with greater depth and lucidity. (More on this topic in Hutcheon, 1986).

6. This strong claim merits serious consideration in the light of studies such as Harrison (1984), Kenton (1984) and Bliss (1985), all of which render a clear and convincing account of the body's innate potential to maintain a *permanent* healthy state when nurtured appropriately.

7. The Human Potential Movement emerged in the early 1970s owing much inspiration to the Esalen Institute in California. It incorporates a wide variety of groups and individuals exploring personal growth and the development of hidden, personal potential.

8. Homosexuality has had a long presence in the human community. While not wishing to inflate its significance few can deny that it has taken on a new cultural prominence in recent times. In good measure, the scorn and stigma of former times has disappeared. Much has been done

to enable people individually and humanly, to interpret and integrate their homosexual or lesbian experience. My contention is that this 'new awareness' has also a social/cultural dimension; it may indicate a subconscious, cultural desire to expand the context of human, sexual relationships providing yet another articulation of the transition from closed to open systems.

In the light of this tentative (rather than speculative) interpretation, two extremes are transcended, one which considers homosexuality to be a perversion needing psychiatric attention, and the other, which argues that we should consider it normal behaviour on par with heterosexuality. I do not wish to underestimate the personal sensitivities surrounding this delicate subject, but I cannot accept that our analysis must focus primarily (or exclusively) on personal behaviour. There are also social and cultural ramifications in the light of which we may understand the personal issues quite differently.

9. The European Economic Community (EEC) consists of twelve European countries who strive to work towards greater unity and cooperation, especially in the political and economic spheres.

10. Wine-lakes and butter-mountains refer to the surpluses of dairy and horticultural produce stored in warehouses, especially in Europe, quantities of food which are withheld from the world market so that prices can be kept at a desired level. Attempts by Bob Geldof and others to persuade European governments to send the surpluses to the Third World have met with much resistance, indicating that economic considerations (geared to productivity and profit) often take preference over human well-being.

Reference Bibliography

Atkins, G. D. (1983), *Reading Deconstruction: Deconstructive Reading*, University Press of Kentucky.

Balasuriya, Tissa (1984), *Planetary Theology*, Orbis Books (New York).

Bateson, Gregory (1979), *Mind and Nature*, Fontana (distributed by Watts, Franklin Inc., Danbury, CT).

Bausch, William J. (1975), *Positioning Belief in the Mid-Seventies*, Fides Books (Indiana).

Berdyaev, Nicolas (1935), *Freedom and the Spirit*, Bles.

Berger, Brigitte & Peter (1984), *The War Over the Family*, Penguin.

Bliss, Shepherd (1985), *The New Holistic Health Handbook*, The Stephen Greene Press (USA).

Bohm, David (1980), *Wholeness and the Implicate Order*, Boston & London: Routledge and Kegan Paul.

Bohr, Neils (1934), *Atomic Theory and the Description of Nature*, Cambridge University Press (GB) and AMS Press, New York (1978).

Boissevain J. & Clyde, J. (1975), *Network Analysis: Studies in Social Interaction*, The Hague: Mouton & New York: Hawthorne.

Bott, Elizabeth (1971), *Family and Social Network*, Tavistock (distributed in USA by Methuen, New York).

Bradbury, Malcolm (Ed) (1977), *The Novel Today*, Fontana (distributed by Watts, Franklin Inc., Danbury, CT).

Brown, Norman O. (1966), *Love's Body*, New York: Random House.

Buhlmann, Walbert (1986), *The Church of the Future: A Model for the Year 2001*, St. Paul's/Orbis Books.

Burrell, G. & Morgan, G. (1979), *Sociological Paradigms and Organisational Analysis*, London & Portsmouth (New Hampshire): Heinemann.

Cada, Lawrence & Alia (1979), *Shaping the Coming Age of Religious Life*, Seabury Press.

Campbell, Anthony (1976), *Seven States of Consciousness*, Victor Gollancz.

Campbell, Joseph (1959), *The Masks of God: Primitive Mythology*, Viking Press.

Capra, Fritjof (1976), *The Tao of Physics*, Fontana (GB) & Shambhala (USA).

(1982), *The Turning Point*, Fontana (GB) & Simon & Schuster (USA).

Cazenave, Michael (Ed) (1984), *Science and Consciousness: Two Views of the Universe*, Oxford & New York: Pergamon Press.

Clarke, Robin & Hendley, Geoffrey (1975), *The Challenge of the Primi-*

tives, Jonathan Cape.

Clarke, Roger (1982), *Work in Crisis*, Edinburgh (Scotland): St. Andrew Press.

Cohen-Richards, Fred & Ann (1973), *Homo Novus: The New Man*, Shields Publishing Inc. (Colorado).

Collins, Michael (1974), *An Astronaut's Journey*, Farrar, Strauss & Giroux (USA).

Cooper, J. C. (1981), *Yin and Yang: The Taoist Harmony of Opposites*, The Aquarian Press (G.B.).

(1982), *Symbolism: The Universal Language*, The Aquarian Press (GB).

Cox, Harvey (1965), *The Secular City*, Penguin.

(1970), *The Feast of Fools*, Harper & Row.

(1973), *The Seduction of the Spirit*, Simon & Schuster.

(1977), *Turning East: The Promise and Pearl of the New Orientalism*, Simon & Schuster.

(1984), *Religion in the Secular City: Towards a Postmodern Theology*, New York: Touchstone Books.

Davies, John & Yates, Tim, 'Too Early for the Factory of the Future', in *New Scientist*, 2/1/1986, pp. 40-42.

de Beus, J. G. (1985), *Shall We Make the Year 2000?*, Sedwick & Jackson (GB).

Dubos, René (1976), *The God Within: A Positive View of Mankind's Future*, Abacus Books.

Einstein, Albert (1950), *Out of My Later Years*, Thames & Hudson (GB), US distributer: W. W. Norton & Co. Inc., New York.

(1954), *Ideas and Opinions*, Crown Publishers (New York) & Alvin Redman (London).

Eliade, Mircea (1964), *Shamanism: Archaic Techniques of Ecstacy*, Pantheon Books.

(1969), *The Quest: History and Meaning in Religion*, University of Chicago Press.

Erikson, Erik H. (1965), *Childhood and Society*, Pelican (first published, 1950).

Fawcett, Thomas (1973), *Hebrew Myth and Christian Gospel*, SCM Press (distributed in USA by Fortress Press, Philadelphia).

Ferguson, Marilyn (1982), *The Aquarian Conspiracy: Personal and Social Transformation in the 1980s*, Los Angeles: Tarcher & London: Routledge & Kegan Paul.

Fowler, James W. (1981), *Stages of Faith*, Harper & Row.

Fox, Matthew (1984), *Original Blessing: A Primer in Creation Spirituality*, Bear & Co Inc. (USA).

Frankl, Victor (1959), *Man's Search for Meaning*, Clarion Books.

Freud, Sigmund (1955), *Beyond the Pleasure Principle* in *The Complete Psychological Works of Sigmund Freud*, Vol. 18 edited by James

Strachey and published by the Hogarth Press, London & Honolulu (HI).

Goldbrunner, Josef (1955), *Individuation: A Study of the Depth Psychology of Jung,* Hollis & Carter, (London)

Goode, William (1963), *World Revolution and Family Patterns,* New Jersey & London: Collier MacMillan.

Griffiths, Bede (1976), *Return to the Centre,* London: Collins.

Hague, William (1969), 'Personal Identity and Community', from *Vita Evangelica* (Canada), No. 3, pp. 145-158.

Handy, Charles (1984), *The Future of Work,* Oxford & New York: Blackwell.

Harrison, John (1984), *Love Your Disease,* GB and Australia: Angus & Robertson.

Hart, Ray. L. (1968), *Unfinished Man and the Imagination,* Herder & Herder.

Heisenberg, Werner (1963), *Physics and Philosophy,* Winchester (MA): Allen & Unwin.

Holland Joe & Henriot, Peter (1983), *Social Analysis: Linking Faith and Justice,* Orbis Books.

Hutcheon, Linda (1986), *A Theory of Parody,* London & New York: Methuen.

Janis, Irving L. (1982), *Groupthink: Psychological Studies of Policy Decisions and Fiascoes,* Houghton Miffin Co., Boston. (First published, 1972).

Jantsch, Erich (1980), *The Self-Organising Universe,* Oxford & New York: Pergamon Press.

Jaques, Elliot (1970), *Work, Creativity and Social Justice,* London & Portsmouth (New Hampshire): Heinemann.

Jung, Carl G. (1944), *Psychology and Alchemy* in *The Collected Works of Carl Jung* (Editors: Gerhard Adler, Michael Fordham and Herbert Read), London & Boston: Routledge & Kegan Paul.

(1966), *The Spirit in Man: Art and Literature,* Pantheon Books, (Vol. 15 of *Collected Works).*

(1968), *Man and His Symbols,* New York: Dell.

Kenton, L. & S. (1984), *Raw Energy,* A Century Arrow Book.

Kilpatrick, William (1975), *Identity and Intimacy,* New York: Delta Books.

Knitter, Paul F. (1985), *No Other Name? A Critical Survey of Christian Attitudes Towards the World Religions,* SCM Press (Distributed in USA by Fortress Press, Philadelphia).

Kroeber, A. (1944), *Configurations of Cultural Growth,* Berkley & Los Angeles.

Kubler-Ross, Elizabeth (1970), *On Death and Dying,* Tavistock (Distributed in USA by Methuen, New York).

(1982), *Living With Death and Dying,* Souvenir Press (GB).

Kuhn, Thomas (1970), *The Structure of Scientific Revolutions,* University of Chicago Press.

Laing, R. D. (1969), *The Politics of the Family,* Penguin.

Lake, Frank (1981), *Tight Corners in Pastoral Counselling,* London: Darton, Longman & Todd, (distributed in USA by South Asian Books, Columbia, MO).

Lane, David (1985), *Soviet Economy and Society,* New York & Oxford: Blackwell.

Leech, Kenneth (1981), *The Social God,* London: Sheldon Press.

Levy-Bruhl, Lucien (1975), *The Notebooks on Primitive Mentality,* New York & Oxford: Blackwell.

Lovelock, James, (1979), *Gaia: A New Look at Life on Earth,* Oxford and New York: Oxford University Press.

Lukes, Steven (1973), *Individualism,* Oxford & New York: Blackwell.

Lunn, Pam (1985), 'New Physics and Old Mystics: Some Points of Contact', *Christian,* Vol. 9, pp. 16-23.

Marris, Peter (1974), *Loss and Change,* Rutledge & Kegan Paul.

Martin, David (1978), *A General Theory of Secularisation,* Harper & Row.

Mead, Margaret (Ed.) (1937), *Cooperation and Competition among Primitive Peoples,* McGraw-Hill.

Miller, James (1978), *Living Systems,* McGraw-Hill.

Murchie, Guy (1979), *The Seven Mysteries of Life,* London: Rider/Hutchinson, (distributed in USA by Methuen, New York).

McDermott, J. (Ed.) (1967), *The Writings of William James,* Random House.

McGinnis, T. C. & Ayers, J. U. (1976), *Open Family Living,* London & Boston: Routledge & Kegan Paul.

McKenzie, A. E. E. (1960), *The Major Achievements of Science,* Simon & Schuster.

McLuhan, Marshal (1967), *The Medium is the Message* Random House.

Olson, David & McCubbin, H. I. (1983), *Families: What Makes Them Work,* Beverly Hills (CA): Sage publications.

Ó Murchú, Diarmuid (1986), *The God Who Becomes Redundant,* Cork (Ireland): Mercier Press.

Panikkar, Raimundo (1982), *Blessed Simplicity: The Monk as Universal Archetype,* Seabury Press.

Pelletier, Kenneth R. (1978), *Towards a Science of Consciousness,* New York: Delta.

Pennington, Basil (1982), *On Centering Prayer,* Image Books.

Polak, Fred (1973), *The Image of the Future,* Elsevier Scientific Publishing.

Pribram, karl (1971), *Languages of the Brain,* Prentice-Hall.

Prigogine, Ilya (1980), *From Being to Becoming,* Freeman (San Francisco).

Rabb, T. K. & Rotberb, R. I. (Eds.) (1971), *The Family in History,* Harper

Torch Books.

Rifkin, Jeremy & Howard, Tim (1984), *Entropy: A New World View*, Viking Press.

Robinson, J. A. T. (1967), *Exploration Into God*, SCM Press.

Rogers, Paul (1972), *The Education of Human Ecologists*, London: Charles Knight & Co.

Roszak, Theodore (1978), *Person/Planet*, Doubleday/Anchor Books.

Russell, Peter (1982), *The Awakening Earth: Our Next Evolutionary Leap*, London: Routledge & Kegan Paul; Los Angeles: Tarcher.

Sagan, Carl (1981), *Cosmos: The Story of Cosmic Evolution, Science and Civilisation*, London & Sydney: McDonald & Co.

Salvadori, M. (1975), *The Rise of Modern Communism*, Dryden Press (Illinois).

Savells, J. & Cross, L. J. (Eds.) (1978), *The Changing Family*, Holt, Rinehart and Winston.

Schmidt, Roger (1980), *Exploring Relgion*, Wadsworth Inc. (California).

Segal, Lynne (Ed.) (1983), *What is to be Done About the Family*, Penguin.

Shea, John (1978), *Stories of God*, Thomas More Press (Chicago).

(1980), *Stories of Faith*, Thomas More Press (Chicago).

Sheehy, Gail (1976), *Passages: Predictable Crises of Adult Life*, Bantam Books.

Sheldrake, Rupert (1981), *A New Science of Life*, Paladin Books.

(1985), 'Religion and Biology', *Resurgence*, July/Aug., pp. 34-37.

Sim, Stuart (1982), 'De-composing in Bad Faith: Its Cause and Cure', *Critical Quarterly*, Vol. 24, pp. 25-36.

Sorokin, Pitrim (1950), *Modern Historical and Social Philosophies*, New York: Dover publications.

Speck, R. V. & Attneave, C. L. (1973), *Family Networks: A New Approach to Family Problems*, Vantage Books.

Spengler, Oswald (1961), *The Decline of the West*, Allen & Unwin (abridged edition).

Stace, Walter (1960), *The Teachings of the Mystics*, New American Library.

Starcke, Walter (1974), *The Gospel of Relativity*, Thurstone Books.

Stevens, Edward (1973), *An Introduction to Oriental Mysticism*, Paulist Press.

Suppes, Patrick (1984), *Probabilistic Metaphysics*, Oxford & New York: Blackwell.

Thompson, Kenneth (Ed.) (1984), *Work, Employment and Unemployment*, Open University Press.

Toffler, Alvin (1980), *The Third Wave*, London: Collins.

Toynbee, Arnold (1960), *A Study of History* (Vols 1-10, abridged version), Oxford & New York: Oxford University Press.

Walter, Tony (1985), *Hope on the Dole*, London: SPCK.

Watson, Lyall, *Supernature*, GB and Australia: Hodder & Stoughton.

Wilber, Ken (1982), *The Holographic Paradigm and Other Paradoxes*, London & Boulder: New Science Library.

(1983), *Up From Eden*, London & Boston: Routledge & Kegan Paul.

Williams, Raymond (1983), *Towards 2000*, London & Honolulu (HI): Hogarth Press.

Wilson, Bryan (1982), *Religion in Sociological Perspective*, London & New York: Oxford University Press.

Wildgoose, Jean (1985), *Radical Jesus Manifesto*, Ashram Community Trust, Sheffield, England.

Zukav, Gary (1980), *The Dancing Wu Li Masters: An Overview of the New Physics*, Fontana, (distributed in USA by Watts, Franklin Inc., Danbury, CT).

Index

The God who becomes redundant
Diarmuid Ó Murchú

Current divisions and conflicts in the church are alarming and deeply disturbing to many. For many people, religion is irrelevant, religious practice is in decline and all the major religions seem to be in a state of crisis. Yet people continue to discuss religious topics, question religious meaning and even experiment with religious ritual.

A new religious search is under way, exhibiting a desire to move away from institutional religion towards a more open-ended, unstructured and globally-based set of beliefs. In taking this broader perspective, not alone do the "searchers" tend to abandon institutional religion but find themselves lured into a new spiritual vision, creating an expanded religious awareness and a whole new context for religious belief itself.

This seems to be a new discovery but it is also deeply rooted in man's religious story as it unfolded over 70,000 years. Contemporary explorations in the physical and social sciences are also sharing this discovery and there is a clear move towards a more holistic approach to knowledge and the development of a new *Global Vision*. This gives faith and religion a credibility hitherto unknown. *Homo Religiosus* seems to be approaching a new evolutionary threshold. Not merely does it guarantee the survival of religion but it poses a profound challenge to believer and non-believer alike.